Hugh MacDiarmid's Epic Poetry

For my mother and father:
Janette Greig Cunningham Riach
and James Alexander Riach

Hugh MacDiarmid's Epic Poetry

ALAN RIACH

Edinburgh University Press

© Alan Riach, 1991

Edinburgh University Press
22 George Square, Edinburgh

Typeset in 10/12 pt Linotron Sabon Roman
by Intype, London, and
printed in Great Britain by Robert Hartnoll Ltd, Bodmin

British Library Cataloguing in Publication Data

Riach, Alan
  Hugh MacDiarmid's epic poetry.
  I. Title
  821

ISBN 0 7486 0257 7 (cased)

The publisher acknowledges subsidy from the Scottish Arts
Council towards the publication of this volume.

Contents

Poetry can only be a valid and valuable activity when we recognise the value of the artifice which makes it different from prose. Indeed, it is only through artifice that poetry can challenge our ordinary linguistic orderings of the world, make us question the way in which we make sense of things, and induce us to consider its alternative linguistic orders as a new way of viewing the world.

Veronica Forrest-Thomson

A Brechtian maxim: 'Don't start from the good old things but the bad new ones.'

Walter Benjamin

Acknowledgements

My first acknowledgements must be of the hospitality, kindness, and generosity with which I was received by Christopher Murray Grieve and Valda Trevlyn Grieve, and, later, Michael and Deirdre Grieve. As this book evolved from work completed for a doctoral dissertation in the Department of Scottish Literature at the University of Glasgow, I should like to thank my supervisor and readers, Kenneth Buthlay, David Daiches, and Roderick Lyall. For their teaching, conversation, and friendship I thank T.J. Cribb, C.T. Larsen, Peter McCarey, and Edwin Morgan. I should also like to thank Sorley MacLean and Norman MacCaig, Cairns Craig and Nancy Gish. Colin Hamilton and Kulgin Duval allowed me access to private manuscript sources for which I am very grateful. And my colleagues at the University of Waikato, John Jowett, Mark Williams, and Marshall Walker read and commented on parts of the manuscript with incisive wisdom. For Angus Calder's comments and for the support of my publisher, Martin Spencer, I am also grateful. My thanks are due to the staff of the Mitchell Library (Glasgow), Glasgow University Library, Edinburgh University Library, the National Library of Scotland (Edinburgh), the British Library (London), and the University of Waikato Library (Hamilton, New Zealand). And also to the forbearance and good spirits of those who typed the book: Sonia Wells, Lorraine Brown, Gaye Miller, Bev Campbell, Inger Cox-Smith, Jennifer Thorpe, and Chris Mackness. Finally, I would like to acknowledge the support of the family I come from. Books have a fate of their own, according to the readers that find them. This book is also theirs.

A.R.

Introduction

Objections, non-sequiturs, cheerful distrust, joyous mockery —
all are signs of health. Everything absolute belongs to the realm
of pathology.

Nietzsche, *Beyond Good and Evil*, maxim 154

Throughout the course of the composition of this book, its purpose
has remained clear: to direct critical attention towards Hugh Mac-
Diarmid's later poetry and to provide a variety of approaches which
would both broaden and sharpen our reading of that poetry.

MacDiarmid's status amongst critics, teachers of poetry, and poets
themselves has never been absolutely secure. So, in a project of this
kind, where I am breaking new ground in difficult areas, there is little
enough to be taken for granted. Readers familiar with MacDiarmid's
Scottish context are often less familiar with, or indeed hostile to, the
introduction of literary theory. Those familiar with developments in
theory are often ignorant of the Scotland MacDiarmid took as his
stage. Influential critics whose grasp of modern poetry is international are often strangely silent when it comes to Scottish literature, as they follow the political constitution and subscribe to the
identities it confers. Irish literature is thereby distinct from British
literature, but the national identities of Scotland and Wales are
subsumed in the 'British' rubric. Different critical assumptions are
already held by readers of different nationalities. Because MacDiarmid remained a stubbornly national figure, his achievement might
seem to be a quite different thing to readers in England and in
Scotland, South Africa, or Eastern Europe (not to mention Nicara-
gua, New Zealand, or the Caribbean). But if nationality means
borders, literature insists upon the possibility of communication
across them.

However, the readership which exists for what I have called Mac-
Diarmid's 'epic poetry' is limited, even among scholars. Where the
American poets Ezra Pound, William Carlos Williams, and Charles

Olson have been well served by critics, textual scholars, and exegetes, MacDiarmid's later poetry remains relatively neglected, despite a number of remarkably insightful essays and articles. I have therefore presented as much information as I felt was necessary, and while avoiding jargon as far as possible, I have attempted to deal with the complexities of MacDiarmid's later poetry in both Scottish and international terms.

This book is both a critical introduction to MacDiarmid's later poetry and a source for further research. I have adapted elements of biography, historical exegesis, close textual criticism, speculative discussion, comparative studies, and simple explication. I have also provided a number of source-texts for critical comparison with the uses MacDiarmid made of them in his verse, and some of these I have discussed in detail. I am aware that the disclosure of the amount of source-material runs the danger of prompting a dismissal of MacDiarmid's work as merely 'chopped-up prose'. It should not need to be said that this is not my intention. My defence of Mac-Diarmid's use of unacknowledged 'quotation' is made not only with reference to T.S. Eliot but by invoking the work of Barthes, Foucault, Derrida, and Lacan, though I have avoided any extensive use of the terminology these theorists employ. This allows an internationalism of approach for which MacDiarmid himself set a precedent and which, I hope, does more justice to his work than efforts to explain him in relation to mainstream English poetry as a belated Romantic or to locate him in a purely autonomous Scottish context.

The book is intended for those who have read MacDiarmid but remain unconvinced by his later poetry and reluctant to engage with it critically. It is also intended for those who know Pound, Joyce, and Brecht but who are less familiar with MacDiarmid. I do not intend that it should replace or supersede more general introductory works, but I believe it will complement and challenge them usefully. Though there is a cumulative argument which foregrounds Mac-Diarmid's achievement in *In Memoriam James Joyce* and thereby challenges conventional acceptance of MacDiarmid's work, my intention has been to discuss the issues discretely rather than to provide an encompassing chronological trajectory. This is not only the most stimulating and interesting way to get into MacDiarmid's later work but is also in keeping with the methodology most appropriate to the texts themselves. The result, however, is not a single, simple, linear argument, so it would be as well to explain at the outset the structure of the work as a whole, for it has been carefully deliberated.

There are three chapters. The central chapter offers a reading of *In Memoriam James Joyce*, a book-length work of 1955 first published in a large format volume of over 140 pages, and a paradigm of MacDiarmid's 'epic' poetry. Chapter 1 provides the intellectual and historical introductions to that work, and explores a variety of contexts in which it might be considered. Chapter 3 begins from the point of *having read* the Joyce poem, and considers the question of MacDiarmid's first person singular and 'plagiarism', taking a retrospective view from the lyrics of *Sangschaw* through to 'Dìreadh III'. This structure might appear wilfully serpentine, but I believe it will be clear enough as we move through it. There are loops, digressions, and *non sequiturs*: but none of these, I trust, is damaging to the essential project. Indeed, it seems to me crucial that the project should present itself as something being enacted rather than absolutely concluded. *In Memoriam James Joyce* is a major work of twentieth-century literature and its complex, transgressive nature means that any real attempt to come to terms with it will involve an invigorating struggle. But of course, that is not to excuse ourselves or lessen the rigour with which we read the work, and I hope I have been as scrupulous in my close reading of particular passages as I have been accommodative in the span of the complete book.

The book begins with the historical panorama of 1928, the founding of the National Party of Scotland and the dawning of MacDiarmid's ambition to write an epic poem superseding his past work. That ambition developed and was demonstrated in ways that show how the practice of literature and the practice of politics are inextricable. It was therefore necessary to interweave biographical, historical, literary, and theoretical strands throughout Chapter 1, and to present a mosaic of information. But the tesserae are connected. The term 'epic' offers a special kind of coherence, and deserves some comment here.

'Epic' is easily one of the woolliest of literary terms. Classical scholars usually allow only one sense to the word: that of a long narrative poem containing some fighting. Literary sociologists would insist that the term signifies a performance dependent upon certain assumptions and conventions that are shared amongst a tribe, society, or nation. Yet the word has been applied meaningfully to texts as different as Patrick White's *Voss*, Salman Rushdie's *Midnight's Children*, and Keri Hulme's *The Bone People*. All of these are modern examples of national awakening and important works in the establishment of the identities of Australia, India, and New Zealand in terms of cosmopolitan literature. There are ways in which these works could be linked back at least as far as Virgil. But any strict definition of 'epic' is going to beg a whole set of questions. Some of these I have dealt with at greater length in Chapter 1, but the primary reason why I have used the word should be stated clearly now.

This book is intended to shift the focus of MacDiarmid studies, and the sense of magnitude the word 'epic' conveys helps to emphasise the significance of MacDiarmid's later poetry in a sweeping, general way. It brings in, on the one hand, the traditional notion of epic work (Homer, Dante, Melville) and, on the other hand, the theoretical use of the term by Brecht. To begin with a sense of *In Memoriam James Joyce* as something similarly great is, I believe, a necessary extravagance, and I hope, also, that some of my enthusiasm for the work comes through in the word. Many readers of MacDiarmid have a shared experience of first reading him, usually his early lyrics or *A Drunk Man Looks at the Thistle*, with a shocking recognition of quality. Frequently, this experience takes place outside of the educational establishments and it has happened in every decade since these works were published. A similar experience of exhilaration is shared by many of those whose early reading of MacDiarmid included *In Memoriam James Joyce*. That sense of quality, exhilaration, and serendipity: the magnitude of MacDiarmid's achievement is what I would like to acknowledge and begin from.

Part of the confusion the word 'epic' causes derives from the fact that it is both a noun and an adjective, and that ambivalence is sidestepped by my title. The *Iliad* is, legitimately, an *epic*; but *The Divine Comedy* is an epic *allegory*, and *War and Peace* is an epic *novel*. As soon as one starts to get more precise, the complexities of MacDiarmid's texts open up, and the questions raised in Chapter 1 — or some of them at least — will have to wait until the end of the book before they can be resolved. I am *not* saying that *In Memoriam James Joyce* is an epic in exactly the same way as *The Iliad*, although I could argue, if I wanted to use the term in a strict sense, that it is an epic eulogy (containing passages of epic elegy). But, clearly, more than one meaning of the word is involved. Saddening as it might be, it must be admitted that no single meaning nor even any single fixed set of meanings will be sufficient to allow us the security of a formal definition of the word as it applies to a poem.

The ambivalence of the term is most evident at that point where one's sense of a poem as object (epic as artifice: noun) and poetry as process (epic as invention: adjective) coalesce. This raises the crucial question of whether the focus of our discussion is an object — a poem — or a practice — a kind of poetry in a continually developing state. Further questions arise in turn, about the political nature of the practice of poetry and the inseparability of the practice of poetry and politics. The convenience of being able to consider *In Memoriam James Joyce* as a work (because it was published as a book, rather than left in fragments and 'unassembled') should not obscure the fact that it is part of, and partakes of, other texts. There are other texts that claim MacDiarmid's authorship; and there are other authors who have claimed that they have provided MacDiarmid's texts. This question — the whole question of 'plagiarism' — is also introduced in Chapter 1, because it is an aspect of the theoretical discussion. The fact that it has serious legal and ethical implications has led some critics to devote myopic attention to it, or else to sensationalise it at the expense of reading. I have tried to avoid those extremes.

So Chapter 1 moves in a discontinuous fashion from one area of enquiry to another, raising rather than answering questions, developing contexts for those questions, and suggesting ways in which those contexts could be further explored. Underlying the discrete sections of the chapter are two main areas of enquiry: balancing the traditional notion of 'epic' poetry, there is the modern, Brechtian notion of 'epic' theatre. Again, the term will only help us if we allow for its capacity. What Brechtian theatre shares with oral poetry is a capacity for curiosity; for shifts of deportment; for questions to be asked. These are qualities which mark both off from traditional bourgeois forms of literary art. To put it crudely (and so, not entirely accurately), in both cases the epic requires the self-conscious participation of the audience or readership in the creation of a social event, rather than their private consumption of a finished product. And in that sense, as we shall see, *In Memoriam James Joyce* is quite clearly epic work.

Chapter 2 closes in on the work itself, dealing first with its composition and publishing history then going through each of the six sections in a fairly straightforward way. This linear method of explication is interrupted by discussions of the key concepts which inform the poetry: language, world literature, and Marxism, for example. Since the work is dedicated to the memory of James Joyce, there is a comparative study which continues the process begun in the first chapter of bringing MacDiarmid more firmly into the constellation of the great writers of the modern age. Moreover, as provincial intellectuals whose complex literary and political worlds fuse in their sense of the word *English*, Joyce and MacDiarmid are both similarly concerned with language as a question in itself. They inherited extremely different national histories, despite a shared Celtic heritage, but the similarities and differences in matters of political commitment and personal behaviour (exile, energy, and radical equanimity) — as well as how they came to write what they did — are genuinely revealing.

The bulk of Chapter 2 is devoted to close readings of *In Memoriam James Joyce*, particularly sections two ('The World of Words') and six ('Plaited Like the Generations of Men'). These readings are supplemented by examples of source-texts, and throughout the chapter a growing theme is the *extent* to which MacDiarmid's epic poetry is actually composed of 'other people's words'. This reaches its fullest development at the end of the chapter in the analysis of 'Plaited Like the Generations of Men'. I give a number of these sources and look at the ways they are transcribed into the verse, arguing that what emerges is not merely a spontaneous collage but a poetry whose material construction is both superficially appealing and profoundly yearning for a metaphysical as well as material complementation. In a sense, this gets us to the heart of the political problem of MacDiarmid's poetry: the struggle between materialism and ontology, between the belief in spirit as always and only the product of matter and the belief in spiritual identity, an essence, or a 'pure being'. Whenever ontology is victorious, its victory is absolute. But, as we shall see, wherever that happens in Mac-Diarmid's work, it is bound to be followed by a reassertion of materialism; so any attempt to describe the 'character' of that work must also describe its movement.

Having come through *In Memoriam James Joyce*, we are ready to take a fresh look over MacDiarmid's *œuvre*, bearing in mind certain qualities of character which are only fully revealed in that epic work. So in Chapter 3, I cast back to MacDiarmid's earliest poetry in Scots and come back more or less chronologically through a selection of poems from different moments in his career. The object here is to trace the development of MacDiarmid's first person as it pluralises itself, both in accommodating 'other texts' and in acting as a 'public speaker' for a plurality of people (a clan, tribe, or nation).

I do not think it is possible to provide a resolution at the end of the book which would neatly reconcile all the arguments that have been raised. However, the relations between 'epic' and Mac-

Diarmid's understanding of language are discussed in this final chapter as I come tentatively to some conclusions — and conclusively to some affirmations.

Note

I have been careful in my use of the word 'MacDiarmid' to refer to 'the author' of a body of work, a fiction whose existence arises from that work but whose influence extends beyond it. And I have assumed the word 'Grieve' will be understood to refer to the historical person whose patronymic it was. That Hugh MacDiarmid and Christopher Murray Grieve sometimes shared the same skin makes for occasional confusions, but I trust readers will be aware of the fact that MacDiarmid was Grieve's *nom de plume* (or *nom de guerre*), born fully-grown in 1922, the year of *Ulysses* and *The Waste Land*, when Grieve was in his thirty-first year.

1.

Hugh MacDiarmid's Epic Poetry

Notes Towards a Supreme Faction

On 28 September 1926 C.M. Grieve wrote of *A Drunk Man Looks at the Thistle*: 'The thing as a whole is really a trial run. I shall do better next time. I have a big programme in front of me and all my deepest difficulties to solve.'[1] The germ of Hugh MacDiarmid's epic poetry was nourished by that programme and those difficulties. The difficulties were personal, social, professional, and political, as well as literary. The programme was revolutionary.

MacDiarmid's ambitions were matched by his confidence. In 1928 he wrote to R.E. Muirhead, the 'Father of Scottish Nationalism': 'My task is to be unpopular — a fighter — an enemy of accepted things; not in any captious fashion but out of profound conviction, and while I may often mistake the promptings of my heart and be merely fac-titious, I have reason to know that the best of my work at all events is proving a powerful influence because it springs from the deeps of the destined.'[2] In context, it is clear that the word 'work' in that letter refers both to literature and to politics. In the same letter, we read: 'I am unquestionably doing far more for Scotland when my activity issues in poetry rather than in any other form.' But we also find: 'I want to help carry the [Scottish Nationalist] Movement . . . forward into the sphere of practical politics.'[3]

It was also in 1928 that the National Party of Scotland (NPS) was founded, unifying the various parties (the Scots National League, Scottish National Movement, Scottish Home Rule Associ-ation, Glasgow University Scottish Nationalist Association) who were all campaigning for Scottish Home Rule. Plaid Cymru, the National Party of Wales, had been founded in 1925. Behind both the Welsh and the Scottish nationalist movements lay the Irish War of Independence (1919–21) and Ireland's emergence among Euro-pean nations. Behind that lay the Russian Revolution, itself scarcely ten years old, an inspiring example to those struggling towards

1

independence. It had inspired other uprisings. In the wake of the First World War, workers' soviets had been established in Munich and Budapest; factories were occupied by workers throughout Italy; and in Berlin there was the Spartacus revolt. Social revolution was contagious. The social order of European capitalism was torn apart. These uprisings were all violently put down, but the cultural values by which the old order had been structured were profoundly shaken.

The connections of these nationalist and socialist revolutionary movements with Scotland were direct. James Connolly, one of the martyrs of the Easter Rising in Dublin in 1916, was a Scottish socialist before going to Ireland, and had a crucial influence on the young Sean O'Casey, who became secretary to the Citizen Army of which Connolly was the principal founder. In Glasgow, Connolly also exerted an influence on John MacLean, the revolutionary Marxist teacher and advocate of Scottish Republicanism, who was appointed Soviet consul in Scotland by Lenin himself. In this international context, we can best understand the coincidence of Hugh MacDiarmid's political activism and his poetic project. When he recalled the Easter Rising in a radio interview in 1977, a year before his death, it was in these terms: 'I was in barracks, in Sheffield of all places, in 1915, and I was there when the Easter Rising took place in 1916. If it had been possible at all I would have deserted at that time from the British Army and joined the Irish.'[4]

In 1928 Bertolt Brecht was producing *The Threepenny Opera* in Berlin. Pablo Neruda, then twenty-four, was acting Chilean consul in Colombo, Ceylon. Another Marxist, Louis Zukovsky, also twenty-four, began in New York to write a hermetic poem called '*A*', which would take him about 800 pages and forty-six years to complete. Vladimir Mayakovsky, thirty-five, who would commit suicide within two years, had set off for Paris, where he met Marina Tsvetayeva and Louis Aragon, proclaimed his solidarity as a 'Proletarian Poet' and asked Dimitri Shostakovich to write the music for his play *The Bed Bug*; Shostakovich agreed. James Joyce was also then living in Paris, checking the proofs of *Anna Livia Plurabelle*. Ezra Pound had settled down in Rapallo; *A Draft of Cantos XVII–XXVIII* had appeared and a *Selected Poems*, with an introduction by T.S. Eliot. Eliot himself, having become a Christian and a British subject the year before, was living in London, working for Faber and Gwyer, editing *The Criterion*. Parts of *Ash-Wednesday* were being published. W.B. Yeats, after convalescence in Cannes and with Pound in Rapallo, returned to Ireland and finished his term in the Irish Senate. *The Tower* was published and well received.

He was sixty-eight years old. He and his wife went back to Rapallo for the winter. William Carlos Williams, having returned to Ruther-ford, New Jersey, in 1927 after a European journey, was writing *A Voyage to Pagany*. And in Scotland, in Stirling, on 23 June, the Inaugural Demonstration of the National Party of Scotland took place, with C.M. Grieve, a thirty-five year old veteran of the First World War, rising to second the Resolution of the Party's formation, but pointing out that what would be required was 'the Resolution of the people who are going to support the Resolution'[5] and that there was a great deal of leeway to make up.

He lost no time himself. By the end of August he had returned from a two-week visit to Ireland (along with another of the founders of the NPS and former president of the Scots National League, the Honourable Ruaraidh Erskine of Marr) and was writing to the novelist Neil Gunn (himself an active nationalist) elatedly about his interview 'with De Valera and his chief henchmen'; about having tea with the Minister of Defence; about a long discussion with Yeats, A.E., F.R. Higgins, and others, 'after which Yeats and I perambulated the deserted streets until 2.15 a.m.'[6]

Whatever the talk of the small hours, the Irish example struck deep. Compton Mackenzie — another founder member of the NPS — remembered feeling worried in 1929 by what seemed to him the mistaken preoccupation of the National Party leaders with get-ting into the Westminster Parliament. He suspected that if any NPS candidates did succeed in getting into Parliament, 'they would be content with the same dilution of Home Rule as Northern Ireland. I did not want to see a glorified county council in charge of Scotland's destiny. I felt that nothing less than the status of the Irish Free State was imaginable for Scotland's future.'

> Ruaraidh Erskine of Marr and Christopher Grieve were both in sympathy with my fear of parochialism and we discussed the possibility of forming a society to be known as Clann Albain, the members of which would be pledged to do all they could to foster the Celtic Idea with a vision, on a far distant horizon at present, of rescuing the British Isles from being dominated by London.[7]

In April of that year, Grieve was writing to Mackenzie from Mon-trose to report on the progress of the party:

> The party is steadily eliminating the moderatist, compromising, democratic, element, and all the young people are coming

round to the realisation for the need of — and readiness to institute — a species of Scottish Fascism.[8]

That last word should not surprise us too much, for the extreme of fascism arises from nationalism just as the extreme of Stalinism was to arise from socialism, and it is MacDiarmid's usual procedure to go with characteristic thoroughness to the furthest limits of such contradictory impulses in what T.J. Cribb has called a struggle 'to reach surer ground below or beyond them'.[9] But the immediate attempt to end the domination of the British Isles by London was not to be military. Radio broadcasting was then in its early days, and Mackenzie (at a time when the press were bent on denigrating radio as a serious rival) had come up with the idea of launching a weekly journal devoted to radio criticism. Grieve was asked to move to London to take up the editorship. The first number of *Vox* carried an editorial translated into English, Scottish and Irish Gaelic, Welsh, Cornish, and Manx. No clearer statement could have been made about the implications of linguistic imperialism and the metropolitan and centralising character of the then fledgeling BBC; as Pound put it in Canto LXXIV: 'free speech without free radio speech is as zero'. After fourteen weeks, the magazine collapsed.[10]

In May 1930 'Clann Albain' gained wide publicity through a series of articles and letters in the *Daily Record* ('Scotland's National newspaper . . . both in circulation and in breadth of appeal'). On 10 May a piece by Grieve called 'Sinn Fein Movement for Scotland' appeared, noting how the left wing of the NPS was 'making towards' a 'wholesale Sinn Fein policy' and 'will not keep within conventional political methods'. Allowing that 'financial control has very largely passed from England to America' Grieve claimed 'the younger pro-European and anti-Imperial groups in Ireland, Scotland, and Wales are all anti-American'.

Compton Mackenzie contributed a front-page article on 12 May on 'Independence for Scots'. When asked 'What is the good of Home Rule when women and children in Dundee are starving?', he replied: 'Women and children in Dundee would not be starving if we had self-government.' In the same paper, Grieve was reported at the second annual NPS Delegate Conference in Glasgow, after which a *Daily Record* reporter caught up with him: 'The possibility of the existing Government getting a trifle annoyed over the operations of such a movement [as 'Clann Albain'] in Scotland, and acting as Governments do in such circumstances, was suggested to Mr Grieve.

With a smile, he replied that it might be the best thing that could happen.'

On Friday, 16 May, the *Record* carried banner headlines: 'Scotland's New Secret Society. / Mystery Chief With Full Powers. / Duke of Montrose's Repudiation. / Land Raiding Among Professed Aims.' 'The *Daily Record* only publishes this article to show how far the extremists in this movement profess themselves as willing to go.' Grieve's article claimed that the organisation had been building up for two years and is 'on a militaristic basis, and in this resembles the Fascist movement.'

> It ought to be realised that the Clann is working in concert with the most advanced wings of the Irish and Welsh Movements, and that its ultimate aim in this connection is to destroy English ascendancy internally and imperially. . . . No form of devolution will meet its requirements. Even the existing Irish Free State Government is regarded as a betrayal of what ought to be the Irish policy. . . . Concurrently with the first active steps of Clann Albain, which will consist of land-raiding activities on a large scale . . . Clann Albain believes that supporting activities can be organised amongst the unemployed in Glasgow and elsewhere, and holds that the working classes have only to be taught the true significance of the 'Southward Trend in Industry' and the causes which have led, or are leading, five of the largest shipbuilding firms on the Clyde, including Beardmore's . . . to close down for good, to rouse themselves in no uncertain fashion and insist upon an effective recognition of the differences between English and Scottish interests.

Grieve's claim that one of the most distinguished of living Scotsmen was the Chief of 'Clann Albain' led to Compton Mackenzie being interviewed by a senior police officer and investigated by the Special Branch.

On 17 May the *Record* divulged 'Rumoured Plans of Scots Secret Society': 'The island of Rum is rumoured to be one of the objectives of Clann Albain's proposed land-raiding.' But the name of the 'Mystery Chief' remained a secret, although the *Record* did note that 'the prime movers are mainly poets or poets in prose'. The article — again, front-page news — was countered by a piece by the Duke of Montrose, who was of the opinion that 'the supposed secret society' was not something to be taken seriously. 'The lunatic ideas adumbrated by Mr Grieve in your columns can have no sympathy or support of sensible people . . . '. Lewis Spence, another founding member of the NPS, added his own blast: 'Mr Grieve and his fellows are associated with Ireland. The whole idea is to work for Ireland and Scotland. I have nothing against Ireland, though I deplore the entry of thousands of Irish into Scotland, and I don't want to see the Irish paramount in Scotland.' (In 1927, in his small book *Albyn, or Scotland and the Future*, Grieve had already welcomed the incursions of Irish men and women that had happened in the 1920s.)

John MacCormack, Secretary of the NPS, also wrote in to the *Record* claiming that Grieve's poetic imagination had distorted the facts. 'Mr Grieve refers to Clann Albain as "Scotland's new secret society." Mr Grieve evidently is not good at keeping secrets.' MacCormack went on: 'I am able to say definitely that there is no such active and secret organisation in existence, except, perhaps, in Mr Grieve's imagination.'

As long as the NPS had been silently behind Grieve's contentions, they had carried some threat. With MacCormack's dismissal the opportunity arose for making fun of the matter, and the *Record* published, on 21 May, a letter from Compton Mackenzie: 'I wish to contradict the rumour that I am proposing to loosen the Shiant Islands from the Minch and sail up the Clyde in them, accompanied by a thousand Scottish Fascists, all in black kilts and armed with rolled-up copies of the *Daily Record*. Just as I am writing these words, I have received a message on my portable wireless set that the marine contingent of Clann Albain, which had been ordered to seize the Shetland Islands, has seized Iceland by mistake and has been arrested for illegal trawling.'

But Mackenzie was cautious enough to add 'You may point out that it was Mr C.M. Grieve who contributed the information, and, of course, I realise that I am not in a position to give an authoritative contradiction, because if such a secret society does exist it will try to keep a few of its secrets even from the Press.' And when Lewis Spence, in the same edition, added his comments, he began: 'On the 10th May, 1930, as some Scottish political historian of the future may in a weak moment record, six men foregathered in a Glasgow hotel and resolved on the formation of a Scottish secret society — Clann Albain.' Spence did not name these men but asserted that their 'ultimate aim' was 'to make Dublin the metropolis and cultural nucleus of a pseudo-Celtic Britain, to establish a false pan-Celticism in the islands rather than a British Commonwealth.' Spence was openly hostile to the Irish connection and expressed astonishment that Grieve should be so sympathetic to the Hibernian element, picturing him linking hands with 'Fianna Fail and a handful of pedantic zealots in Wales'. But what is remarkable about Spence's final contribution is the concrete statement that 'Clann Albain' did exist, that those six men in a Glasgow hotel room had met, that — potentially if not in fact — a larger organisation of people might have been brought about. It would have been possible for the *Record* to let the matter drop with Compton Mackenzie's 'Humorous Sally', but Spence is quite serious, and quite impassioned. While Grieve's imagination was invariably mixed with his aspiration, it would be rash to consign 'Clann Albain' entirely to a realm of fantasy.

Now separated from his first wife and having completed another poem even longer than *A Drunk Man Looks at the Thistle*, Grieve had found work in Liverpool and on 14 June he was writing to Helen Cruickshank, then Secretary of Scottish PEN, that he could not yet manage to get back up to Scotland, but 'Mums [*sic*] the word about *C.A.* in the meantime. I'm earnest there; and having a deuce of a lot of correspondence thereanent with young people (for the most part) all over Scotland.'[11]

Later the same month, he wrote to Neil Gunn that he had sent the new poem, *To Circumjack Cencrastus*, off to his publishers, but that he was also 'very busy in other directions — intending, *inter alia*, to have a hell of a say — a much bigger say than ever — in Scottish affairs shortly. And don't you sniff about Clann Albainn [I have observed the erratic spelling of these words, which changed almost every time they were used] — *it is going O.K.*'[12]

While he advised Helen Cruickshank to say nothing of '*C.A.*', a periodical called *The Modern Scot*, edited by James H. Whyte (a bookshop owner, patron of the arts, the dedicatee of 'On a Raised Beach' and the co-dedicatee of *In Memoriam James Joyce*) was starting up. It was to run from Spring 1930 to January 1936. Its second issue included an article entitled 'Clan Albainn and Other Matters' by C.M. Grieve, a public announcement alerting readers to the existence of a politically motivated 'secret society' being organised specifically in order 'to act'. Informed by the then fashionable economic theories of Major C.H. Douglas (who had found favour with Grieve as with Pound through the columns of *The New Age* in the early 1920s), Clann Albain, Grieve claimed, was an overtly militant nationalist 'society.' He added: 'Scotland will never secure a measure of independence worth having without being forced to adopt means similar to those taken by the Irish.'

By October Grieve was again writing to Helen Cruickshank of a proposed two-day trip to Scotland during which he would address the Glasgow University Scottish Nationalist Association. 'I am in eruption again — definitely getting on now with the organization of Clan Albainn, and also with the Douglas Economic Proposals Enquiry Committee of the Scottish National Party . . . '[13] 'Clann Alban' is mentioned again in January 1931, in volume I, number 4 of *The Modern Scot*, in Grieve's review of *La langue des relations interceltiques* by Louis Le Roux. Grieve notes primarily that the book is dedicated to the memory of Padraic Pearse, underlines M. Le Roux's references to Sinn Fein, and praises the book for being 'in the front line of militant Celticism': 'I commend it to the especial attention of Clann Alban'.

Padraic Pearse was the Irish revolutionary leader who read out the proclamation of the Irish Republic from the steps of the General Post Office in Dublin, on Easter Monday 1916. He was executed along with James Connolly and other rebel leaders. It was Connolly, the man who planned for a socialist Ireland, who impressed on Pearse that there was more to revolution than the Gaelic Revival. The Irish critic Seamus Deane has recently discussed Pearse's ideas in terms which suggest that they influenced MacDiarmid's own ideas and intentions.

> The claim of the Revival was that Ireland was culturally distinct from England. Pearse took this notion to its literal conclusion, that Ireland should also become politically distinct. His idea was that the achievement of political separatism could only be produced by the recovery of a nobler and more spiritual ideal than that which prevailed in the lower-middle-class Ireland which he knew. The source of this spiritual authority was in the old Celtic civilization; its modern prophets were the revolutionary leaders of the last century; its modern inheritor was the contemporary generation. Pearse's evangelism against mean-spiritedness, cowardice, caution, commercial wisdom, is precisely the old Victorian-Romantic crusade against the spiritual atrophy of middle-class rule.[14]

Behind Pearse lies Matthew Arnold's conviction that there was a Celtic element in European culture; that it was visible more in literature than in political institutions and was naturally hostile to that practical and unimaginative English spirit embodied to perfection by the middle classes. MacDiarmid was undaunted by the fictive nature of these ideas. He claimed in an essay, 'The Caledonian Antisyzygy and the Gaelic Idea', that the dynamic myth of a Celtic commonwealth need have little or no relation to facts. As a creative myth, like Dostoevsky's Russian Idea, it would retain its volatility, and provide the vision with which the facts must be confronted.[15] Like Pearse or Arnold, MacDiarmid made 'fictions which had a regenerated society as their aim'. All three were essentially pedagogues, 'with society as their audience, and the idea of civilization as their subject'.[16] Grieve, in fact, had been introduced to Pearse's work as a boy, by his schoolteacher, T.S. Cairncross. It is no coincidence that Pearse's one disciple amongst literary critics — Daniel Corkery — was singled out for high praise by MacDiarmid and noted as an influence. He figures crucially, for example, in MacDiarmid's seminal essay 'English Ascendancy in British Literature', which T.S. Eliot accepted for publication in *The Criterion* of July 1931. Writing to Neil Gunn on 13 March, Grieve referred to this forthcoming publication as 'carrying the War into the enemies' camp'. And in a postscript, he added 'Delighted at progress of Inverness Branch SNP. But intend shortly to put the "cat among the pigeons". Fed up with SNP policy altogether — and SNP personnel too. Nothing for it really but Clann Albann.'[17]

Volume II, number 1 of *The Modern Scot* (April 1931) included an article on Scottish National Development by Grieve, with a section titled 'Clann Albann'. Here he affirmed the value of the role to be played by 'the left wing of the younger generation' in the development of 'militant methods' to achieve nationhood, denigrating the politics of compromise and the methods of the National Party (although he was not expelled from that party until 1933). Yet the 'secret society' remains curiously intangible, and the terms in which Grieve described it were both threatening and cautious: 'Clann Albann is surely if slowly growing and maturing its plans', he said, going on to mention 'one significant instance' where militant action had actually taken place, but where the event had been hushed up by the popular press and the media.

In the next issue (July 1931), MacDiarmid (not Grieve) had a poem published under the title 'From Work in Progress' which appears in the *Complete Poems* as 'Kinsfolk'.[18] This, he explained in a footnote, is 'the first few stanzas of Part I of Mr MacDiarmid's big new poem, "Clann Albann" the complete scheme of which is as follows: — Dedicatory Poem, Prologue; Part I. The Muckle Toon, First Interlude; Part II. Fier Comme Un Ecossais, Second Interlude; Part III. Demidium Anima Meae, Third Interlude; Part IV. The Uncanny Scot, Fourth Interlude; Part V. With a Lifting of the Head. Epilogue.'

'Clann Albann' had ceased to refer to a secret militant nationalist political society and had come to signify a long, structurally conceived but incomplete poem. From this point on, MacDiarmid's comments on 'Clann Albann' referred to this projected poem, parts of which were published in the books MacDiarmid produced in the early 1930s. *First Hymn to Lenin and Other Poems* appeared in 1931; *Second Hymn to Lenin* and *Scots Unbound and Other Poems* appeared in 1932.

What happened? Why does the existence (or even possibility) of the nationalist activist group disappear at this point? And by what transformation of intentionality does its name come to entitle a poem?

One answer might be that it did not disappear, but MacDiarmid stopped talking about it. It would have been a very astute move, to label a poem with the title and let the secret society develop its activities in secret. But little evidence survives in any form to suggest that militant Scottish nationalism achieved anything of material significance through the action of such a group in the 1930s, although 'Clann Albainn' did resurface in 1948 with the actual land seizures on Lord Brocket's Knoydart estates, and the name was used on various occasions in connection with land occupations in the late 1940s and early 1950s. But of greater interest to us here is MacDiarmid's shift of intention. If, in the late 1920s and early 1930s, 'Clan Albann' was merely a Miss Jean Brodie-type of fantasy, what led to its becoming a 'poetry of fact'?

Consider, for a moment, the meaning of the words. MacDiarmid himself said they meant 'The Children of Scotland' (past, present, and future). Note the protective, bonding sense that comes through the phrase; the sense of essential potentiality; and of national identity. In the first section of the poem's plan, as outlined above, the poetry is to be centred on Langholm, in Dumfriesshire, the 'Muckle Toon' where MacDiarmid (or rather, Grieve) was born. And among the poems surviving as individual pieces which were to be part of this section, many deal affectionately and evocatively with Grieve's birthplace, celebrating boyhood delights in its rivers and landscapes. There is a sense here of a primary constituency, a world of one's earliest knowing, an audience one encounters in early youth. In *A Drunk Man*, MacDiarmid had talked about the order in which identities could be established between husband and wife: first, themselves; secondly, their children; beyond that, their race. And that suggests another fictional constituency, which, it is hoped, might be transformed by the action of poets like MacDiarmid himself. Or better, it suggests a world in which a citizenry might transform and transcend itself, in an act of surmounting, and create out of itself a better society.

The conjunction of political desire and poetic intention is most clearly felt at exactly this point. The aspiration of a nation's children, or youth — remember the letter to Helen Cruickshank, mentioning 'a lot of correspondence . . . with young people (for the most part) all over Scotland' — coalesces with a sense of what that nation might be. And frustrated in the practical political sphere, MacDiarmid's production of verse increased drastically. Writing to Gunn on 14 June 1932, he said he had composed more poetry in the last two months than in the previous two years: and '*Clann Albann* will be some book.'[19] Ten days later, he wrote to Gunn once more hoping to be able 'to finish Vol. I of *Clann Albann* (which — at present rate of progress — won't take me more than another month)'.[20] When, in 1933, MacDiarmid discussed the project at length, little enough progress had been made. *The Scots Observer* ('A Weekly Review of Religion, Life and Letters') of 12 August 1933 carried an article called 'Clann Albann: An Explanation' — but it offered no explanation whatever of the relation between the political activist group, the poetic project, and the vision of a renaissant society. Instead, it offered an exposition of the projected poem in reply to the criticism that his last three books had consisted of 'detachable items'. MacDiarmid admitted he had no idea when the 'very long poem' they were part of would be published and that, in any case, he was doubtful if it could ever be written in any satisfactory form. 'Even at the best the scheme as realized must fall short of the conception.'

The conception was affirmed, the ambition undiminished, but the confidence was faltering. He went on in the same article to describe the various sections of the projected poem, emphasising the autobiographical detail and the progressive development of the work from birth to a spiritual awakening. He insisted that 'in many cases — some of which have raised questions — the opinions expressed do not correspond with my own views, but are balanced against the opposite views expressed elsewhere in the poem'. (This insistence was to be echoed in an explanation of *In Memoriam James Joyce*, where MacDiarmid claimed to be using Joycean precepts rather than his own unalloyed convictions.) He went on: 'it should also be noted that it is part of the plan that each volume [of *Clann Albann*] consists of different kinds of poetry, and that the whole series is thus designed to represent a systematic progression in the techniques and kinds of imagery and subject matter hitherto employed.'

He said that the poems that had already appeared were mainly from the first, preliminary, 'boyhood' section, and may suggest (since the poem is to be, in a sense, allegorical) that mankind is only in its boyhood, and that all its ideas are as provisional and susceptible of change as those between a boy and a man. He also drew attention to the title, 'Clann Albann', the children of Scotland, 'past, present, and future': 'the aspects from which they are envisaged from book to book are intended to correspond to past, present, the double present (i.e. the apparent and the real), future and finally, *sub specie aeternitatis.*'

Clann Albann was never written.[21] For MacDiarmid, the desire to impose an order retrospectively on the poems he had published by insisting on a grand plan underlying them suggests his own recognition of a loss of formal control. Criticism has followed this recognition. Remarking on the difference between *A Drunk Man Looks at the Thistle* and *To Circumjack Cencrastus*, Kenneth Buthlay noted how 'one feels, not so much that MacDiarmid has lost his power, but rather that he has lost his grip'.[22] But if MacDiarmid's grand plan was in part a rearguard action (and it is clear from the 'Explanation' that he is defending himself), it was also a *projected* idea, both in the continuing desire to write a long poem and in the sense that the *Clann Albann* project had a definite structure. In applying or trying to apply that structure, MacDiarmid was attempting to impose coherence upon a constantly growing number of fragments. The contradictions inherent in the project proved impossible to reconcile.

It is a commonplace of MacDiarmid criticism that contradiction or paradox is at the heart of his vision, but there are different kinds of contradiction, different kinds of paradox. Two opposite opinions may be equally true, and there are contradictions which, when explored and understood, go on enriching each other by their difficult relationship. As Dr Johnson's Imlac remarked, 'Inconsistencies cannot both be right, but, imputed to man, they may both be true.'[23] *Transformation* is as central to MacDiarmid's work as contradiction. It is the event which unties conflicts and isolates items, while recognising and at times representing their capacity for change. In poetry, MacDiarmid understood this to have a political as well as an aesthetic dimension: 'what Socialist poets in particular must know — if they are to be poets of any value as poets — is the difference between "critical realism" which is the depicting of present evils or the acceptance of even the best of "things as they are," and "Socialist realism," which should concentrate on the germ of transformation.'[24] It is exactly that 'germ of transformation' which is essential to poems like 'The Watergaw', 'The Eemis Stane', 'Scunner', 'Harry Semen', and 'Perfect', or in the climactic turn of the Great Wheel, the First World War, in *A Drunk Man Looks at the Thistle*, or in the moment of '*ek-stasis*' towards the end of *In Memoriam James Joyce*.[25]

There are some contradictions, however, which cancel out, where the relations represented are too difficult to bear or too complex to carry through. In MacDiarmid's plan for *Clann Albann*, there are contradictions at the most basic level. He was already (by 1933) aware of the point at which he wanted the poem to end, a Dantean point of spiritual achievement and realisation. He declared his desire for an allegorical poem which would relate the physical history of his own life to the spirit of national unification. However, what we have, in the pieces that were printed as part of *Clann Albann*, is an overtly autobiographical poetry with a first person singular constantly shifting. Unlike the persona of the drunk man, this protagonist is undefined by any kind of full, coherent, developed expression, and appears only in fragments.

There remains one point to consider a little further: the adoption of the title from the provisional nationalist militant group to the desired but unrealised poem. It may be doubtful if *Clann Albann* in either sense was anywhere near the point of revealing itself fully, but the relation between what we might call a 'Supreme Faction' and the proposed poem is striking. MacDiarmid was determined to organise and produce both society (within the nation) and poem (within the international literary world), and he brought to the attempt his characteristic mixture of ambition, faith, and urgency. He claimed that *Clann Albann* was a faction of people being organised in order 'to act'. Concurrently, he was nurturing a deep and growing desire to write a more 'effective' poetry — not simply verse which would 'win through to the man in the street,/The wife by the hearth'[26] but poetry which would, at the very least, show an awareness of their condition and address the task of changing it. 'The poetry of the past', he wrote, 'can only be properly appreciated when it is seen in its proper historical setting. The whole position of poetry has been menaced by the insistence in schools and elsewhere on the poetry of the past, divorced from vital current interests . . . and by our insistence that the general public must have things made as simple as possible for them. This, to my mind, is simply not true, and only a "superior" bourgeois assumption.'[27] That being so, he could hardly see the effect and value of the poem as anything but political, and pragmatic at that: 'Poetry has nothing to do with religious mysticism but is entirely an affair of the practical reason. Our mind is part and parcel of terrestrial nature, in which it is immersed, and there and only there can it meet with requitals and fulfillments.'[28]

At this period in his career (with the 'First Hymn to Lenin' and 'The Seamless Garment' published in 1931, and the 'Second Hymn' and 'On the Ocean Floor' in 1935) MacDiarmid was beginning to examine the contradiction in his commitment to both an extreme élitism and an extreme sense of solidarity. 'On the Ocean Floor' is a perfect example:

> Now more and more on my concern with the lifted waves of
>   genius gaining
> I am aware of the lightless depths that beneath them lie:
> And as one who hears their tiny shells incessantly raining
> On the ocean floor as the foraminifera die.

Here is Edwin Morgan's comment:

> MacDiarmid is saying that he has been too self-centred, too concerned with the individual genius, the outstanding person, he had forgotten the great mass of ordinary mankind; but now, in the thirties, in the period of economic and political crisis, he suddenly becomes aware of what as a Communist he should be aware of — the masses themselves, dying and falling anonymously like foraminifera, but from whom something is going to rise up, a new society, like the chalk cliffs rising from the depths of the sea.[29]

The change that takes place in MacDiarmid's poetry in the 1930s, from the 'parts' of *Clann Albann* contained in *First Hymn to Lenin and Other Poems* (1931) through to a poem like 'Island Funeral' from *The Islands of Scotland* (1939), is a change in attitude and concern and subject, but it is also a change of technical procedure, a change into a different kind of poetry altogether. It is a change, in fact, in the function of the poetry itself.

Epic

The overt espousal of communism which was made evident in the essay of 21 January 1933 for *The Scots Observer*, 'Not Merely Philosophical Piety: Communism Means a Clean Sweep', was paralleled in the poetry in specific praise of Lenin, in the recognition of mankind as just that suffering and unrealised force Edwin Morgan describes, but also most importantly in the kind of poetry being written and projected. For the poetry MacDiarmid wanted was a communist poetry, neither dismissive of the pre-Marxist cultural heritage nor devoted to 'hothouse proletarian' philistinism of the 'boy-meets-tractor' variety, but a 'poetry of to-day, not of the past';[30] which is to say, a poetry not afraid to be dated and placed, having a local and timely application.

It was still to be 'long' poetry. In the middle of the decade, in 1936, MacDiarmid wrote and published the essay 'Charles Doughty and the Need for Heroic Poetry', which first appeared in *The Modern Scot*. He wants, he says, poetry which consciously presents national characteristics, poetry which is in itself 'monumental' and 'heroic', poetry which actively involves historical knowledge rather than impressionistic detail, and which accords a heroic position to the poet.[31] Doughty and his poetry are conceived in imagery evocative of the desert and the heroic self, when MacDiarmid writes of the long poem being the only work 'equal to the perspectives of modern life and the horizons now opening before us'. The poet is defined as one in opposition to received literary values: 'Doughty has gone unrecognized or obstinately opposed'. The essay opens by making a generalisation about the connection between political activity and the form of poetic production: 'Only in the U.S.S.R. today is the trend of poetic effort towards epic — in keeping with the great enterprise afoot in that country . . . '. As for Doughty, his genius too lay 'in the direction of epic'. That connection between political and poetic activity was something MacDiarmid repeatedly announced and demonstrated. His epic poetry is not merely 'political' in the narrow sense of being connected to political action by ties of commitment. Rather, it engages its readers in such a way as to alter the nature of their interpretive reading of the text.

In much literary criticism, the word 'poetry' is taken to signify 'lyric poetry'. In *Lyric Time: Dickinson and the Limits of Genre*, Sharon Cameron writes:

> Unlike the drama, whose province is conflict, and unlike the novel or narrative, which connects isolated moments of time to create a story multiply peopled and framed by a social context, the lyric voice is solitary and generally speaks out of a single moment in time. . . . The lyric's propensity [is] to interiorize as ambiguity or outright contradiction those conflicts that other mimetic forms conspicuously exteriorize and

then allocate to discrete characters who enact them in the manifest pull of opposite points of view.[32]

There is a tacit assumption here, as Marjorie Perloff has suggested, that the lyric is to be opposed to 'drama' or 'the novel or narrative'; but the possibility of non-lyrical poems is not considered. It is that assumption which MacDiarmid (like his American contemporaries Pound, Williams, and Olson) blasts. MacDiarmid's early Scots lyrics in *Sangschaw* and *Penny Wheep* are justly renowned; *A Drunk Man Looks at the Thistle* is a subtle extension and reorganisation of lyrical impulse, accommodating itself to satirical intention and abstract speculation in a way that implicitly includes the dramatic (or gestural). But it maintains a lyric ability to 'interiorise', and in its climax, the speaker undergoes a kind of 'Romantic Agony'. This is not the procedure of MacDiarmid's later poetry.

If MacDiarmid had abandoned the idea of the structured poem sequence *Clann Albann* was to have been, he none the less fostered the intention and affirmed the desire to write an 'epic' poetry. It was to be 'Not like epics of the past, except in scale' (as he wrote in an essay on Ezra Pound).[33] And yet, he insisted on the applicability of the term 'epic' and the immediate need for 'Long poems . . . poems *de longue haleine* — '.[34] If we are to attempt a reading of his epic poetry we must explain *our* use of the term 'epic' first. How should we understand MacDiarmid's later poetry in relation to epic literature? What connects it generically to epics of the past?

To present a retrospective view of epic literature is to confront the task of placing in an ongoing tradition texts as disparate as *Beowulf* and *Moby Dick* or writers as different as Dante and Doughty. The primary difficulty for such a reconciliation is the fundamental distinction between oral and written epic. As Albert Lord reminds us:

> There is no direct line of literary development from the *chansons de geste* to the *Henriade*, or from *Beowulf* to *Paradise Lost*. Our Western literary tradition of epic stems from Homer through Apollonius and Virgil. Virgil did not write in Saturnians, nor in any direct descendant of them; nor did Milton write in alliterative Germanic verse, nor in any direct descendant of it, because there were no real direct descendants of these native oral traditional meters. Oral tradition did not become transferred or transmuted into a literary tradition of epic, but was only moved further and further into the background, literally into the back country, until it disappeared.[35]

Be that as it may, writers and critics have often sought to establish a continuity, a tradition of epic which, in Lord's words, 'stems from Homer'. When Erich Auerbach began his great survey of Western literature, *Mimesis*, he took Homer, and a theory of epic poetry, as his starting point. His treatment of the Homeric poems as readable texts illuminates an aspect of epic literature which is directly reflected in the technical necessities of oral transmission: the way in which the externalising of events retards the progress of the narrative. Auerbach, following the arguments of Goethe and Schiller, considered that the distinction between epic and tragic writing lay in the lack, in the former, of suspense.[36] If events are to be suspenseful, to be hanging, dependent on an event in the future, the possibility and increasing proximity of that approaching event must always be kept at the back of the mind. In Homer, this does not happen. The story of the fall of Troy is known; but the immediate effect of what might be called digressions from the narrative is not to illumine the narrative: for the time of their duration, the narrative is forgotten.

What Auerbach perceived as a relaxation of tension, what Goethe and Schiller referred to as 'the retarding element', is a quality of written texts, texts to be read. (Auerbach began his essay with, 'Readers of the *Odyssey* will remember . . .'.) Yet it is also a quality of the poems in their historical location as oral performances. Undirected by aesthetic considerations, it resulted from a need to leave nothing that is mentioned 'half in darkness and unexternalised.' Each line of the Homeric poems brings out, externalises, its action. There is a fundamental similarity between this mode of oral epic delivery and MacDiarmid's 'plotless' epic poetry: their stark distinction from the mode of narration of the realist story, where the end is foreknown only by the narrator, according to whose laws suspense can be generated by a balancing of narrative strands. Only if the reader concedes that authority from the beginning can such suspense be generated. In this respect, there are interesting affinities between the classic realist story, with its ultimately dominant authorial control, and the lyric poem, with its unified structure and coherent, normally solitary, voice. In a song, for instance, the end is 'seen from the beginning'. But with epic there is no urgent need — which is to say, no lawfully prescribed way — to end, and so there are important connections with procedures of journalism (by its nature, a continuing process, a 'work in progress').

The poet implied in *The Kind of Poetry I Want* is (like Doughty) isolated and opposed: 'a Tarzan among apes all/Suddenly murderously inimical'.[37] When MacDiarmid's rallying cry for heroic poetry is raised, it is worth remembering Galileo's remonstrative reply to Andrea Sarti in Brecht's play. Andrea's 'Unhappy is the land that has no heroes' prompts Galileo: 'No. Unhappy is the land that is in need of heroes.'[38] Yet a quality of the term 'epic' is that it involves a largeness of scale, an inclusiveness. The word itself can connote heroism. In Europe, in fact, the epic came to be termed the heroic poem in the seventeenth century, and the classic retrospective discussions of the genre by H.M. Chadwick, W.P. Ker, and C.M. Bowra all discuss the heroic element.[39] Bowra (*Heroic Poetry* was published in 1952) exemplifies this:

> The fate of Achilles or Sigurth or Roland is the fate not of an abstract Everyman but of an individual who is both an example of pre-eminent manhood and emphatically himself . . . The hero who champions a people's rights has taken a new form in modern times when the word 'people' is used less of a race or a nation than of the nameless masses who are helpless to assert their rights without a leader . . . In Northern Russia the Revolution of 1917 has inspired poems in which Lenin is a hero in this sense.[40]

Epic oral poets were, and were understood to be, essential to their society. Eric Havelock points out that Plato's relegation of poets from the ideal Republic may have had less to do with what we have come to understand as the ideal tenets of Platonic philosophy than the act of a philosopher committed to the transformation of a society out of an oral culture and into a culture where writing would supersede the functions of the epic oral poets. Plato was describing and attacking the oral culture out of which Greek abstract thought — Plato himself — was struggling to extricate itself.[41]

Epic poets of the twentieth century, however, are essential, and understood to be essential, only to themselves, and to that small number of people who constitute their readership. The most monumental forerunner (MacDiarmid called him a 'harbinger') of twentieth-century epic poetry, Doughty (in 1906, *The Dawn in Britain* ran to six volumes), remains, despite MacDiarmid's praise, consigned to oblivion in social and literary-historical terms, and read by few even of the learned. In *The Pisan Cantos* Pound poignantly recalls Yeats and himself, 'at Stone Cottage in Sussex by the waste moor' and asks:

> did we ever get to the end of Doughty:
>   The Dawn in Britain?
>   perhaps not[42]

Where the last ironic phrase refers not only bathetically to the failure of his own and Yeats's attempt to finish the poem (Pound read it out aloud to Yeats in the evenings, after the day's secretarial work was over) but also bitterly to the failure of the dawn in Britain to arrive. Pound's own epic, *The Cantos*, remains to literate readers more attractive than Doughty's, but its lack of influence upon the social, political, and common uses of language has not effectively lessened through the course of the century. And yet, having said that, one must acknowledge that the point was not merely to influence the political world. Pound certainly hoped to do that, visiting Mussolini to explain his economic theories point by point. But just as important was the desire to alter the provenance of poetry, to return to the domain of poetry those areas of concern which had fallen into the hands of historians, philosophers, priests, and novelists. (And we should note the appropriateness of the vocabulary of territorial conquest there.)

There are three ways in which heroism is involved in Mac-Diarmid's epic poetry. There is a sense of 'the poet', the poem's first person singular, as 'heroic' (which we shall deal with in more detail later). Secondly, there is a sense of heroic quest, of the 'impossible and imperative job'[43] to which poet and poetry both are obliged to address themselves. (At the heart of this lies the hero's function in epic as a representative of 'the people'. When asked what was the 'controlling principle' of *In Memoriam James Joyce*, MacDiarmid replied: 'There's the absolute coherence of the writer's intellectual quest into all the possibilities of the language. . . . '[44]) There is, thirdly, a kind of heroism in the achievement of the poetry itself, in the very fact that it was written at all. As Basil Bunting said of *The Cantos*: 'There are the Alps.'[45]

If the poet was a solitary figure and the poem a solitary achievement, they proclaimed a social function for themselves in national terms. Since the early 1930s, when he elaborated theories of a federation of Celtic nations, linking Scotland with Wales and the new Irish Republic, MacDiarmid's work implicitly maintained (and often explicitly stated) a dogmatic nationalism. This he considered to be in accordance with his Marxist beliefs. It may appear that MacDiarmid's vision of Scotland and his idea of a 'Celtic dynamic' were, in the 1930s, direct descendants of the nationalisms rampant in Europe in the nineteenth century. These had led to the use of oral epics for nationalist propaganda, glorifying national heroes and depicting the struggles of the nation against outside foes. The hero was a 'national' hero, the poems 'national' epics; and in some of the Slavic countries the word *narodni* exercised a useful ambiguity, since it meant both 'folk' and 'national'. Finland's national poet Elias Lönnrot, for example, created an epic cycle from a mass of scattered folk verses, and stitched together the *Kalevala*, Finland's national epic (published in 1849). One might also consider the *Nibelungenlied*, which had been written down about the year 1200 in 9000 lines of four-line stanzas, but was recycled by Richard Wagner as *Der Ring des Nibelungen* in the second half of the nineteenth century, and has a notorious place in the rise of fascist Germany.

MacDiarmid's nationalism, however, did not merely aspire to the nineteenth-century ideal of a national state in which the commodity market could be controlled through a homogenised economy and language. The entire effort of MacDiarmid's work is opposed to such linguistic homogeneity as is fostered in the bourgeois nation state. The theoretical grounds for MacDiarmid's nationalism in Marxist terms are to be found in Lenin's articles of April to June 1914, published as *The Right of Nations to Self-Determination*.[46] Once again, it is the Irish example from which MacDiarmid takes off. Lenin quotes the discussion of Marx and Engels on the Irish Question, drawing attention to their reconsideration of the assumption that revolutionary national liberation movements are bourgeois by nature, and showing how they came to understand that Irish nationalism was vitally important not only for Ireland but for England too. Paraphrasing Marx, Lenin concluded: 'The English working class will never be free until Ireland is free from the English yoke.'[47] There was, of course, a strong component of MacDiarmid's nationalism which unquestioningly accepted ideals of separate political identity and economic autonomy, but there was also an understanding that national identity would involve federation, and, in British terms, was part of the struggle of proletarian emancipation. The one most crucial condition of that struggle for MacDiarmid was not economics but language.

Traditionally, epics deal with epic subjects: the foundation of great states, the epic journey, the fall of civilisations or their beginning; they celebrate acts of significant magnitude. It is in that sense, exactly, that MacDiarmid's 'subject' is language. But, in so far as his poetry is written in language, language cannot function in the poetry merely as a 'subject'. It has to enact what it represents; it must embody and enliven the political thrust of MacDiarmid's argument while it is the instrument by which that argument is articulated. An example might help here. A remarkable passage in

In Memoriam James Joyce likens the exploration of the polar ice-cap to the exploration that can be done through dictionaries:

When climbing on to the ice-cap a little south of Cape
    Bismarck
And keeping the nunataks of Dronning Louises Land on our
    left
We travel five days
On tolerable ice in good weather
With few bergs to surmount   5
And no crevasses to delay us.
Then suddenly our luck turns.
A wind of 120 miles an hour blows from the East,
And the plateau becomes a playground of gales
And the novel light gives us snow-blindness.   10
We fumble along with partially bandaged eyes
Our reindeer-skin kamiks worn into holes
And no fresh sedge-grass to stump them with.
We come on ice-fields like mammoth ploughlands
And mountainous séracs which would puzzle an Alpine   15
    climber.
That is what adventuring in dictionaries means,
All the abysses and altitudes of the mind of man,
Every test and trial of the spirit,
Among the débris of all past literature
And raw material of all the literature to be.   20

                                                    C.P., p.823

The immediacy of the descriptions and the force of the metaphor are startling. The passage as a whole is remarkable because no privilege is being given to one description over another. It is a similar quality to that which Auerbach discerned in the Homeric poems. No tension is set up between the traversal of the ice-fields and the traversal of the dictionaries. Rather, they are each foregrounded in their turn and presented as things of equal significance. That supplies the power to the 'meaning' referred to in line 16. There is no 'passive' reality presented by means of a vivid image. The word 'means' refers both to 'adventuring in dictionaries' and to the word 'That' at the beginning of the line, so the juxtaposition is effected semantically rather than imagistically. MacDiarmid does not present a mimetically petrified vision of 'reality'; his poetry enacts a dynamic understanding of literature and reality, in which struggle is unceasing. The passage conveys the excitement of exploration as an exhilarating consequence of understanding truth to be not correspondence but struggle.

There is, furthermore, a sense in which the passage works as metaphor in a more transparent way, and in this it will prove typical of *In Memoriam James Joyce*. The entire description of the journey across the ice-cap is transcribed from John Buchan's 1933 novel *A Prince of the Captivity*.[48] It consists of two passages, skilfully interleaved and run together. I have italicised the significant sentences.

> At first fortune had been with Adam and his party. *They climbed on to the ice cap a little south of Cape Bismarck, and, keeping the nunataks of Dronning Louises Land on their left, travelled for five days on tolerable ice in good weather, with few bergs to surmount and no crevasses to delay them. Then suddenly their luck turned. A wind of 120 miles an hour blew from the east, and the plateau became the playground of gales. They came on ice fields like mammoth ploughlands*, where they scarcely made three miles in the day, *and mountainous seracs which would have puzzled an Alpine climber.* They found valleys with lakes and rivers of blue ice out of which they had to climb painfully. There was trouble, too, with the dogs.
>
> Book I, Chapter 3, Part II
>
> It was hard travelling for both men, for *their reindeer-skin kamiks had been worn into holes, and there was no fresh sedge grass with which to stuff them. The novel light induced snow blindness in both, and they had to fumble along with their eyes partially bandaged.* Adam felt his strength steadily ebbing. Tasks which on the outward journey he would have made light of were now beyond his power.
>
> Book I, Chapter 3, Part IV[49]

MacDiarmid takes lines 1 to 9 of this part of the poem from the first passage, grafts in lines 10 and 11 from the second passage, follows them with what precedes them in Buchan's prose (lines 12 and 13 in the poem), then returns to the first passage of Buchan for lines 14 and 15. His rearrangements are deft. It is not a simple transposition of material from prose to verse but a careful reordering of constituent elements. He knows what to leave out. Moreover, there are characteristic alterations in pitch. MacDiarmid is not writing a narrative: tense in *In Memoriam James Joyce* is constantly shifted from past to present to future, and the characters of Buchan's novel in the passages quoted above are telescoped into an inclusive first person plural, which implies the reader's participation as much as the poet's. The poem does indeed reflect a 'novel light', and our eyes are half-blind to it if we do not realise the extent to which traditional, print-bred notions of copyright and literary property are undermined by MacDiarmid's practice.

When MacDiarmid asserted that the scale of the modern epic poem was the only thing it had in common with epics of the past, he provided a rubric under which all the categories I have been considering might be included: the senses of heroism and nationality, the epic subject, and the notion that identity and struggle are inseparable. The term epic itself implies magnitude, inclusiveness, aspiration. Epic poetry is full of beginnings and endings, arrivals and departures; it is advocating and enacting, full of self-proclamation and oppositions. As Wole Soyinka says in *Myth, Literature and the African World* (writing from a situation where oral epic persists and affects written work directly): 'The epic celebrates the victory of the human spirit over forces inimical to self-extension. It concretises in the form of action the arduous birth of the individual or communal entity, creates a new being through utilising and stressing the language of self-glorification to which human nature is healthily prone.'[50] Thomas Greene noted in his study of 'epic continuity' that 'the energy of epic breathes a kind of excitement like the basic human excitement of living bodily in a physical word. . . . The language which imparts epic energy must be itself in some sense *alive*. . . . Language can do more than denote, it can possess, exorcise, invoke, bind with a spell . . . it has magical demonic properties transcending its concern with statement.'[51] For MacDiarmid, language itself exists in the political struggle:

> There lie hidden in language elements that effectively
>   combined
> Can utterly change the nature of man
>
> C.P., p.781

From Homer to Brecht

Since Homer the metaphor has borne that element of the poetic which conveys cognition; its use establishes the *correspondences* between physically most remote things — as when in the *Iliad* the tearing onslaught of fear and grief on the hearts of the Achaians corresponds to the combined onslaught of the winds from north and west on the dark waters (*Iliad* IX, 1–8); or when the approaching of the army moving to battle in line after line corresponds to the sea's long billows which, driven by the wind, gather head far out on the sea, to roll to shore line after line, and then burst on the land in thunder (*Iliad*, IV, 422–3). Metaphors are the means by which the oneness of the world is poetically brought about ... Linguistic 'transference' enables us to give material form to the invisible — 'A mighty fortress is our God' — and thus to render it capable of being experienced.[52]

Thus Hannah Arendt introduces Walter Benjamin's *Illuminations*. Benjamin suggests a further sense of 'epic' applicable to MacDiarmid's poetry: that is what was made of the term by another major, revolutionary writer, Brecht. If anyone can bring us succinctly from Homer to Brecht it is Benjamin. In Benjamin's essay 'The Work of Art in the Age of Mechanical Reproduction' we get an astonishingly precise summary of the ground bases of the forces affecting our appreciation and our critical sensibilities, and a clear exposition of the way those forces are at work on artists themselves, both as restrictive and yet also as potentially liberating principles. It was first published (in *Zeitschrift fur Sozialforschung*, V, [1]) in 1936 — the year of MacDiarmid's essay on Doughty.

> '*Fiat ars — pereat mundus,*' says Fascism, and, as Marinetti admits, expects war to supply the artistic gratification of a sense perception that has been changed by technology. This is evidently the consummation of '*l'art pour l'art.*' Mankind, which in Homer's time was an object of contemplation for the Olympian gods, now is one for itself. Its self-alienation has reached such a degree that it can experience its own destruction as an aesthetic pleasure of the first order. This is the situation of politics which Fascism is rendering aesthetic. Communism responds by politicizing art.[53]

Brecht and MacDiarmid

Raymond Williams's critical account of the modern theatre, *Drama from Ibsen to Eliot*, first published in 1952, was revised in 1964 and reissued in 1968 under the title *Drama from Ibsen to Brecht*. The alteration is significant of the degree to which the influence of Brecht on English-speaking critics was growing. In the 1940s, Brecht was not well known in Britain at all, and there is only a cluster of critical articles in English on his work before the mid-1950s.[54] MacDiarmid himself does not mention Brecht very much. There is a reference in *Lucky Poet* (1943), where Brecht's name occurs among a list of other writers. MacDiarmid recalls, approvingly,

> Heinrich Mann, Julien Benda, Bert Brecht, Oscar Maria Graf, Jean Cassou, Emil Ludwig, Hans Marchwita, Karin Michaelis, Gustav Regler, Stefan Zweig, H.G. Wells, Karel Capek, and Romain Rolland saying: 'And before going to sleep in the anarchic and cruel world chaos where I hear the shock of colliding masses of diverse nations and differing spirit, I recall the wise and clear thought of Lenin, and I know that our freedom is secured for we are right.'[55]

There is very little in that to suggest MacDiarmid had been profoundly impressed at this stage by Brecht's work. There is, however, a telling reference in the poem 'Glasgow' quoted in *Lucky Poet*, not to Brecht but to Marc Blitzstein, whose satirical reviews and cabaret language influenced Brecht as effective anti-Nazi propaganda:

> It's a far cry from the *Jolly Beggars* of Robert Burns
> To Mark Blitzstein's *The Cradle Will Rock*,
> The measure of the leeway Scottish poets must make up.
> Mr Blitzstein's unjolly proletarians are not beggars
> But demanders . . .
>
> > C.P., pp.648–9

The contrast, the poem goes on to make clear, is between the compelling urgency of contemporary issues for poetry and the satirical aptitude a poet like Burns had in his day, which is no longer useful in dealing with steel strikes. Blitzstein translated *The Threepenny Opera* for productions in 1954 in New York and 1956 in London. MacDiarmid also produced a version (first performed in London in 1972) after a meeting with Helene Weigel (fondly remembered in *The Company I've Kept*). Stefan Brecht wrote to MacDiarmid in 1965: 'I have long urged Mr Cullen of Methuen's and Dr Czech, to approach you about translating such work of my father's as the Caucasian Chalk Circle . . . '. However, nothing seems to have come of this.[56]

It is often forgotten that an important part of the Scottish literary renaissance at its earliest stages was the demand for a Scottish national drama, and where MacDiarmid describes what he has in mind, the effects he seems to be after bear a striking similarity to Brechtian effects. As early as November 1922, in the 'Causerie' or editorial section of the *Scottish Chapbook*, MacDiarmid discusses the lack of an authentic Scottish drama:

> I do not attach the slightest importance to the present Scottish Players' movement. Blake, Brandane, Neil Grant, J.J. Bell, Hugh Robertson, and others are writing plays superficially Scottish — or at any rate superficially subscribing to the stock conception of what is Scottish — but, apart from the fact that these plays are in every respect inferior to English or Irish plays in their respective *genres*, and are entirely destitute of literary distinction or significance, it must be emphasised that in embodiment and effect they are not only not Scottish but anti-Scottish . . .
>
> There has never been a Scottish drama. If there is ever to be one the psychological factors which prevented its developing naturally as in other countries must be overcome. I believe that the temperament and tendencies of the Scottish nation have so radically altered within recent years that the inhibiting agencies have been removed, and that the creation of a genuine Scottish drama is now feasible. It will have to create its own forms and, hypothetically, at any rate (for the actuality will remain commercially impossible for some years yet — the commercial success of the Scottish Players proves this) its own theatre. The difference in form and production will be equivalent to the stupendous and tremendously underrated difference between Scottish and English psychology. The extension of the theatre into the midst of the audience, or the abolition of the platform and scenic detachment altogether — the extensive readaptation of the method of progress by soliloquy along lines appropriate to Scottish self-disclosure — the deliberate extirpation of English influences and rejection of English expedients of all kinds and the search for effective Continental affinities — all these must be considered.[57]

It was too early (in 1922) for such a Scottish theatre to be erected, but the attention to the relations of psychology, economics, and nationalism with the desire for radical political theatrical development was certainly there, and a strong desire for political effect was registered. It took half a century, a world war, Tyrone Guthrie's re-entrenchment of middle-class theatre, and the eventual rise to prominence of the 7:84 Theatre Company before that desire found anything like an articulate expression in Scotland. MacDiarmid helped.

The polemic quoted above overlooks traditions of early Scottish drama, such as the humanist tradition which produced the Latin tragedies of George Buchanan, or the popular tradition of morality plays. Conspicuous by his absence from MacDiarmid's reckoning is Sir David Lyndsay (1486–1555), who was at the centre of both the literary and the political culture of his time. Lyndsay's great political allegory, *Ane Satyre of the Thrie Estaits*, had an enormous public impact in Scotland on the eve of the Reformation. If MacDiarmid forgot to mention Lyndsay in 1922, he corrected himself in 1943, noting, 'The vital thing about Lyndsay to-day is the fact that he opposed great established powers, spoke to (and for) the great mass of the working people, and in circumstances in many ways not dissimilar to those the latter are now facing, succeeded in discharging to tremendous effect and with great historical results something very like the task to which the satirical poets and poetic dramatists of the Left are to-day addressing themselves in this and other countries.'[58]

However, when MacDiarmid reviewed Brecht's *Collected Poems* in 1976, it was to approve Brecht's genius 'not as a dramatist, but far more importantly, as a great poet'.[59] The difference between the two writers was essentially that between a playwright and a poet. MacDiarmid lacked the dramatist's single most important qualification: the ability to create *others*. The first person of MacDiarmid's poems is protean, similar to the Brechtian survivor, the character who has suffered much and travelled far, who changes his role to suit his circumstances, who, through being empty, consenting, pliant, adaptable, can exchange roles and identities (the drunk man, the victim of *Cencrastus*, Lenin's praise-singer, the madman in the 'Ode to All Rebels', the metaphysical chemist of *The Kind of Poetry I Want*). Yet MacDiarmid's first person is alive and vital in the same way as Azdak or Galileo. He is engaged and exhilarated by experience, in a way that that more famous 'disinterested' sage of twentieth-century poetry, Tiresias, is not. The sense of progress which MacDiarmid gives us, the survivor-sense of an Azdak, the ability both to adapt and to provide, suggests the concern shared with Brecht in the possibility of future development, and here we might recall the project of *Clann Albann*, and the children of Scotland. Brecht's work is full of children. They are there in the poems and the plays, learning, reading, playing, asking questions, and teaching their elders. There is nothing really comparable in Pound or Eliot to MacDiarmid's sense of unborn humanity and children — the future generations, whether revealed in the image of the growing foetus at the end of *In Memoriam James Joyce* (which reappears at the beginning of *The Kind of Poetry I Want*) or in the raging realism of 'In the Children's Hospital'.[60] The safeguarding of life for those yet to arrive and the provision of qualities outrunning present needs but considering future developments are central concerns to MacDiarmid, and, as with Brecht, they afford no opportunity for solemnity. MacDiarmid is the least solemn of twentieth-century poets. Laughter, always on the point of breaking through, continually abets a serious argument. It is laughter with a gleeful prospect, that is in profound and mischievous agreement with what Brecht wrote in the *Organum*: 'There is a great deal to man, we say; so a great deal can be made out of him. He does not have to stay the way he is now, nor does he have to be seen only as he is now, but also as he might become. We must not start with him; we must start on him. This means, however, that I must not simply set myself in his place, but must set myself facing him, to represent us all.'[61]

In conversation with Walter Benjamin in 1934, Brecht outlined a distinction between two kinds of artist, two literary types: the visionary artist, who is in earnest; and the cool-headed thinking artist, a man who is not completely in earnest. He considered himself to be 'not completely in earnest'.[62] A case might be made for MacDiarmid as a visionary artist — the Joyce poem is after all, from 'A Vision of World Language' — but it would be mistaken to consider MacDiarmid as anything other than an experimenting artist, a writer who could adapt to many forms and write in many ways. Consider the racy doggerel written to celebrate a production of *The Good Woman of Setzuan* at Glasgow's Citizen's Theatre in 1962:

> No subtle means of self-indulgence here!
> Are you afraid it'll blow up in your face?
> It's explosive enough, but smug complacence
> Will be the only casualty in this case.   C.P., p.1413

Or the poem which was published under the title 'Credo' in *A Clyack-Sheaf* (1969) but which had already appeared untitled, embedded in *In Memoriam James Joyce* (1955). With the multiple ironies and final pun, is this the work of a 'wholly serious' man?

> As a poet I'm interested in religious ideas —
> — Even Scottish ones, Wee Free ones even — as a matter of
>   fact
> Just as an alcoholic can take snake venom
> With no worse effects than a warming of the digestive tract.
>   C.P., p.798

In Memoriam James Joyce can easily accommodate a joke like this and turn immediately to a different tone. Parts of it are very earnest indeed, but there are also moments like 'Credo'. The point to recognise is that this is an accommodative poetic which proceeds by what Brecht called a radical separation of its elements.

To what extent this radical separation of elements was performed self-consciously remains debatable. In Brecht's case, we can be fairly certain about the intelligence engaging with and operating wilfully, and playfully, upon the arguments. But with MacDiarmid, there is a degree of ambiguity: there *is*, despite or alongside the humour, a sense of the light that never was on land or sea. There is a puritan aspect (which we shall have cause to return to) which breaks upon the materialism with consoling visions of liberation. It would be wrong to imply that MacDiarmid was a Marxist, pure and simple. We know that Brecht began writing from a position of philosophical anarchism, but that (especially after conversations with Karl Korsch) he became a committed socialist. MacDiarmid's communism was never as *reasonable* as Brecht's. It always maintained polemic. This was, arguably, a strategic necessity. The polemic was needed in Scotland: reasoned argument would not have achieved as much. And, to that extent, MacDiarmid's political career was enormously successful. He significantly altered the way Scots might understand themselves, and what we understand to be the limits of our ability. But there is a deeper contradiction between communism and nationalism than MacDiarmid allowed for, and there are reasons why MacDiarmid espoused fascism (as we have seen) and Major Douglas's proposed system of 'Social Credit'.

Brecht's opinions of C.H. Douglas's economic theories, if they exist, are unknown to me: but one can imagine something scathingly dismissive. The economist who exerted such an influence upon Mac-Diarmid, Ezra Pound, and other contributors to A.R. Orage's journal *The New Age*, would have been dealt with sharply by the Marxist playwright. MacDiarmid's approval of Douglas can be understood as a means of bringing economics into the world of human relationships in a way that would be liberating, but it cannot be maintained that Douglas's economic theories are reconcilable with Marxist economics, or that they are applicable in such a way as to help bring about a society whose structure would be communist. Douglas believed that taxation, credit, and the authority to create money was what empowered capitalist governments. Since the value of currency was alterable by bankers, the banks effectively controlled the government. The working class was systematically denied fair distribution and purchasing power in such a system. In order to change this, Douglas believed that 'credit' should be give to workers and producers, according to the nation's 'real wealth'; the capacity of the nation's people to produce needed goods and services. That the banks and government together had the power to print paper money independent of production was, according to Douglas, the single most important reason why the social system was so wasteful.

Douglas's vigorous attack on usury fuelled the moral outrage felt by MacDiarmid, Pound, and others, at the moneylenders. It also fuelled Pound's (and to a much lesser extent, MacDiarmid's) anti-Semitism. Douglas's warning about the existence of great secret organisations bent on the acquisition of world power appealed to Pound and MacDiarmid: after all, they considered their literary work was taking place in a global theatre. Moreover, Douglas actually thought about the necessity of artists in society. He accorded their work a place of practical efficacy, according to the guild socialism in which he believed. A better economic system would release more energy for artistic creation.

It is clear from even such a cursory look at Douglas's thinking that he believed that reform was possible 'from above', that the class structure of British society would be reformed by the application of his proposals (but not revolutionised), and that, in fact, the very idea of social revolution was not an integral part of his economic thinking. These are major departures from orthodox Marxism. (In fact, Pound was keen to suggest that Douglas's economics could be happily reconciled with orthodox fascism.) MacDiarmid, in his approval of Douglas and his occasional advocation of a 'Scottish Fascism', was clearly not always a committed, doctrinaire Marxist. He was a party member, but he did not *subscribe*.

But then neither did Brecht, entirely. Brecht's anti-Stalinist writings contrast strongly (especially in their humour and reductive tone) with MacDiarmid's pro-Stalin poetry. So that while Brecht seems, in retrospect, to have been the better Marxist, MacDiarmid seems to have been an adherent of various different causes — causes whose constitutions and aims were in real conflict. The conflict (of interests and desires and understandings and resolutions) is made evident in MacDiarmid's later poetry by just that 'separation of the elements' which Brecht describes in terms of drama. So, in MacDiarmid's case, what we are dealing with is not only a technique but also an effect. It is not only a method of composition but also the unfinished outcome of a creative struggle.

In the notes to the opera *Mahagonny*, Brecht stated that integrating the elements of opera, words, music, and production, results in a muddled 'fusion' — 'Witchcraft' — by which the spectator is befuddled. 'Whatever is intended to produce hypnosis, is likely to induce sordid intoxication, or creates fog, has got to be given up.' This means, in effect, that there has to be 'a radical separation of the elements.' It was a principle of epic theatre that it should be made up of isolable units, quotable *gestures*. 'Epic theatre is gestural', wrote Walter Benjamin. The 'gest' is separate and isolable by virtue of the interruptions between each 'gest'. 'The general educational approach of Marxism is determined by the dialectic at work between the action which is shown on the stage and the attitude of showing the action on the stage.' That dialectic could be shown at work through 'gests' and the interruptions between them. If a play proceeds in this way, it is likely not to present an organic growth of action and development, but an unfolding sequence of relationships which, whenever they are interrupted, present a number of ways in which the action could develop. This form of narrative development eschews the sense of *inevitable* progression. It demands the reasoned reflection of the spectator: where do we go from here? In *The Good Woman of Setzuan* the audience is left with exactly that question. The movement of the work itself is no straight line of development but a zigzag course.

This, being a retrospective assessment or overview of how the play proceeds (made after we have seen or read it), implies the vital importance of experimentalism in its creation. The playwright has collaborators (co-writers, fellow producers, the actors themselves) as the revolutionary has confederates, and in the very construction of the play the author and his collaborators have to experiment with various alternatives until the one that serves their purpose is discovered. There should be no hesitation in replacing one alternative with another if the occasion demands it. The implications of Galileo's recantation were extensively revised after the atom bomb was dropped on Hiroshima.

> Brecht stressed the indispensable need for experimentation in the arts, and the necessary freedom of the artist to be allowed to fail, or only partially to succeed, as the price of the invention of new aesthetic devices in any transitional epoch of history. Interior monologue, montage, or mixture of genres within a single work were all permissible and fruitful, so long as they were disciplined by a watchful truthfulness to social reality.[63]

The nature of the theatrical experiment must depend on the audience for whom it is designed, and of increasing importance to Brecht was the establishment of a theatre in which the kind of audience he wanted could be brought about. This involved a number of practical considerations such as the use of lights, make-up, stage-effects, film: considerations of dramaturgy. It also involved literary consider-ations. While it was desirable to keep the audience relaxed and capable of reasoned consideration, it was also necessary to maintain the immediate reality of the public event: 'You don't just see things in the theatre, you share an experience.'

Likewise, reading MacDiarmid's epic poetry cannot be under-stood simply as passive consumption. (For one thing, to get any-where with his references and allusions, you need the resources of a pretty good library — or at least a dictionary and an encyclopedia.) Neither Brecht's drama nor MacDiarmid's poetry invite you to stay 'inside' the texts — as a classic realist novel does. The event of reading MacDiarmid's epic poetry involves the simultaneous estrangement and participation of the reader. It involves an irregular, but continuing series of contradictions and recognitions, and its desired effect is to relocate the reader, both as a reader and also as an agent in the world, and to bring about the recognition that these are one. The denial of a completely empathetic response is part of the effect desired — in Benjamin's words, 'not so much to fill the audience with feelings — albeit possibly feelings of revolt — as to alienate the audience in a lasting manner, through thought, from the conditions in which it lives'.[64]

The desire for alienation through thought springs from didactic intentions, and Brecht and MacDiarmid are pedagogues. A funda-mental tenet of Marxism is that the point is no longer just to interpret but to alter, and it is crucial in the work of both writers, bearing directly on the forms chosen for expression. In 1934 Benja-min made this point clearly in an address delivered at the Institute for the Study of Fascism in Paris. He quotes Sergey Tretyakov's distinction between 'operative' and 'informative' writers. The 'oper-ative' writer's job is not to report but to fight; not to assume the spectator's role but to intervene actively. In 1928, in the period of total collectivisation of Russian agriculture, Tretyakov went to the 'Communist lighthouse' commune and was engaged in a variety of activities: in calling meetings, contributing to newspapers, radio, film shows, working towards the subsequent organisation of collec-tive farms. Benjamin's point is that if Tretyakov's activities are those of a journalist or a propagandist and have little to do with literary creation, then 'we must rethink the notions of literary forms or genres if we are to find forms appropriate to the literary energy of our time'. He concludes that literary forms are being melted down in a process in which many seemingly contradictory terms will lose their relevance.[65]

In a letter written in 1949 to Maurice Lindsay, MacDiarmid commented that compulsory education is always directed to ends acceptable to the economic system — whether British or Russian. 'But there is no question of the reproduction here of the Russian state of affairs; we have a very different background and are at a very different stage of historical development; our application of Communism will differ accordingly from the Russian.' He went on:

> I cannot, however, see that it is possible, let alone desirable, to keep our arts and our politics in watertight compartments; and certainly the major danger to our arts now is not from the Communists, who are a small and largely a cultural minority, but from the forces of reaction which are, as in America, engaged in an incessant witch-hunt and eager, and able, to keep us under a statute of Mortmain. It is this equating of artistic values with the extent to which they are 'safe' to the existing order and to which they stuff themselves with religious, moral, social and other anachronisms of the most infantilist and vicious character that I am up against.
>
> Above all, it must be insisted that a man who uses his literary gifts as a weapon in the social struggle and makes his means of artistic expression a vehicle for Communist propaganda, cannot be said to have no real concern for literature (Scottish or any other). These two things are not necessarily exclusive, and to suggest that they are implies the assumption that Communism in this respect is in a different case from Conservatism or any other brand of politics. And, of course, the pretence of being 'non-political' or 'above politics' is the worst form of political partizanship.
>
> I set out all these considerations simply because it is inevitable that this issue will become more and more important, and I want you to realise that I have chosen my side and am utterly and irrevocably opposed to Christianity, capitalism, and all the social *and artistic* forms these have produced or that are compatible with them.[66]

By this stage MacDiarmid had made the most radical changes in the formal nature of his artistic production. The general critical response to this has been to regret it. Iain Crichton Smith, for example, complained of having 'difficulty with MacDiarmid's longer poems, more so than with his lyrics' and it seemed to him that the 'poetry of "fact" requires some new form of criticism that we haven't as yet got'.[67] I want to question this, partly because it seems to be leading away from a reading of the poetry, and partly because it is not really the case. 'New' forms of criticism have been available for a long time, the thing is to use them. We shall have to be less divisive than Crichton Smith, who concluded: 'If we want logic we should go to a logician. If we want sociology we should go to a sociologist. If we want politics we should go to a politician. That is not the poet's job.'[68]

If we want to avoid the rigidities of such distinctions and declare our own critical position, it will be, in Benjamin's words, to help 'rethink the notions of literary forms or genres' and 'to find forms appropriate to the literary energy of our time'.[69]

'A machine full of shortcomings'

In *Stony Limits* (1934), the pivotal volume of MacDiarmid's poetic career, brilliant and beautiful lyrics such as 'First Love' or 'With the Herring Fishers' are printed alongside foretastes of the epic poetry to come. 'Lament for the Great Music' is there, for example, as is 'In the Caledonian Forest' — part of which was to be accommodated in the Joyce poem later on. At the centre of the book there is the axial confrontation — to which we shall return — 'On a Raised Beach'.[70] In this period MacDiarmid's poetry becomes, as we have noted, more outward-turning, more concerned with humanity at large. One of the dilemmas in 'On a Raised Beach' is precisely that conflict between 'great poetry' and 'the crowd':

> It will be ever increasingly necessary to find
> In the interests of all mankind
> Men capable of rejecting all that all other men
>   Think, as a stone remains
> Essential to the world, inseparable from it,
>   And rejects all other life yet.
> Great work cannot be combined with surrender to the crowd.
>
> C.P., p.429

This reflects upon a personal dilemma but declares its interests to be those of 'all mankind'. While MacDiarmid is relatively unconcerned with personal immortality, there is an opposition here between the 'Essential', the notion of 'Great work', and the sense of 'the crowd'. That opposition is clearly felt in the contrast between the modes of lyric and epic poetry, and the question lying behind it is to do with the durability of works of art, the function of endurance in poetry. The effect of MacDiarmid's lyrics has been admirably described by Norman MacCaig in a short poem:

> The tide goes over.
> Not on my knees
> These poems lie,
> But on the floor of existence.
>
> Whelk and razorshell,
> Delicate weight-lifters,
> Supporting and made by
> The crush of fathoms.[71]

The effect of MacDiarmid's epic poetry takes the tidal sweep into greater consideration, and consequently calls into question the desirability that poems should sink to the floor of existence, if they are to remain there. MacCaig himself has written cautiously of the long poems: 'they are disturbing. I myself will take them to avizandum for some years before making my own judgement with any sort of confidence.'[72]

There is a pertinent poem Brecht wrote in 1932, 'About the way to construct enduring works' which asks

> How long
> Do works endure? As long
> As they are not completed.
> Since as long as they demand effort
> They do not decay.
>
> Inviting further work
> Repaying participation
> Their being lasts as long as
> They invite and reward.
>
> Useful works
> *Require people*
> Artistic works
> Have room for art
> Wise works
> Require wisdom
> Those devised for completeness
> Show gaps

The long-lasting
Are always about to crumble
Those planned on a really big scale
Are unfinished.
Still imperfect
Like a wall awaiting the ivy
(It was once unfinished
Long ago, before the ivy came; bare).

Still short-lived
Like a machine that is used
But is not good enough
But gives promise of a better model
Work for endurance must
Be built like
A machine full of shortcomings.[73]

That seems to me to describe exactly the strengths and weaknesses, the achievement and the 'shortcomings' of MacDiarmid's epic poetry. Brecht clearly refuses to recognise beauty as static. For him, the work of art is necessarily incomplete, necessarily violable. If it demands and repays participation, it cannot be turned into a sacred object to be worshipped. Brecht rejects the idea that the object of art (or indeed the object of society) can ever be inhumanly finalised and complete. He continually refuses to sacralise the text. It is a salutory reminder to those critics whose misgivings towards Mac-Diarmid's long poems hinge on the fact that they seem to be 'unfinished' or 'imperfectly realised'.

In Brecht's *Messingkauf Dialogues* there is a conversation which turns on the idea of perfection, of the inviolable text. It is 'The Second Night' of the Dialogues; the Dramaturg says, 'Shakespeare's plays are extraordinarily full of life. Apparently they were printed from the prompt copy, and took in all the changes made at rehearsal and the actors' improvisations. The way the blank verse is set down suggests that it must in many cases have been done by ear.' *Hamlet* he takes to be full of possibilities depending on values of production for their effect. 'Act IV contains a number of scenes each of which represents one possible solution. The actor may have needed to use the whole lot; or perhaps he only needed one, and the rest were none the less included in the book. They seem to me like so many bright ideas.'

The Actor: From what you've said I'd picture Shakespeare coming along with a fresh scene each day.

The Dramaturg: Exactly. I feel they were experimenting. They were experimenting just as Galileo was experimenting in Florence at that time and Bacon in London. And so it is right to stage the plays in a spirit of experiment.

The Actor: People think that's sacrilege.

The Dramaturg: If it weren't for sacrilege the plays wouldn't exist.

The Actor: But as soon as you alter them in any way you're accused of treating them as less than perfect.

The Dramaturg: That's simply a mistaken idea of perfection.[74]

This last item presents peculiar problems for poetry. Drama is by its very nature concerned with relationships. Poetry — or rather, post-Romantic Western European poetry — is widely regarded as a much more personal thing, largely because of its retreat from the social sphere into a less communal relationship with its readers. It has, perhaps, been assumed that the truth could be mediated only by the poet through poetry, that any other use for poetry was inferior, and that the solitary voice of lyric poetry was supreme. Allied to the *specific* notion of 'lyric poetry' is the function of generic categorisation: but there are texts which transgress the conventional genres. 'Dramas like Geothe's *Faust* and Byron's *Manfred* are agreed to have been more effective as books', Brecht wrote in 1936 or thereabouts, concerned as he was with the different ways of presenting a work to the public and how these effect the methods of the work's construction. And there are transgressive poems, like *Beowulf* (which was an oral poem but also and probably at the same time written down) and *Paradise Lost* (which was certainly written down, but which its author could judge only by hearing). Problematically, the sanction that is afforded by the material actuality of a book usually directs us away from a reading where participation in the text involves an oral and aural response, and affirms the sacral nature and silent authority of the printed text.

Yet it is pertinent to remember that our sense of epic *does* depend upon Homer, and oral poetry is as much a performance art as a literary event. Oral poets re-enacted their performance, recreated their poems at each occasion: they were not constrained to repeat a fixed text but could shift emphases, and narrative devices abounded to allow a fresh interpretation to stories commonly known both to themselves and to their audiences. Only after the advent of written culture could the notions of originality and plagiarism be resolved in enforceable laws of copyright. Brecht regarded any work once in existence as lawful plunder for a subsequent writer. In theatre, he passionately rejected the mania for possession leading to an approach to the classics which treated them as sacrosanct. Yet he was well aware of the political implications of the censorship enacted by bourgeois theatre productions of the classics in the 1920s. The notion of collective ownership was, ironically enough, being promoted in the cutting and paring being done there in the interests of bourgeois society. Brecht's response was to start from the premise that all creative work is a timebound articulation, and that therefore nothing is inviolable. Finding forms appropriate to the literary energies of their time, Brecht and MacDiarmid both shared one great creative principle: 'Bourgeois philosophers make a distinction between the active man and the reflective man. The thinking man draws no such distinction.'[75]

The Unfamiliar Text

The originality of Brecht's theory of estrangement, as Fredric Jameson has written, 'was to have cut across the opposition between the social and the metaphysical in a new way, and to throw it into a completely new perspective'.

> For Brecht the primary distinction is not between things and human reality, not between nature and manufactured products or social institutions, but rather between the static and the dynamic, between that which is perceived as changeless, eternal, having no history, and that which is perceived as being essentially historical in character. The effect of habituation is to make us believe in the eternity of the present, to strengthen us in the feeling that the things and events among which we live are somehow 'natural' which is to say permanent. The purpose of the Brechtian alienation-effect is therefore a political one in the most thorough-going sense of the word. It is, as Brecht insisted over and over, to make you aware that the objects and institutions you thought to be natural were really only historical: the result of change, they themselves henceforth become changeable.[76]

The effects we have been discussing in relation to epic theatre and epic poetry, of retardation, composition by stages, the 'separation of the elements' are all techniques for defamiliarisation. The Russian formalist critic Shklovsky used this term to define art as a process of 'making strange' familiar objects, and there are profound ethical as well as political considerations that emerge from this. The desire to effect renewal of perception reflects the desire to reconstitute the relations between the present and a possible future, or the 'condition' of the present and possible futures. Therefore, the process of 'defamiliarisation' entails a reconsideration of the relation between the present and the past. Benjamin's 'Theses on the Philosophy of History' are lucid on this matter: 'Only that historian will have the gift of fanning the spark of hope in the past who is firmly convinced that *even the dead* will not be safe from the enemy if he wins. This enemy has not ceased to be victorious.'[77]

Benjamin insists that at every retrospective reconstitution of events, the formation of traditions proves that the past is changeable, and history a relative matter of position and intention. The inherent danger for history and its receivers is the possibility of becoming a tool of the ruling classes. The effort to resist the normative and conformist character of ideological control and create the possibility for a different relation to the events of history is an essential part of the dynamic of Benjamin's criticism, as it is of the process of defamiliarisation. When, at the end of Brecht's *Galileo*, we are made painfully aware of how scientific discovery is controlled by the agents of conformism, we are confronted with the problem at one remove: its representation on the stage effects a distancing. When Benjamin wrote the 'Theses on the Philosophy of History' in 1940, that 'distanciation' was understandably felt as part of the social fabric. Nor has this criticism lost any urgency since 1940. 'This enemy has not ceased to be victorious.' We cannot let ourselves pinpoint a moment in history where that victory has not ceased to be imminent. The struggle Benjamin refers to is *present*. Consequently, we must beware of any chronological determination which provides a linear representation of history. We have already encountered this problem with regard to the term epic, as a difficulty arising from methods of definition and determination. Much criticism has been devoted to the establishment of a linear historical development of 'epic' literature. Yet we cannot deny the contemporaneous existence of oral and written epics (chronologically separate in any traditionally retrospective view). For example, Richard Dorson writes in the 'Introduction' to *Heroic Epic and Saga* (1978):

Heroic epics and sagas have enthralled two entirely separate audiences, one of listeners at the time of their oral performance and, much later, one of readers in modern European languages. The appeal in the first instance is tribalistic, or nationalistic, as the listeners identify with a hero of their blood, cast in their mold, and in the second is universalistic, as Western readers respond to the adventures of a champion.[78]

The distinction between these two 'entirely separate' audiences itself is foreign to the dynamic of epic literature. It is the product, as Brecht put it, of the bourgeois philosopher. The result of such a distinction is the inference that the epic is impossible in the twentieth century: it is a genre that can be safely located in the past. This is extremely questionable, suspiciously generalised, and ultimately might serve to dissuade the reader from studying how contemporary literature works in social and ideological terms. 'Western readers' who 'respond to the adventures of a champion' are involved in a process of self-identification suspiciously similar to that of a tribe of listeners identifying with 'a hero of their blood', and there is an arrogant assumption underlying Dorson's use of the word 'universalistic', as if the practice of 'Western readers' were normal. Are these readers — students, perhaps, of *The Kalevala* or the *Iliad* but not *The Maximus Poems* or *The Cantos* — encouraged to consider contemporary literature as part of the vital struggle of which those earlier epics are records? That struggle is, in modern terms, for the structure of society rather than territorial domination, and most typically involves a struggle to control the functions of language in society. MacDiarmid understood the full difficulty of his task, and its thanklessness: 'to take the whole field of knowledge and to assimilate all the diverse components into a general view — establish a synthesis, in fact — is clearly a Herculean undertaking scarcely to be attempted by anyone, and hardly more likely to be understood by anyone else. Yet it is a task of paramount importance . . . on which the whole future of poetry depends.'[79]

The fact that cultures and societies exist in different parts of the world where the term epic can usefully be applied to activities of extremely different kinds raises a number of questions about the normative functions of our own critical literary vocabulary. The advent of a global overview, embracing both literate and pre-literate peoples, is itself a historical phenomenon. It follows the breakthrough made by European modernism. In T.E. Hulme's *Speculations*, there is an account of the crucial advance made in the possibilities of perspective in the early part of this century: that where hitherto the art of distant periods or distant places has been regarded as archaeology or ethnology, today it is possible to understand it *as art*.[80] Picasso's use of African aesthetics is one example of this revaluation of aesthetics and culture. And it is no accident that Picasso, along with Braque, was one of the first to introduce the revolutionary formal innovation of collage to the world of 'high art' in the twentieth century. (We shall return to this point.)

The challenge this revaluation poses is a challenge to values very deeply rooted in Western civilisation, values of belief and identity in the self. Such values began to be widely and deeply held in Western Europe through the Renaissance in ways that still directly pertain to contemporary understanding of them. MacDiarmid, like other great modernists, understood the significance of the challenge posed to these values, and wished to link the evolution of global consciousness to a pre-Renaissance, pagan dynamic. For the effect of this revaluation in artistic terms is to destabilise the values of the self, and to introduce as equal values desire and knowledge of 'the other'.

The threat that exists in tribal or national societies from 'the other' can be defined geographically, and nationalism is one way of dealing with it. But when 'the other' is not bounded by a geographical border but constitutes the threat of what one's identity could *become*, then the very notion of identity is reinterpreted. MacDiarmid's epic poetry raises this question, for while it does not wholly relinquish notions of identity and belief, it interpenetrates them with desire and knowledge.

Not surprisingly, the quality and weight of criticism that has been written about MacDiarmid's poetry diminishes in authority and strength as it approaches the later work. Criticism of *To Circumjack Cencrastus*, for example, registers the poem's failure as an organic unity but does not adequately suggest the implications of this for the poetry which follows from it.[81] To do so would be to relinquish the critical ideal of an organically unified poem and to admit the failure of one kind of critical procedure. For there is no self-enclosing coherence in MacDiarmid's later texts. To single out and extract a lyrical passage from the text of *In Memoriam James Joyce* is an act justified by the nature of the text and, in a way, predicted and sanctioned by the precedent of MacDiarmid's own practice of using bits of the work as, or in, separate poems (like 'Credo'). Yet if this alerts us to the futility of a search for organic unity in the text, it need not keep us from attempting to perform some responsible critical reading, to ask what kind of work this is and to suggest how it can best be read.

One way of doing this has been proposed by Kenneth Buthlay. The 'poetry of fact' he has written 'is mainly a poetry of the Fancy, using the term in its Coleridgean sense . . . it is largely a product of "a mode of memory emancipated from the order of time and space, while it is blended with and modified by that empirical phenomenon of the will which we express by the word Choice. But equally with the ordinary memory the Fancy must receive all its materials ready made from the law of association." '[82]

What Coleridge sought from Wordsworth was a poetry of ideas, but what Wordsworth produced in *The Prelude* was rather a description of the growth of a poet's mind. Such a description was latent in the plan MacDiarmid proposed for *Clann Albann*, developing an autobiographical strain from boyhood to maturity. However, since *Clann Albann* was abandoned, *In Memoriam James Joyce* might well be thought of as just that 'poetry of ideas' which Coleridge imagined but which Wordsworth himself was incapable of producing. There is something very attractive in that kind of achievement.

One counterpoint to this view of MacDiarmid as a latter-day Wordsworth was provided by Walter Perrie, who suggested that *In Memoriam James Joyce* could best be understood as a counteractive measure to the course of European poetry since the Romantic movement: 'a history of successive retreats from the language of social, public usages'.[83] And yet in those terms MacDiarmid's poem is an awesome failure. It has effectively no social or public use, and is distinct from MacDiarmid's earlier poetry by the extent of its commitment to literature and the arts, its bookishness. It does not engage in a social debate; it produces its own interlocutions. Its readership itself is so small as to be socially insignificant and no more general audience is currently available. It is therefore more appropriate to understand it in the company of such works as Pound's *Cantos*, William Carlos Williams's *Paterson*, Charles Olson's *The Maximus Poems*, and, most appropriately, Joyce's *Ulysses* and *Finnegans Wake*.

Pound's *Cantos*, the 'poem containing history' is the model modern verse epic, paradigmatic in its attempt to bring a range of kinds of wisdom into a coherent, public work. MacDiarmid returned to it and praised Pound repeatedly, calling him the most lovable man he ever met: an odd phrase for a member of the Communist Party to use of a supporter of Mussolini. But they were old men in 1971, when they enjoyed each other's company for an afternoon in

Venice. It had been decades since their correspondence in the early 1930s, when they were both contributing to *The New Age*. Pound had advised MacDiarmid then:

> can't write everything
> all at once on the same page

in a letter from Rapallo dated '7 Dec. anno XII'[84] (that is, 1934 according to the fascist calendar, which began from the 1922 March on Rome and the rise to power of Mussolini). Yet who was Pound to talk? *The Cantos* is crammed on every page with references that demand explication, details and facts that are heaped up to such an extent that only the prismatic clarity of Pound's language keeps the attention from drifting too far from the page. The result is a work which catalysed William Carlos Williams and Charles Olson into producing their own epic poems, and, following Pound, to continue the attempt to bring back to poetry the provenance of social discourse. To quote Michael André Bernstein (whose book *The Tale of the Tribe: Ezra Pound and the Modern Verse Epic* is a seminal exposition of the work of these three poets): 'Pound, Williams, and Olson sought to recapture for verse the amplitude and inclusiveness of the novelist. One could go much further and say that it was the entire domain of public, ideological utterances, "the word permeated with confident and categorical social value judgement", that the epic poet was determined to rehabilitate and install at the core of his project.'[85]

To deal adequately with the ways in which Williams and Olson departed from Pound would require a book in itself, but we might characterise the progress made by Pound's successors briefly in this way: Williams focused his attention on the town of Paterson, New Jersey, and built up his poem of that name from a collection of stories, statements, letters, and other kinds of information, so that geographical and historical data interpenetrated with a human quality of care. *Paterson* is a carefully local poem: it is missing Pound's grand and assertive arrogance.

Although Charles Olson's *The Maximus Poems* appears to harness an arrogance akin to Pound's, Olson's directive was to abandon the notion of cultural élitism in an attempt to make poetry attend to the radical egalitarianism which he deemed possible after the cataclysm of the Second World War. Like Williams, Olson focused on a particular place: the New England fishing port of Gloucester, and its environs of Cape Ann. He dug deep into its local history and speculated with marvellous, wild abandon on the significance of that local history to the national condition of the United States. He attempted (and the pun suggests the hubris involved) 'to write a Republic'. And in the attempt, he evolved a theory of poetic production and described his verse as 'projective'. 'Projective Verse', Olson claimed, was a new evolutionary development in poetry. The idea was to allow the poet a more immediate and direct access to the reader. The poem was something Olson understood to be an enactment of energy, a charge erupted from the poet and only concluded in its proper reception by the reader, or listener, and from that point on it might help bring about action. The poem itself was necessarily unfinished, inevitably a 'work in progress', a bridge from thought to social action. Described in this way, Olson's 'Projective Verse' differs from traditional, print-bred notions of poetry as formally complete, or 'closed' and (although there are greater complexities and subtleties which we cannot dwell on here) the significance this confers upon poetry as an act of social rhetoric is easy to see.

What distances MacDiarmid's work from Pound and Olson, and brings him closer to Joyce is his rejection of an egocentric lyricism and his embracing of the protean forms of language. MacDiarmid is not a poet of *place* in the way that Williams and Olson are. He had no need to be. The function of *location* in Williams and in Olson is to allow a secure vantage point, a position of relative stability from which to begin. Location, whether in Paterson or Gloucester, encourages, at least provisionally, a rootedness. In this, as in their deliberate use of demotic American idioms, Williams and Olson were distancing themselves from Pound. Pound's notion of the high cultural tradition led him to Italy and away from the 'grounded' culture of America. Williams more than any other modern American poet simply accepted where he was and got to work. Olson went out from Gloucester, but constantly *with* Gloucester as referent and starting point, to take in larger and larger spans of geography and time.

> I have this sense
> that I am one
> with my skin
>   Plus this — plus this:
> that forever the geography
> which leans in
> on me I compell
> backwards I compell Gloucester

```
to yield, to
change
      Polis
is this
```

As *The Maximus Poems* develop, Olson discusses shifting conti-
nents, transatlantic migrations, pre-Christian mythologies. But he
remains, as he puts it himself, 'astride the Cabot fault' — a North
Atlantic man, standing on the eastern seaboard of America. And
both Olson and Pound, despite the enormity of their efforts and
the greatness of their achievements, return in similar ways to the
vulnerable and solitary ego. It was from the wreckage of Europe
that Pound saw himself emerge alone: 'ego scriptor'. And when
Olson reflected on his own subsequent enterprise, he distanced himself from Pound's egotism by remarking upon the difference between
their poetics:

> I love Ezra for all the boxes he has kept. . . . This is where he
> really is a canto maker. And I ain't got nothing to do . . . with
> cantos. I couldn't write a canto if I sat down and deliberately
> tried.[86]

Olson's preferred form in *The Maximus Poems* was the letter, or
series of letters, a mode intended to initiate dialogue and effect
action directly. It was therefore dependent on the speed of transmission rather than the sustained assertion of the lyrical ego that is
implicit in a 'canto'.

Yet, just as Pound maintains a singleness of understanding and
expression in the fragments which end his great work, Olson's final
volume of *The Maximus Poems* discloses more and more the vulnerable, fated author himself. The *polity* Olson sang shrinks into the
voice of its author alone. The difference between these poets and
MacDiarmid is of some consequence, therefore. A fundamental difference lies in the fact that in Scotland, MacDiarmid had a literature,
culture, and history, which, however fragmented it was in the
modern age, however broken or submerged it had been in periods
during the past, stretched back to a pre-Christian era. He had an
ancient civilisation, and was aware of it from his boyhood and
youth. The struggle in Williams to build up from the immediate
things around him, not to use ideas that come from anything but
the facts of his situation; or the struggle in Olson to produce a new
social vision and bring it about as reality — these republican ideals
are dependent on the individual who holds them. They are projects

of the individual's vision, and the precedent of Pound and before him of Whitman is not the same thing as a national culture of real antiquity.

What makes the end of *The Cantos* and the last of *The Maximus Poems* so deeply moving is the reduction and impending loss of their authors' selves. In Joyce and MacDiarmid (and one should note the depth of social history from which Joyce emerges too), the self is extended at the same time as it is broken up and destabilised. This is also, inevitably, a matter of form. *Finnegans Wake* is famous for its circularity, its final words running on into its opening words. As Peter McCarey has shown, MacDiarmid's most characteristic myths figure sets of concentric circles. This accords with MacDiarmid's sense of Scotland in its variety as microcosm, related to the world as a small circle to a great one. The figure is self-repeating, self-confirming and ever-widening.[87] How might we appraise the quality of that figure more accurately? Can we describe the dynamic within it?

'Synaptic verse'

MacDiarmid's epic poetry can be characterised as 'synaptic verse'. The words on the page are like the progression of an impulse-instruction going along the neurological paths of a body. Each cell has a single *axon* but each neuron has a number of *dendrites* — that is, the ways in which the message can be taken up are various. When the impulse-instruction arrives at the end of a nerve, at an axon, it must make a leap to another neuron, it must make a synaptic connection with (at least) one of a number of possible dendrites. It thus progresses by a number of such synaptic connections until its course is run. The impulse stops when its instruction is carried out, or when its instruction is cancelled or altered by the brain. The movement itself is both cyclical (the impulse denied by or returning to the brain), and terminal — being released in external action. However, if this describes the progress of the words down page after page, there is implied in the analogy an organic body which houses the neurological system represented. This body is never visible, 'since ecdysis is never complete'[88] but it is implicit in the text (or rather, *from* the text, *around* the text) in the same way as the city of Dublin in *Ulysses* is never directly described but always present, always assumed to be there in all its intricate detail. The reader supplies it as far as he or she can, but part of the excitement of reading MacDiarmid is the discovery that as you proceed, that organic body can never be *finally* realised. If this suggests that the text is in danger of etherealising itself out of existence, we should emphasise that its material presence is affirmed again and again by the repeated 'baring of the device', the recurrent instances by which the reader is alerted.

The 'synaptic leap' is most often found in the poetry at points where MacDiarmid seems about to make an analogy. For example, between pages 759 and 764 of the *Complete Poems*, we find the phrases: 'And so on to . . . ', 'And to . . . ', 'Even as . . . ', 'Even as we know how . . . ', 'Even as we know that . . . ', 'Even as we delight in . . . ', 'And even as we know . . . ', 'Even as we know . . . ', 'Or even as we know . . . ', 'And rejoicing in all . . . ', 'Or even as . . . ', 'Or like . . . '. Within the verse-paragraphs we find lists of languages, lists of linguists, examples of the particularity of vocabularies, a 'philological parenthesis' on the world history of the dance and an extended simile likening 'our' knowledge of abstruse languages to the perspicacity of a farmer surveying his fields and distinguishing the crops in each one while they all would look alike to the untrained eye. Then we shift course again, abruptly, with the closure of the parenthesis and yet another 'Even as we know . . . '.

The lists that constitute this part of the poem are arbitrary in any academic sense and in reading through them we receive series of further identities, sets of further divisions. Yet they also seem to suggest the associative and centripetal nature of the mind that sets them down. If the text seems sporadic, then perhaps we can identify the author behind it as the arranger, the assembler of the montage? There are modes and expressions in the text which seem to give him away. One particular way in which proverbial truths are questioned is to assert the *obviousness* of the lie. In the section we are looking at we find:

> Above all I rejoice that we are not
> All 'Joan Thompson's bairns'
> But that there are many, perhaps countless,
> Psychologically incommensurable,
> Even mutually incomprehensible, types . . .
> Of human beings —

> C.P., p.843

My ellipsis after 'types' is in place of a six-line parenthesis and following the dash is a list of seventeen such 'types'. MacDiarmid's overemphasis is itself typical. Just as typical is the frequently recurring use of the small phrase 'of course' which is found throughout MacDiarmid's writing. Such characteristics of technique and phraseology alert us to the procedures of the text, but they also ask us to question what we are told, what we take for granted.

In the crucial essay 'Reply to Criticism' (published in *The Voice of Scotland*, in 1956, as a response to David Craig's criticism of *In Memoriam James Joyce*), MacDiarmid defends his own appraisal of the work and insists that there are many different kinds of poetry used in the book.[89] While all are intended to abet a 'consistent argument which runs throughout not only this poem but all my work', there are nevertheless included many lyrics, two obscene poems, catalogues, and various passages of utterly different character or texture. Before we examine the consistency of the argument by going through the text, the fact that there are a variety of types of poetry present needs some comment in the light of our proposition that the protean nature of MacDiarmid's first person singular constitutes a diversity of authorial postures. The structure of the work allows for no such authorial stance to be *consistently* held and the reader, too, is displaced. We are constantly at work with the poetry since there is no hierarchy ensuring control and distance; authoritative positions which can be allocated to writer, text, and reader are simply not present.

Consider, for example, this passage from 'The Snares of Varuna' section of *In Memoriam James Joyce*. MacDiarmid refers to 'the American angler' who 'is right' when he 'tells how'

First fishing in England with the dry-fly,
He lost fish by striking too soon and too hard.
He deems this due to the difference between
English and American conditions; in our chalk streams
Every movement of the fish is seen   5
While in America, though their rivers
Are apparently clear enough, they have not
The 'gin' clearness of which so much has been written.
But it is not only the American visitor
Who loses the best fish by striking too soon.   10
It requires 'iron nerves' for all fishermen,
English or others, to hold their hands
When the great nose of a four-pounder
Slowly rises to the fly. So Pushkin is clear enough
But he can't be caught. There is a genius   15
In literature too like the Zambesi crocodile
That keeps its powerful jaws wide open
What time a bird hops about in the gape

Picking food from between the teeth.
The bird is never injured. The crocodile   20
Appreciates its service as a toothpick.

C.P., pp.850–1

If the prosody of this passage is conservative, it is also flexible
enough to contain easily some disconcerting shifts of authorial position. The American angler's words are delivered in reported speech
by an intermediary. Though he or she is not specified, and not even
identified by quotation marks, we are surely to assume a source for
a text in MacDiarmid's writing when it equates the possessive of
the first person plural with the adjective 'English' (as in line 4), and
we may detect a slight but certain irony in the use of the word in
line 12. But then what transition is being made in line 14? When
Pushkin rises here we have to refer back to page 849, where a
description of Mozart's lucid, perfect, infinitely protean masterpieces
gives way to the sense that suddenly through the clarity of these
works something demonised and 'completely baffling' arises. Then
we have:

> Pushkin's Salieri who wanted
> To poison Mozart was right.
> He should have poisoned Pushkin too.

So when Pushkin reappears in line 14 of the first extract quoted, we
are meant to understand that he is 'clear' — like a Mozart masterpiece or a cloudless day or the water through which a trout will
rise — but he also resembles the trout in clear water in that he
cannot be 'caught'. He is, in other words, a quality, an object, and
a reference. He stands metonymically for a 'transparent' quality of
creative work, but his name also represents that quality in his own
creative work; furthermore, he is an example of one of the great
writers, whose names drift in and bank up on the pages of *In
Memoriam James Joyce*. There is a transitional move across that
word 'So' in line 14 which is a bigger leap than we ordinarily make
in reading that little word. (It is deployed as if to mean 'therefore',
but that is a *non sequitur*. The required sense is 'in just such a
way' — a literary use of the word, archaic in English but current in
Scots.) Another transition follows immediately with the Zambesi
crocodile (a footnote refers us to 'Herodotus II 68') and a different
kind of phrasing is evident in line 18, with 'What time' and 'in the
gape'.
    Tonally, the passage is coherent. Look how the quotation marks

in lines 8 and 11 add tonal colour; how wonder in lines 13 and 14 is rewarded with a snappy disclosure in lines 14 and 15; and how the humour works in the last six lines. But the coherent pitch and conservative prosody are themselves transparencies through which a number of authorial and textual positions are arranged in a consecutive, but not hierarchical, order.[90]

An agreed position from which a reader can enter this text is missing, or at least held in question. Consequently, an attempt to specify the author of such a text is an attempt to create him, to fictionalise beyond a text which is patently caught up in the movement of other texts, and to assign a definite location for a number of non-authorial voices. The problems thus posed for the reader are caused by the lack of any agreed level at which to enter the text. Without this, the reader's response at its most extreme is initially one of fear, boredom, or laughter. Cast unprepared before *In Memoriam James Joyce*, the reader is like a child listening to its parent's conversation, uncertain of the language, the ways in which to use the language, and what part he or she will play in the situation. (But children, of course, learn the use of words without having any data or fixed points to go upon, so we need not despair.) Rather than fixing an authorial position, the explicitly personal vocabulary ('I remember . . . ', ' . . . as I have often told/My angling friend Norman MacCaig . . . ', and so on) often serves to subvert any promise of the identifiable author. So often the first person singular makes assertions that are outrageously extravagant and at times stunningly fictitious. What does it mean, after all, when he says he has known all the poets and delighted in all the languages in the world?

In his essay 'What is an Author?' Michel Foucault points out some of the consequences of this kind of writing.[91] It is a familiar thesis, he says, that the task of criticism is not to bring out the work's relationship with the author, nor to reconstruct through the text a thought or experience, but rather to analyse the work through its structure, its architecture, its intrinsic form, and the play of its internal relationships. At this point, however, a problem arises: 'What is a work?' The word 'work' and the unity that it designates are probably as problematic as the status of the author's individuality. How does an author's name function? A proper name is not a simple reference; it has other than indicative functions. It describes a work, an *œuvre*, or part of a strain in a work. If we proved Shakespeare and Bacon were one, the function of their names would radically alter. The 'author-function' is therefore characteristic of the mode of existence, circulation, and functioning of certain discourses within a society. Texts, books, and discourses really began to have authors to the extent that authors became subject to punishment, that is, to the extent that discourses could be transgressive. In Western European culture, discourse was not originally a product, it was an act; it was (historically) a gesture fraught with risks before it became goods caught up in a circuit of ownership. Once ownership of texts came into being, once strict rules concerning authors' rights, author-publisher relations, rights of reproduction, and related matters were enacted, the possibility of transgression took on more and more the form of an imperative peculiar to literature. Scientific discourses began to be received for themselves, in the anonymity of an established or redemonstrable truth, and literary discourses became acceptable only when endowed with the author-function. We now ask of each 'literary' text, who wrote it? Where does it come from? When was it written and how? Its meaning is the answers we give to these questions. The anonymous text becomes a game of 'find the author'. 'The author', Foucault concludes, 'is the principle of thrift in the proliferation of meaning.' Not an indefinite source of significations, he does not precede the work, but is rather a functional principle by which, in our culture, one limits, excludes, and chooses, by which one impedes the free circulation, manipulation, composition, and decomposition of material. Given historical modifications in society, however, this author-function may well disappear in such a manner that polysemic texts may once again function according to another mode, still with a system of constraint but one which will have to be determined, or, perhaps, experienced.

With this in mind, we can approach more openly MacDiarmid's epic poetry as texts designed to remain transgressive and transitional. If the notion of a 'work' (such as *In Memoriam James Joyce*) is traditional and thought of in a Newtonian fashion, concrete, occupying book-space, then the 'text' is something else. The work is held in the hand (as, say, the edition of *In Memoriam James Joyce*, published by William MacLellan in 1955), but the text is held in language. These distinctions, devised by Roland Barthes in his essay 'From Work to Text', are highly appropriate here. The text cannot stop at the end of the shelf. Its constitutive method is a *traversal*. It can cut across a work or indeed several works, so that in *In Memoriam James Joyce*, MacDiarmid frequently postulates the kind of poetry he wants, which was the title he gave to a book published in 1961. MacDiarmid justly claimed he was entitled to expect that competent readers will bring to *In Memoriam James*

Joyce a knowledge of all his previous works.[92] Etymologically, the text is a cloth; *textus*, from which the word text derives, means 'woven'. Every text is itself the intertext of other texts, and belongs to the intertextual. This is not to be confused with a text's origins: to search for the 'sources of' and 'influence upon' a work is to satisfy a hierarchical myth of filiation. The function of such a search is to reaffirm authorial presence. By contrast, MacDiarmid insisted that 'The multiplicity of quotations, references and allusions [in *In Memoriam James Joyce*] must be completely understood', not to satisfy any myth of filiation but because 'they constitute the *language* in which it is written . . . '.[93] 'Plagiarism' is too small a grenade to throw against work like this.

Barthes' description of text and work point forward to one more, and perhaps the most important one, of the 'distancing' devices of MacDiarmid's epic poetry. MacDiarmid described the text as 'full of quotations' (in words he once attributed to an old lady's opinion of Shakespeare). This is peculiarly relevant to the textual idiosyncrasies both of Joyce and MacDiarmid. Joyce always refused to use what he called 'perverted commas'. When Valery Larbaud, in translating *Ulysses*, asked him if quotations should go in quotation marks, Joyce replied, in a letter dated 4 June 1928, 'the fewer quotation marks the better' because even without them the reader 'will know early in the book that S.D.'s mind is full like everyone else's of borrowed words'.[94] If MacDiarmid's epic poetry is similar in some vital respects to the train of thought in Stephen Dedalus's mind, there is nothing in it to correspond with Stephen himself. And if we go further and consider Stephen as a linguistic construction made by the historical person Joyce, then we still have to distinguish between Joyce's literary practice as a novelist and MacDiarmid's as a poet — and a poet, moreover, writing a great elegiac tribute to the author of *Finnegans Wake*.

Notes

1. Alan Bold (ed.), *The Letters of Hugh MacDiarmid* (London: Hamish Hamilton, 1984), p.326. Henceforth, *The Letters*.
2. Ibid., p.298.
3. Ibid., p.297.
4. Alan Bold (ed.), *The Thistle Rises: An Anthology of Poetry and Prose* (London: Hamish Hamilton, 1984), p.289.
5. Gordon Wright, *MacDiarmid: An Illustrated Biography* (Edinburgh: Gordon Wright, 1977), p.48.
6. *The Letters*, p.225.

7. Compton Mackenzie, *My Life and Times. Octave Six: 1923–1930* (London: Chatto & Windus, 1967), p.189. Compare the account given by Fionn MacColla in his autobiography *Too Long In This Condition (Ro Fhada Mar So A Tha Mi)* (Thurso: Caithness Books, 1975), pp.80–95.

8. *The Letters*, pp.393–4.

9. T.J. Cribb, 'The Cheka's Horrors and "On a Raised Beach" ', in G. Ross Roy (ed.), *Studies in Scottish Literature*, XX (Columbia, SC: 1985), pp.88–100 (p.89).

10. Cf. Gavin Wallace, 'Compton Mackenzie and the Scottish Popular Novel', in *The History of Scottish Literature Volume 4: Twentieth Century*, ed. Cairns Craig (Aberdeen: Aberdeen University Press, 1987), pp.243–57 (p.254); and Ezra Pound, *The Cantos* (London: Faber & Faber, 1975), p.426.

11. *The Letters*, p.110.

12. Ibid., p.229.

13. Ibid., p.112.

14. Seamus Deane, *Celtic Revivals: Essays in Modern Irish Literature* (London: Faber & Faber, 1985), p.65.

15. Cf. Peter McCarey, *Hugh MacDiarmid and the Russians* (Edinburgh: Scottish Academic Press, 1987), pp.95–6.

16. Deane, op. cit., p.65.

17. *The Letters*, p.232.

18. P.1147. All page references to MacDiarmid's poems are to *The Complete Poems of Hugh MacDiarmid, 1920–1976*, ed. Michael Grieve and W.R. Aitken, 2 vols (Harmondsworth: Penguin Books, 1985); henceforth, *C.P.* It is worth just noting that *Work in Progress* was the name James Joyce used to refer to *Finnegans Wake* during the long course of its composition, and early drafts of the *Wake* had been appearing in little magazines and pamphlets under that title since as early as 1924.

19. *The Letters*, p.232.

20. Ibid., p.243.

21. Cf. W.R. Aitken, 'Hugh MacDiarmid's 'Unpublished' Books: A Bibliographical Exploration', in *Of One Accord: Essays in Honour of W.B. Paton*, ed. Frank McAdams (Glasgow: Scottish Library Association, 1977), pp.57–71.

22. Kenneth Buthlay, *Hugh MacDiarmid (C.M. Grieve)* (Edinburgh: Oliver & Boyd, 1964), p.57.

23. Samuel Johnson, *The History of Rasselas, Prince of Abissinia*, ed. D.J. Enright (Harmondsworth: Penguin Books, 1976), p.56.

24. 'Folk-Song' (a paper read at the Traverse Theatre Club), 16pp. ms in private collection.

25. *C.P.*, pp.17, 64–5, 483–5, 573, 164, 888, resp. By far the best discussion of this quality of MacDiarmid's writing is in Harvey Oxenhorn,

Elemental Things: The Poetry of Hugh MacDiarmid (Edinburgh: Edinburgh University Press, 1984), especially pp.171–82, where 'Harry Semen' is treated to a close analysis.

26. 'Second Hymn to Lenin', *C.P.*, pp.323–8 (p.323).
27. 'The Return of the Long Poem', in *Ezra Pound: Perspectives*, ed. Noel Stock (Chicago: Henry Regnery Co., 1965), pp.90–108 (p.92).
28. Ibid., p.93.
29. Edwin Morgan, *Hugh MacDiarmid* (Harlow: Longman, 1976), p.21. It is worth noting perhaps that on one of the occasions when I visited MacDiarmid, in 1977, shortly after Morgan's book had been published, it was this passage which MacDiarmid singled out for particular praise, reading it to me aloud and commenting on its remarkable acuity.
30. *C.P.*, p.615.
31. 'Charles Doughty and the Need for Heroic Poetry', in *Selected Essays of Hugh MacDiarmid*, ed. Duncan Glen (London: Jonathan Cape, 1969), pp.75–85.
32. Quoted in Marjorie Perloff, *The Dance of the Intellect: Studies in the Poetry of the Pound Tradition* (Cambridge: Cambridge University Press, 1985), p.159.
33. 'The Return of the Long Poem', in *Ezra Pound: Perspectives*, ed. Noel Stock (Chicago: Henry Regnery Co., 1965), pp.90–108 (p.93).
34. *C.P.*, p.608. 'poems *de longue haleine*' are poems for which you have to take a deep breath.
35. Albert B. Lord, *The Singer of Tales* (Cambridge, Mass.: Harvard University Press, 1960), p.138.
36. Erich Auerbach, *Mimesis: The Representation of Reality in Western Literature*, transl. Willard R. Trask (Princeton, NJ: Princeton University Press, 1953), pp.3–23 (p.5).
37. *C.P., p.609.*
38. *Bertolt Brecht, The Life of Galileo*, trans. Desmond I. Vesey (London: Methuen, 1963), pp.107–8.
39. W.P. Ker, *Epic and Romance* (New York: Macmillan, 1897); H.M. Chadwick, *The Heroic Age* (Cambridge: Cambridge University Press, 1926); C.M. Bowra, *Heroic Poetry* (London: Macmillan, 1952).
40. Bowra, op. cit., pp.91 115, 116.
41. Eric A. Havelock, *Preface to Plato* (Cambridge, Mass. and London, England: The Belknap Press of Harvard University Press, 2nd printing, 1982).
42. Ezra Pound, *The Cantos* (London: Faber & Faber, 1975), p.534.
43. 'On a Raised Beach', *C.P.*, pp.422–33 (p.432).
44. Nancy K. Gish, 'An Interview with Hugh MacDiarmid', *Contemporary Literature*, 20 (2) (1979), p.135–54 (p.143).
45. Basil Bunting, *Collected Poems* (Oxford: Oxford University Press, 1978), p.110.
46. V.I. Lenin, *Collected Works, vol. 20: December 1913–August 1914*

(London: Lawrence & Wishart; Moscow: Progress Publishers, 1972), pp.393–454.

47. Ibid., p.440.
48. For this information I am grateful to Edwin Morgan.
49. John Buchan, *A Prince of the Captivity* (London: Pan, 1962), pp.68, 78–9.
50. Wole Soyinka, *Myth, Literature and the African World* (Cambridge: Cambridge University Press, 1976), p.2.
51. Thomas Greene, *The Descent from Heaven: A Study in Epic Continuity* (New Haven and London: Yale University Press, 1963), pp.1–3.
52. Walter Benjamin, *Illuminations*, ed. Hannah Arendt, transl. Harry Zohn (London: Fontana, 1973), p.14; henceforth, *Illuminations*.
53. Ibid., p.244.
54. In *Politics and Letters: Interviews with New Left Review* (London: NLB, 1979), pp.215–16, Raymond Williams recalls that although Brecht had appeared in the *Left Review* of the 1930s and it was possible to have known about his work, he was not widely known until the mid- and late 1950s. Articles had, however, appeared before this; some are listed in the bibliography in Ronald Gray, *Brecht* (Edinburgh: Oliver & Boyd, 1961), p.119.
55. Hugh MacDiarmid, *Lucky Poet: A Self-Study in Literature and Political Ideas* (London: Methuen, 1943; reissued London: Jonathan Cape, 1972), pp.136–7; henceforth, *Lucky Poet*.
56. Letter dated 12.iv.65, in private collection.
57. 'Causerie', *Scottish Chapbook*, I(4), November 1922, pp.90–1. MacDiarmid (or rather Grieve) also advocates a Scottish National Drama in *Albyn, or Scotland and the Future* (London: Kegan Paul, 1927), p.15, and it is a recurring concern in *Contemporary Scottish Studies* (London: Leonard Parsons, 1926; reissued Edinburgh: The Scottish Educational Journal, 1976), pp.55 ff. and 74 ff.
58. *Lucky Poet*, pp.205–6.
59. 'Our Brecht', the *Guardian*, Thursday, 6 May 1976, p.14.
60. C.P., pp.886–8, 1003, 547.
61. 'A Short Organum for the Theatre', in *Brecht on Theatre*, ed. and transl. John Willett (London: Eyre Methuen, 1979), pp.179–205 (p.193).
62. Walter Benjamin, *Understanding Brecht*, transl. Anna Bostock (London: NLB, 1977), pp.106–7; henceforth, *Understanding Brecht*.
63. 'Presentation II', in Ernst Bloch, Georg Lukács, Bertolt Brecht, Walter Benjamin, Theodor Adorno, *Aesthetics and Politics* (London: NLB, 1977), pp.60–7 (p.63).
64. Benjamin, *Understanding Brecht*, p.63.
65. Ibid., pp.88–9. Tretyakov (1892–1939) achieved fame in the West for his play *Roar, China!* (from 1924 to 1925 he was a lecturer in Russian literature at Peking University). Based on a real event, it uses the

reportage style common to much Soviet literature of the 1920s. Meyer-hold's production of 1926 attracted international attention. A poet, prose-writer, journalist, an author of film scenarios, an academic and scholar, Tretyakov collaborated with Meyerhold and Eisenstein and was a close friend and comrade of Mayakovsky on the journal *LEF*. His first play, *Are You Listening, Moscow?!* (1923), subtitled 'agit-guignol', was followed by *Gas Masks*, which was staged in a Moscow gas plant, rather than a theatre. His last play, *I Want a Baby* (1926), proved excessively controversial and was denied permission for per-formance because of its frank treatment of female sexuality, childbear-ing, and eugenics. By 1929 Tretyakov had thrown his energies into the collectivisation of literature. 'We are living in a period of mass organizations', he wrote. 'When the earth is on the move like broken ice, how small-minded seems the argument concerning literary-group interests and slogans. One cannot aim indefinitely, one must finally fire.' Tretyakov was in his forties, exactly contemporary with MacDiar-mid, when he was arrested and executed during Stalin's purges, alleg-edly because his meetings with several non-Russian authors had raised Stalin's suspicion. He was also labelled a Trotskyite and slandered as an English spy. See Harold B. Segel, *Twentieth-Century Russian Drama: From Gorky to the Present* (New York: Columbia University Press, 1979); and Wiktor Woroszylski, *The Life of Mayakovsky*, transl. from the Polish by Boleslaw Taborski (London: Victor Gollancz, 1972).

66. *The Letters*, p.620.
67. Iain Crichton Smith, 'MacDiarmid and Ideas', in *The Age of MacDiar-mid*, ed. P.H. Scott and A.C. Davis (Edinburgh: Mainstream, 1980), pp.157–62, (p.157).
68. Iain Crichton Smith, 'The Golden Lyric', in *Hugh MacDiarmid: A Critical Survey*, ed. Duncan Glen (Edinburgh: Scottish Academic Press, 1972), pp.124–40 (p.124).
69. Benjamin, *Understanding Brecht*, p.89.
70. *C.P.*, pp.434, 437–8, 462–82, 391–2, 422–33, resp.
71. Norman MacCaig, 'MacDiarmid's Lyrics', in Gordon Wright, *Hugh MacDiarmid: An Illustrated Biography* (Edinburgh: Gordon Wright, 1977), p.131.
72. Norman MacCaig, 'A Note on the Author', in Hugh MacDiarmid, *Scottish Eccentrics*, 2nd edn (New York and London: Johnson Reprint Corporation, 1972), p.x.
73. Bertolt Brecht, 'About the Way to Construct Enduring Works'. (Section I, part 1), in *Poems 1913–1956*, ed. Willett and Manheim (London: Eyre Methuen, 1976), pp.193–5.
74. Bertolt Brecht, *The Messingkauf Dialogues*, transl. Willett (London: Eyre Methuen, 1965), pp.59–60.
75. Bertolt Brecht, 'Zu den Lehrstucken — Theorie der Padagogien', *Schrif-

ten II, 129–30, quoted in Frederic Ewen, *Bertolt Brecht: His Life, His Art, and His Times* (London: Calder & Boyers, 1970), p.237.

76. Fredric Jameson, *The Prison-House of Language* (Princeton, NJ: Princeton University Press, 1972), p.58.

77. Benjamin, *Illuminations*, p.257.

78. Richard Dorson, 'Introduction', in *Heroic Epic and Saga: An Introduction to the World's Great Folk Epics*, ed. Felix J. Oinas (Bloomington and London: Indiana University Press, 1978), p.1.

79. Hugh MacDiarmid, 'The Esemplastic Power', *Agenda*, 8 (3–4) Autumn–Winter 1970, p.28.

80. T.E. Hulme, *Speculations* (London: Routledge & Kegan Paul, 1924), pp.54–5.

81. Cf. Kenneth Buthlay, 'The Scotched Snake', in *The Age of MacDiarmid*, ed. Scott and Davis (Edinburgh: Mainstream, 1980), pp.122–56.

82. Kenneth Buthlay, *Hugh MacDiarmid (C.M. Grieve)* (Edinburgh: Oliver & Boyd, 1964), p.109.

83. Walter Perrie, 'Prosody and Politics in *In Memoriam James Joyce*', in *Out of Conflict* (Dunfermline: Borderline Press, 1982), pp.29–52 (p.48).

84. Ezra Pound, letter to Hugh MacDiarmid dated '7 Dec. anno. XII' (1934), Edinburgh University Library, Special Collections Department, C.M. Grieve Collection.

85. Michael André Bernstein, *The Tale of the Tribe: Ezra Pound and the Modern Verse Epic* (Princeton, NJ: Princeton University Press, 1980), p.230.

86. Charles Olson, *M:thologos: The Collected Lectures & Interviews*, II, ed. George F. Butterick (Bolinas, California: Four Seasons Foundation, 1979) pp.121–2.

87. Peter McCarey, *Hugh MacDiarmid and the Russians* (Edinburgh: Scottish Academic Press, 1987), p.98.

88. *C.P.*, p.741. Ecdysis is the act of sloughing (as of the skin of a snake), the process of casting off and renewal, from the Greek *ek*, out of, and *dyein*, to put on.

89. Hugh MacDiarmid, 'Reply to Criticism', *The Voice of Scotland*, 7 (1), April 1956, pp.19–25.

90. There are indeed hierarchies implied by the things referred to in the passage. For example, there is the medieval order of fish and fowl (the fish, a lower object; the bird, gifted with flight and so closer to God but also with a voice, whose song relates it to man). There is also, perhaps, the suggestion of the line 'Shall I at least set my lands in order?' from one 'American angler' (the Fisher King) and the century's most famous poem. Is MacDiarmid saying here (as he said explicitly in *A Drunk Man Looks at the Thistle* [*C.P.*, p.941]) that *The Waste Land* might have been a better catch if its author had held his hand a little longer?

91. Michel Foucault, 'What is an Author?' and Roland Barthes, 'From Work to Text' are collected in *Textual Strategies*, ed. Josué V. Harari (London: Methuen, 1980), pp.141–60; and 73–81, respectively. I have paraphrased some passages and condensed others rather than quoting in full.

92. Hugh MacDiarmid, 'Reply to Criticism', *The Voice of Scotland*, 7 (1), April 1956, pp.19–25.

93. Ibid.

94. James Joyce, *Letters*, I, ed. Stuart Gilbert (London: Faber & Faber, 1957), p.263.

2.

In Memoriam James Joyce

If Chapter 1 has dealt largely with historical and theoretical prelimi-
naries, I wish in Chapter 2 to concentrate more on *In Memoriam
James Joyce* itself. This is more easily said than done. Perhaps the
most characteristic feature of modern literary theory is the notion
that identity or subjective selfhood is lacking in any reliable autonomy. We have seen how this notion applies with peculiar relevance
to 'MacDiarmid' as author. It also applies to *In Memoriam James
Joyce* as text. To simplify matters, I have discussed the text in the
edition published by William MacLellan in 1955 and reprinted in
1956. The same text, with some corrections but without the
Author's Note or J.D. Fergusson's illustrations, is reproduced in
volume 2 of *The Complete Poems*.

I have not been concerned to any extent with cross-referencing
passages from *In Memoriam* which turn up elsewhere in Mac-
Diarmid's *œuvre*, though there are a number of examples. I have,
first, recounted what is known of the composition and publishing
history of the work (a Gordian knot no Alexandrian critic has
adequately dealt with). I have then looked at the terms in which the
first part of the poem describes or refers to itself, and the most
salient features of MacDiarmid's understanding of language, world
literature, and Marxism. These three areas of discourse are crucial
to the work as a whole. Moreover, they are related to each other
in MacDiarmid's understanding, so I have discussed them together
as forming a 'nexus' of ideas. There follows an extended comparison
of MacDiarmid and Joyce, drawing some of these concerns together
(in particular, the political relations of language and literature).

The second part of *In Memoriam*, 'The World of Words', is then
given a reading and commentary which pays attention to the relation
between the millennial nature of MacDiarmid's poetic and political
ambitions. His use of source-material is also selectively considered.
The three central parts of *In Memoriam* ('The Snares of Varuna',
'The Meeting of the East and the West', and 'England is Our Enemy')

are then discussed, first by reading through them in a linear fashion, then by placing them in a more general argument about the primary (if often only implicit) consideration of modern epic poetry: the coming into existence of the masses. Finally, in 'Plaited Like the Generations of Men' the practice of constructing the text from a variety of sources is considered extensively and in detail.

Composition and Publication

Composition

'This poem was written in the Shetland Islands where I was then living immediately after James Joyce's death.'[1] A curiously ambiguous sentence opens the Author's Note to the first editions of *In Memoriam James Joyce*. Does MacDiarmid mean that he was living in the Shetlands when Joyce died on 13 January 1941 or that the poem was written after that date? Both? Or is the ambiguity deliberate, meant to suggest the sincerity of the work as elegy, intended to 'produce' it as a wake?

That Joyce's death supplies that function for the poem, defining its purpose and adding a tonal resonance, is true, but the composition of the work known as *In Memoriam James Joyce* is more complex. 'As early as 23rd February 1936', as Ruth McQuillan has pointed out,

> MacDiarmid [as C.M. Grieve] wrote to John Purves, Reader in Italian in the University of Edinburgh: 'You would gather of course that what interests a synthetic Scots poet is what Vossler calls Folengo's "improvisation of his own 'gibberish' out of Latin, Italian, and Mantuan", and you may be interested to know that I have written what I consider one of my best poems surveying the whole field, Occidental and Oriental, of linguistic experimentation and interaction — an *In Memoriam Teofilo Folengo* running to three or four hundred multilinguistic lines.'[2]

Teofilo (or Teophilo) Folengo (1496?–1544) was an Italian monk who wrote, under the pseudonym Merlin Coccai, a long burlesque-heroic poem 'Opus Macaronicum', which influenced Rabelais. He was one of the best-known writers of macaronic verse (that is, verse in which vernacular words are introduced into a Latin context, or, more loosely, any form of verse in which two or more languages are mingled together). The relevance of his work to MacDiarmid and the precedent he set need no comment. But one wonders how MacDiarmid came across him in the Shetland Islands. From Mac-Diarmid's description, *In Memoriam Teofilo Folengo*, this poem of three or four hundred lines, seems to have become part of *In Memoriam James Joyce*. So the problem we have as textual critics is not only the instability of the content of the work but the changeability of the work's title.

On 7 April 1937 MacDiarmid wrote to the poet William Soutar that he was at work on his 'monumental *A Cornish Heroic Song*, which is now about five times as long as *Cencrastus* and not yet completed'.[3] 'Cornish Heroic Song for Valda Trevlyn'[4] was published by T.S. Eliot in *The Criterion* in January 1939, after Eliot had read it as an 'Appendix' to *Mature Art*, a manuscript of 'between 4,000 and 5,000 lines' which MacDiarmid had sent Faber in 1938. This work had been typed by Henry Grant Taylor, a young man then in his twenties, who had volunteered to act as MacDiarmid's unpaid secretary and who stayed with the Grieves in the Shetlands. But this typescript proved too much for Eliot to take. He wrote to MacDiarmid saying that he thought it should be published but 'the question is how and by whom'.[5] Taylor, on a visit to Paris in 1939, talked to Jack Kahane, an Englishman from Manchester who had started a publishing company, the Obelisk Press, for English language books that would not otherwise have appeared in the puritanical climate of British publishing. He hoped to rival Sylvia Beach and Eugene Jolas, who were publishing important and daring contemporary American and British writers. He had already published Frank Harris and Henry Miller, and the press also produced the work of Alexander Trocchi, the Scottish novelist. Kahane agreed to publish *Mature Art* (which had grown in size in the interval), but he died that autumn. His son, Maurice Girodias, wanted to carry on and publish the book.[6]

In October 1939 MacDiarmid wrote to the artist William Johnstone: 'I think the Obelisk Press, Paris, will be publishing my big new poem — *Cornish Heroic Song for Valda Trevlyn* (over 20,000 lines) — ere long.'[7] According to MacDiarmid's biographer Alan Bold, MacDiarmid sent out prospectuses for *Mature Art* on 18 December:

> It is an enormous poem of over 20,000 lines, dealing with the interrelated themes of the evolution of world literature and world consciousness, the problems of linguistics, the place and potentialities of the Gaelic genius, from its origin in Georgia to

its modern expressions in Scotland, Ireland, Wales, Cornwall, Galicia and the Pays Basque, the synthesis of East and West, and the future of civilization.

It is a very learned poem involving a stupendous range of reference, especially to Gaelic, Russian, Italian and Indian literatures, German literature and philosophy, and modern physics and the physiology of the brain, and while mainly in English, utilises elements of over a score of languages, Oriental and Occidental.

The Fall of France made publication of the poem in Paris impossible. MacDiarmid then tried Methuen, and then the Hogarth Press. Both firms declined to publish the work. MacDiarmid revised enough of the manuscripts to retitle a portion of them 'dealing with linguistic matters and the limitations of the human mind'[8] *In Memoriam James Joyce*, and sent this to Eliot two months after Joyce's death, in 1941. This manuscript must have been substantially different from that which was published in the book *In Memoriam James Joyce*, as we shall see. Eliot returned it, having read it, and said he wished Faber could have published it. He called it 'a very fine monument to Joyce though I am afraid that it gains no advantage from the association until such time as Joyce's later work is properly appreciated. I not only enjoyed the poem but there is a great deal in it that has my sympathy as well as admiration, but in this time when we are really being starved for paper it is works like this which must suffer.'[9]

Even in the thick of London in war, Eliot might have been more helpful, I think, in securing publication elsewhere or getting other parts of MacDiarmid's poem into print. As it was, fourteen years passed before a publisher took it on. But Eliot's sympathy was genuine. In 1945, at the end of the war, he wrote to MacDiarmid asking for a copy of the manuscript to read again. MacDiarmid sent it but once more had it returned, in 1946. Eliot wrote to him:

I found my Board indisposed to take it on but I am afraid I have been hanging on to it and brooding over it by myself from time to time to try to think whether anything could be done. It is a magnificent tribute to language and even the least sympathetic critic could not deny that it is an astonishing piece of work. I don't believe that more than a few people would read it . . . But I still don't see what can be done . . . [10]

What MacDiarmid did was continue to supplement, rearrange,

and plot further extensions, updating references, adding allusions to and taking quotations from more contemporary sources, and changing the title again to *Impavidi Progrediamur*, the apt sense of which is 'Let Your Progress be Unimpeded' or 'Keep Going'. MacDiarmid later decided to change this title into Scots and call the whole thing 'Haud Forrit' (or, 'Hold Forward').

In Memoriam James Joyce was published as a book in 1955. *The Kind of Poetry I Want* appeared as a book in 1961 (in a limited edition omitting large sections of verse which had appeared in *Lucky Poet* in 1943, so that in *The Complete Poems* we find 'Further Passages from "The Kind of Poetry I Want"' on p.607 and *The Kind of Poetry I Want* itself on p.1001). MacDiarmid's autobiography, *Lucky Poet*, which contained long passages from all these works, was published in 1943 but had been ready for publication since 1939.

The confusions all this produces are notorious, and scholarly attempts to find order in the chaos are always partly doomed to failure. W.N. Herbert has concluded that MacDiarmid has left us with 'an unclosable text'.[11] And in the Author's Note to *The Complete Poems*, MacDiarmid said he had 'abandoned the whole project' of *Impavidi Progrediamur* and the 'Cornish Heroic Song' and 'other large scale projects . . . were either abandoned or subsumed in other works'.

Different senses of pitch and address can be identified in various parts of the texts that were published. There is *The Kind of Poetry I Want*: a goal and a practice, a demonstration and a depiction, an extended series of metaphors, and an exultation. There is the love-song addressed to the poet's second wife, the Cornishwoman Valda Trevyln, a celebration of sexual and sensual delight. There is also the funeral oration addressed primarily to Joyce, either directly or by implication, as if MacDiarmid was holding a wake at which the guests arrive and depart with an unaccountable sense of timing. But these different modes of address are not absolutely distinct in the texts we have. Ruth McQuillan puts this succinctly:

> Hugh Kenner said of Yeats: 'he was an architect, not a decorator; he didn't accumulate poems, he wrote books.' Hugh MacDiarmid, especially the older, post-1935 MacDiarmid, wrote not individual books but a life's work, and it is entirely suitable that the margins of his unpublished, and even his published volumes should remain blurred, one book shading off into another, as in *In Memoriam* he frequently postulates

the kind of poetry he wants — which is the governing theme of the volume that apparently succeeds this book.[12]

The editors of *The Complete Poems*, Michael Grieve and W.R. Aitken, stated that *Impavidi Progrediamur* was 'the unpublished third volume of the huge poem of which *In Memoriam James Joyce* and *The Kind of Poetry I Want* are the first two volumes'.[13] So the sanction of print and binding allows some categorical structure, perhaps — but only some. MacDiarmid's epic work achieves a kind of inchoation that should not be understood as a failure but as the necessary outcome of the accommodation he attempts.

Publication

Hugh MacDiarmid, or rather C.M. Grieve, supplied the most concise version of the book's history in a 1956 letter to D.G. Bridson, Assistant Head of Features at the BBC. Bridson arranged a BBC broadcast reading from *In Memoriam James Joyce* on Radio 3 in 1956 (31 May) and asked MacDiarmid to supply further material from his proposed subsequent book, then to be called *Impavidi Progrediamur*. Extracts from this (unpublished) book were later broadcast and published in MacDiarmid's *Collected Poems* and are noted in the index of *The Complete Poems*. MacDiarmid replied to Bridson's request by asking him for six weeks to collect, collate, and prepare his manuscripts.

> The position is this. I wrote the whole immense thing in the Shetland Islands just before the war. Then I had to come to Scotland and go into engineering for a year or so, and subsequently, for another year or so, into the Merchant Service. Towards the end of that period my wife packed up all my books and papers and brought them down. We were in digs at first and had no room for a huge mass of trunks, boxes etc. and had to store them. Later we succeeded in renting a house and later again moved here. In both of these moves we were obliged to leave a large amount of our stuff still in storage — and have not yet recovered a large proportion of it.
>
> When I prepared the Joyce poem for the printer I had great difficulty in recovering my mss — and did not recover it all. So I had to write fresh stuff to fill these gaps. Also in the interval some of my ideas had changed — and there had been developments in linguistic thought; so I had to do a considerable amount of amending, adding, etc.

The same thing will happen with the unpublished sections of the whole poem when I lay my hands on the original drafts.[14]

This is noteworthy because of the attention given to the amount of work done in the Shetlands before the war (and so, years before Joyce's death); because of the open admission that this work was never wholly recovered; because of the imperative and immediate sense of having to 'write fresh stuff' (a journalist's sense as well as a poet's); because of the admission that he had, in some respects, changed his ideas; and especially because it suggests he was keeping abreast of contemporary debates in linguistics and wanted to maintain a quality of timeliness and appropriateness in the poem.

The four men most involved in the publication of *In Memoriam James Joyce* were the poet's son Michael Grieve, the poet's best friend Norman MacCaig, the poet's publisher William MacLellen, and the poet himself. Michael Grieve's role in preparing *In Memoriam* for publication was to type the manuscript his father presented to him.[15] MacDiarmid did not type or use a typewriter in the writing of *In Memoriam* and the manuscripts were all in longhand.

Despite the fact that internal evidence in the text demonstrates that passages were transcribed long after MacDiarmid had left the Shetlands, Michael Grieve told me he believed that a substantial, relatively coherent, body of work was written in the Shetlands (which would have been the text sent to T.S. Eliot at Faber). Michael Grieve's memoir of the Shetland years, published in *The Hugh MacDiarmid Anthology*, is a clear and moving account of that period of composition.[16] In the move from the Shetland Islands back to the mainland, the manuscripts of parts of this work, being transported in leaky tea-chests, were soaked and unreadable and the texts were lost. Consequently, much of what was written after the move was written to 'fill out' (to use Michael Grieve's phrase) the gaps between the parts already written which had survived.

Norman MacCaig, who became Grieve's best and closest friend, had first met him in 1946: that is, after Grieve had left the Shetlands, and after much of the text of *In Memoriam* had been written, but before the text that was published as *In Memoriam James Joyce* had been completed: there is, in fact, a reference to MacCaig himself in the published text. MacDiarmid refers (accurately) to 'my angling friend Norman MacCaig'; but this part of the poem also exists in typescript as a separate poem titled 'On Going Angling' with everything else intact, but missing MacCaig's name.[17]

When *In Memoriam James Joyce* was being prepared for publication, Chris Grieve asked MacCaig if he would read over the text and check for any misplaced accents in the Greek phrases used in the poem.[18] MacCaig (whose first degree was in Classics) told me that the accents were everywhere and anywhere, and there were even letters where a tail would be on the wrong side or the letter would be back-to-front. 'I did my level best', he said and then commented astutely that MacDiarmid was not, in such practice, really interested in *languages* at all; he was interested in vocabulary.

The extent of MacCaig's involvement with the preparation of the text was, he said, limited to the corrections he made in this way. Although his description of the awry Greek letters suggests that MacDiarmid had transcribed the words in longhand, MacCaig also said that he thought that most of the script he read was typed, since he had no recollection of reading the mass of material in MacDiarmid's own handwriting, which was distinctive and well known to him.

William MacLellan published *In Memoriam James Joyce* in 1955 and then in 1956 reprinted it. Born in Glasgow in 1917, he was educated there and at the London School of Printing, and in 1934 took over the family printing business. Throughout the 1940s and 1950s he published many of the leading Scottish poets: George Bruce, W.S. Graham, William Jeffrey, Sydney Goodsir Smith, George Campbell Hay, Sorley MacLean, and MacDiarmid himself; as well as plays, stories, novels, books of art criticism and art design, and periodicals. In conversation he told me he remembered that Michael Grieve had collected the manuscripts and provided the typescripts.[19] There was over a year between the first proofs of *In Memoriam James Joyce* being ready and the book's publication.

In 1954 the proofs were given to MacDiarmid, who then returned them with 25 per cent more material to be added, much of it handwritten and including a long passage dealing with the Austrian satirist Karl Kraus, which had been transcribed from Erich Heller's (anonymous) *Times Literary Supplement* article of 8 May 1953.[20] Footnotes were put in on the pages of the text but then additional notes had to be added as an Appendix (after the newly composed poetry), because it was too late at that stage to include them in the body of the book.

The first edition of 1955 ran to 500 copies, MacLellan said; the second edition ran to 1500 copies. Dozens of copies were distributed throughout Europe and America, and in lower New York one bookshop put on a Joyce evening in 1971 with *In Memoriam James Joyce* used in the celebrations. But there was no attempt at a mass circulation. MacLellan was still taking orders for copies of the second edition from his home in Glasgow in the 1970s.

MacLellan had published the artist J.D. Fergusson's book *Modern Scottish Painting* in 1943.[21] MacDiarmid's opinion of Fergusson was high. He referred to him as 'my friend, that splendid octogenarian and doyen of Scottish painters, who knew James Joyce in Paris' in the Author's Note to *In Memoriam*, and he later wrote a warm Preface to Margaret Morris's biography of Fergusson and opened a Fergusson exhibition in Glasgow's Kelvingrove Art Gallery and Museum on 11 October 1974. MacLellan had arranged for various illustrations by Robert Frame, William Crosby, George Bain, Denis Peploe, Andrew Taylor Elder, William Halliday, and other Scottish artists in the *Poetry Scotland* series he was publishing in the 1940s. He invited Fergusson to illustrate *In Memoriam James Joyce*; but it was, MacLellan said, Fergusson's idea to use the ancient Celtic ogam script as a decorative motif. Fergusson provided a series of 'decorations' for the book which appeared in the MacLellan editions. These are based on the letters of the name James Joyce in the ogam alphabet, which is glossed in the book as 'an indigenous script of old Ireland named after Ogma the Celtic God of Literature and Eloquence'. This obsolete alphabet contains twenty characters, each of which is composed of a number (from one to five) of thin strokes arranged and grouped above, below, or across a horizontal line. The word 'ogam', according to Brewer's *Dictionary of Phrase and Fable*, is linked with Ogmius, a Gaulish god who was associated with Hercules by the Latin writer Lucian, and who performed great feats through eloquence and the gift of languages.

MacDiarmid and MacLellan had known each other since the early 1940s, when MacDiarmid was living and working in Glasgow, writing introductions for books and editing journals which Mac-Lellan was publishing. *In Memoriam James Joyce* was still a 'work in progress' in the 1940s, according to MacLellan, and he knew it would be a major work and indeed publishing it must have been a substantial undertaking. The first edition was helped into publication by about one hundred subscribers. The subscription price for the de luxe edition in full morocco signed by the author was five guineas; for the cloth edition, one guinea. It made very little money for MacLellan; very little indeed for MacDiarmid.

'In Memoriam James Joyce'

'*This collection of* fonds de tiroir'
In Memoriam James Joyce has six sections. The first and longest has
the actual title 'In Memoriam James Joyce' and, in Edwin Morgan's
words:

> aims to describe, by every direct and indirect means, the kind
> of poetry MacDiarmid likes and would like to write; and it is
> a poetry which he relates specifically to the major work of
> Joyce. Particularity of language, and range of knowledge and
> of reference, are important to it. Plenitude and richness of the
> linguistic texture, however, should not be so continuous as to
> rule out moments of silence, absence, abstracted vision, black
> holes in the text through which we can suddenly peer into
> alternative worlds:

> So beyond all that is heteroepic, holophrastic,
> Macaronic, philomathic, psychopetal,
> Jerqueing every idioticon,
> Comes this supreme paraleipsis,
> Full of potential song as a humming-bird
> Is full of potential motion

C.P., p.771

> ('So beyond all that is of non-standard pronunciation, that
> compresses many ideas into a single word, that combines dif-
> ferent languages, that loves learning, that homes in on the
> mind like a target, that ransacks every dialect and jargon
> dictionary, comes the supreme emphasis of non-emphasis, of
> omission, of absence, which is full of potential song as a
> humming-bird is full of potential motion.')[22]

There are four more passages in 'In Memoriam James Joyce' where
the verse explicitly describes itself, mingling and co-ordinating practice and intention, subject and object. The first telescopes the idea of
poetry as journalism into the actual practice of poetry as journalism.

> I agree with the Swiss littérateur:
> 'Let us regard modern poetry
> As one of the signs of the times
> In which men formerly read
> The fate of their century . . .
> To maintain it has little influence

Today is to be blind to the fact
That since romanticism,
And especially from 1912 to 1927
Poetry has often performed
The function of the looker-out aboard ship.
It is true it may have few readers;
Nevertheless it registers the slightest change
In the atmosphere, and makes the gesture
Others will imitate and develop'

C.P., p.744

The quotation marks suggest that MacDiarmid is transcribing material here, and in a footnote he refers us to 'Marcel Raymond, in *From Baudelaire to Surrealism* (Wittenborn, Schultz, 1947)'. In actual fact, it was Peter Owen (London, 1947) not Wittenborn, Schultz. Turning to that book, we find the last paragraph of the last chapter has provided the source:

> Let us regard this poetry, of which I have traced some essential features (there are others, and the pictures vary according to the light cast upon them), as a myth rather than a historical reality. Many works give us a glimpse of it, in none of which is it positively embodied; it is an airy dream, a mirage, which attracts pilgrims to the horizon. Let us regard it as one of those signs of the times in which men formerly read the fate of their century. Some critics repeat that it has but little influence in our day, that it occupies only a limited place in literature as a whole. To maintain this is to be blind to the obvious fact that since romanticism, and particularly from 1912 to 1927, the poet has often performed the function of the looker-out aboard ship. It is true that this poetry has few readers, and that it sometimes discourages readers; nevertheless, it registers the slightest changes in the atmosphere, it makes the gestures that others will imitate and develop (in writings that will be read and rewarded), and it is first to utter the long awaited word.[23]

MacDiarmid condenses and re-emphasises slightly, but Raymond's image and the cultural-historical point are lifted over without comment. There is one crucial change. MacDiarmid makes it 'poetry' and not 'the poet' who is the looker-out on board ship, and at the same time, by breaking up the prose into verse, puts the transcription into the same category and, by extension, not only this passage but the whole poem.

Another source lies behind Marcel Raymond, carrying the connections even further afield. Consider the following:

> Live literature does not set its watch by yesterday's time, nor
> by today's, but by tomorrow's. Live literature is like a sailor
> who is sent aloft; from the masthead he can descry sinking
> vessels, icebergs, and maelstroms which are not yet visible
> from the deck. You can drag him down from the mast and
> put him to work in the boiler room or on the capstan, but
> that won't change a thing: the mast is still there and from the
> masthead another sailor will be able to see what the first sailor
> has seen.
>
> In stormy weather you need a man aloft. And right now the
> weather is stormy. SOS signals are coming in from all direc-
> tions. Only yesterday the writer was able to stroll calmly on
> deck, taking snapshots of 'real life'; but who wants to look at
> pictures of landscapes and scenes from daily life when the
> world has taken on a forty-five-degree list, when the green
> waves are threatening to swallow us up and the ship is breaking
> up? Right now we can look and think only as men do in the
> face of death — and what then? How have we lived? If we
> are to live all over again in some new way, then by what shall
> we live, and for what? Right now we need in literature the
> vast philosophical horizon, the vast sweep from the masthead,
> from the sky above, we need the most ultimate, the most
> fearless 'Whys?' and 'What nexts?'[24]

This is from an essay by Evgeny Zamyatin (whom MacDiarmid
also quotes directly elsewhere) entitled 'Literature, Revolution and
Entropy'. It was first published in Moscow in 1924 and again in
1926, but Zamyatin emigrated to Paris in 1929 and died there in
1937, only five years before the first French edition of Raymond's
book was published. It is not unlikely that the image MacDiarmid
spotted, collected, and used so pertinently in his own poem had
come to Scotland from Moscow by way of Paris.

Such internationalism is typical. A little later, MacDiarmid
describes *In Memoriam James Joyce* as:

> . . . this *hapax legomenon* of a poem, this exercise
> In schablone, bordatini, and prolonged scordatura,
> This *divertissement philologique*,
> This Wortspiel, this torch symphony,
> This 'liberal education,' this collection of *fonds de tiroir*,

This — even more than Kierkegaard's
'Frygt og Baeven' — 'dialectical lyric,'
This rag-bag, this Loch Ness monster, this impact
Of the whole range of *Weltliteratur* on one man's brain,
In short, this 'friar's job', as they say in Spain . . .

C.P., p.755

In these ten lines MacDiarmid has used languages and colloquial idioms from at least nine countries (Greece, Italy, France, Germany, Scotland — 'this Loch Ness monster' — England, Denmark, the United States, and Spain). To gloss:

hapax legomenon — the last word, the final utterance (*hapax* is an adverb meaning once and for all, *legein* is an infinitive meaning to tell or to speak);

schablone — presumably the transliterated plural of *sciablona*, a template, model, or pattern;

bordatini — presumably the plural of *bordatino*, meaning striped cloth, ticking, and therefore something like 'coats-of-many-colours' or patchwork quilts;[25]

scordatura — a term used for the alteration in the manner of tuning some stringed instruments to produce discordant effects:

divertissement philologique — a diversion or entertainment in the study of languages;

Wortspiel — word-game;

torch symphony — a 'torch dance' was music provided for a torchlight procession — a survival from medieval tournaments — which took place at some German courts on state occasions, but a torch *symphony* suggests a marshalling of all the orchestral resources to celebrate an occasion of great ritual significance — like a great man's funeral;

'liberal education' — an education not bound by the authority of traditional orthodoxy;

fonds de tiroir — the things that are left in the bottom of the drawer, a mess;

Kierkegaard's 'Frygt og Baeven' — Kierkegaard, the Danish philosopher and theologian, his major work, 'Fear and Trembling';

rag-bag — a motley collection of material, a bag in which scraps and rags are collected. In the first version of Canto I, revised several times after its appearance in *Poetry* 10 (3) in June 1917, p.113, Ezra Pound wrote: 'Hang it all, there can be but one *Sordello*! / But say I want to, say I take your whole bag / of tricks / Let in your quirks and tweeks, and say the / thing's an art-form, / Your *Sordello*, and that the modern world / Needs such a rag-bag to stuff all its thought in.' Fifty years later Pound said: 'I picked out this and that thing that interested me, and then jumbled them into a bag. But that's not the way to make' — and here he paused for a moment — 'a *work of art*.';[26]

'friar's job' — Cassell's *Spanish Dictionary* gives 'frailada' as a colloquial term meaning the 'rude or unbecoming action of a monk'. A little later, we find the verse:

> Other masters may conceivably write
> Even yet in C major
> But we — we take the perhaps 'primrose path'
> To the dodecaphonic bonfire.

C.P., p.758

C major is the traditional Romantic key of triumph and achievement in melodic music. The 'dodecaphonic' reference is to Schoenberg's twelve-tone system of composition. MacDiarmid is emphasising that here there will be an understanding of tonality quite different from that which we might expect of traditional melody. It is typical also that this should be announced with a wry irony conveyed by that echo of Shakespeare. We recall the Porter in *Macbeth*:

> Knock, knock, knock. Who's there? Faith, here's an English tailor come hither for stealing out of a French hose: come in, tailor; here you may roast your goose. Knock, knock. Never at quiet! What are you? — But this place is too cold for Hell. I'll devil-porter it no further: I had thought to have let in some of all professions, that go the primrose way to th' everlasting bonfire. Anon, anon: I pray you, remember the Porter.[27]

If the Porter is referring to a linear movement, MacDiarmid's 'dodecaphony' takes place on more than one level. So does the irony of this particular allusion, for MacDiarmid is not only invoking the Shakespearian source, he is also distancing himself critically from the arch-Victorianism 'primrose path'. We might also recall another phrase, from *Hamlet* (i.iii.50): 'the primrose path of dalliance'. Mac-Diarmid is certainly pleased to introduce as many 'of all professions' as he can in the course of his 'dallying' and 'dodecaphonic' progress.

One further passage where MacDiarmid describes his own work picks up the allusions to music and journalism. He declares his desire to have

... all sorts
Of excruciating *bruitist* music,
Simultaneist poems,
Grab-bags and clichés, newspaper clippings,
Popular songs, advertising copy,
And expressions of innocence,
And abstract sounds — taking care
That one of them never turns out to be
Merely the Rumanian word for *schnapps*;
And all dada, mertz, fatagaga.

C.P., p.796

It is, then, a poetry noι entirely or uncritically inclusive. For all its ragged, ill-sorted ingredients, it is not merely careless. It carries 'expressions of innocence': a capacity for wonder. It is a poetry in which themes, ideas, facts, names, languages, cultures, sources, and quotations are let loose from any imperial centrality and occur in a free, but not directionless, movement. If that movement involves correspondence through more than a simply horizontal plane, then the complexity of the texts need not blind us to the fact that they have such purposive direction.

A Nexus: Language, World Literature, Marxism

MacDiarmid's understanding of language, world literature, and Marxism informs the whole procedure of *In Memoriam James Joyce*, and these three areas of discourse are, for him, closely braided together. They form a crucial nexus which empowers the entire text. MacDiarmid takes the trouble to define language as 'the instrument / For the progressive articulation of the world / In spatial and temporal terms', since 'the space-time network' is 'the distinctive character of human consciousness'. And this is significant enough for him to repeat it twice in *In Memoriam James Joyce* (*C.P.*, pp.778 and 794). It is suggestive of Maud Ellman's words: 'Language constantly confuses time with space. The very structure of the sentence separates the subject and the object from the movement which constitutes them both.'[28] And we will have cause later in this chapter to consider other theoretical understandings of language at greater length. For MacDiarmid, however, language is not conceived in purely abstract terms, and he contrasts himself with the French poet and aesthete Paul Valéry in this regard. 'All language!', he exclaims: 'Not like Valéry with an occasional doling out / Of a word like "*pur*" used as the chemists use it . . . '. By contrast, MacDiarmid claims to have

> . . . understood throughout the organic nature of
>   communication,
> And the relations of words to a whole, and of that whole
> To the whole of our mind and personality.

C.P., p.778

He is not a specialist in linguistics in any academic sense; but he frequently displays an uncanny accuracy. In a review of *In Memoriam James Joyce* in *The New Statesman and Nation* (10 September 1955), G.S. Fraser took him to task for writing ' . . . what is the word / They have in Peru for *adios*! — *Chau*, that's it.' Fraser commented: 'I know nothing about surviving Indian Languages but there are large Italian colonies all over Latin America, and I am willing to bet that the word Mr MacDiarmid has in mind is "Ciao!". Nearer the very end there is something worse: "And in Guatemala they use '*vos*' instead of 'tu' / As they would say '*che*' in Argentina." The Spanish second person plural is not '*vos*' but '*vosotros*': '*che*' is not a Spanish word, it is the Italian connective 'that' of which the Spanish spelling is '*que*' and it could in no conceivable circumstances be substituted for '*usted*' or 'ustedes.'" Fraser called the book 'a ragbag of linguistic information, much of it, where I can check on it, inaccurate.' On 17 September a letter from a certain F.B. Hills of Pinner, Middlesex, corrected Fraser's 'perfunctory' checking:

> The facts are that (1) in Peru they do say chau and that is how they write it, too. (2) In Guatemala they do use 'vos' in the place where [Fraser's] textbook would give him 'vosotros', or, as Mr MacDiarmid says, instead of 'tu' which is also second person plural. (3) In Argentina they *do* use 'che', which has nothing whatever to do with the Italian connective 'that' of which, as [Fraser] pontificates, the Spanish spelling is 'que'. The Argentine uses 'che' as a friendly appellation in somewhat the same context as an Englishman might use 'chum'. For example, 'como no, che'? Why not, chum?
>
> Mr MacDiarmid has observed closely at first hand; and . . . [Fraser] has probably turned up a couple of foreign dictionaries. Latin-American colloquialisms are not to be checked from an armchair as easily as that, and it is an unsafe method by which to attempt a show of erudition.

It would be simple-minded to infer that F.B. Hills imagines Mac-

Diarmid, notebook in hand, wandering through the Peruvian Andes or Cordillera-Real in search of first-hand experience of native colloquialisms, for it is quite possible that among his range of acquaintances MacDiarmid might have gained a first-hand experience of these linguistic forms. But Hills is, of course, wrong to say that it could not have been done from an armchair. If he is somewhat severe on Fraser, he does dramatically emphasise the credit MacDiarmid was due: he is perfectly right to say that MacDiarmid 'observed closely'. And the final point is that it is not MacDiarmid but Fraser who is attempting 'a show of erudition': MacDiarmid is attempting something that is both more exalted and less pompous.[29]

Exactly this point is made by MacDiarmid's transcription from *The Wrong Box*, by R.L. Stevenson and Lloyd Osborne (first published in 1889). In the first verse-paragraph of 'In Memoriam James Joyce', MacDiarmid opens a lengthy parenthesis by recalling

> . . . R.L. Stevenson's Joseph Finsbury
> 'With a polyglot Testament in one hand
> And a phrase-book in the other,
> Groping his way among the speakers of eleven
>   European Languages,'
> — Joseph discoursing in the Tregonwell Arms
> To the inmates of the public bar
> On nine versions of a single income,
> Placing the imaginary person
> In London, Paris, Baghdad, Spitzbergen,
> Bassorah, Heligoland, the Scilly Isles,
> Brighton, Cincinnatti, and Nijni-Novgorod
> — Only an Englishman yet much to my liking
> And one I resemble in a little way perhaps

C.P., p.743

Here what MacDiarmid has transcribed has created an entirely different character for 'Joseph Finsbury'; in the first chapter of *The Wrong Box* he is heavily ironised:

> With a polyglot testament in one hand and a phrase-book in the other, he groped his way among the speakers of eleven European Languages. The first of these guides is hardly applicable to the purposes of the philosophic traveller, and even the second is designed more expressly for the tourist than for the expert in life. But he pressed interpreters into his service — whenever he could get their services for nothing — and by one

means and another filled many note-books with the results of his researches.

In 'The Lecturer at Large', Chapter 3 of the novel, Finsbury (who is referred to as 'Mr Finsbury' or 'Joseph', with a degree of affection but with a stronger degree of sharply sardonic familiarity) is shown to the 'Tregonwell Arms' where (after a meal and 'a big pewter mug of ale from the tap') he sits himself by the fire and begins to examine the other guests 'with an eye to the delights of oratory. There were near a dozen present, all men, and (as Joseph exulted to perceive) all working men. Often already had he seen cause to bless that appetite for disconnected fact and rotatory argument, which is so marked a character of the mechanic.' To court his audience, he spreads his papers before him and after a while the customers turn their eyes towards the unusual stranger ('and certainly it is unusual to see any one immersed in literary and scientific labours in the public apartment of an inn', he remarks, congratulating himself). He proceeds to read out his researches.

> Whereupon the old gentleman, with less compassion than he would have had for brute beasts, delivered himself of all his tedious calculations. As he occasionally gave nine versions of a single income, placing the imaginary person in London, Paris, Bagdad, Spitzbergen, Bassorah, Heligoland, the Scilly Islands, Brighton, Cincinnati, and Nijni-Novgorod, with an appropriate outfit for each locality, it is no wonder that his bearers look back on that evening as the most tiresome they ever spent.

Indeed, when Finsbury reaches the Scilly Isles only the proprietor is left with him, and next morning, when Finsbury is faced with a bill he cannot pay, the same proprietor insists that he leave without paying, and offers him ten shillings to be rid of him.

MacDiarmid likens himself to a Joseph Finsbury derived from this character, but one he has made different, from whom the meanness, tedium, self-satisfaction, and blindness have been almost (but not, I think, quite completely) removed. Finsbury in *The Wrong Box* is a comic or semi-comic figure, a close relation of Flaubert's Bouvard and Pécuchet. MacDiarmid was clearly aware of this, as he takes the trouble to emphasise the adventurous range and sensitivity of the Finsbury with whom he identifies, and elsewhere in the poem distinguishes himself and his poem from Bouvard and Pécuchet and their *Dictionary of Received Ideas*. And although MacDiarmid is risking the comparison, he is cautious: Finsbury, he says, he resembles 'a little in a way perhaps'; and after all he is only 'an Englishman'.

The sub-text *The Wrong Box* provides here (and aside from the reference in the poem to Stevenson, MacDiarmid does not direct you to the book), supplements our sense of what MacDiarmid's polymathic, polylinguistic fictions take as their dynamic. It alerts us to the solipsisms MacDiarmid is at pains to avoid (even if a number of critics, like G.S. Fraser, have concluded that he does not always avoid them). One last point to make about MacDiarmid's extract from *The Wrong Box* is how it foregrounds the proximity of linguistic ability ('Groping his way among the speakers of eleven European languages') with economic understanding (discussing 'nine versions of a single income').

The result of MacDiarmid's relativistic sense of language is that any emphasis on the specific meaning of a word is balanced by an awareness of variations across languages in different parts of the world. Yet it is an implicit factor of Marxism that historical materialism is a method for explanation in which finalism has a place, in which a place is set aside for the human ability to distinguish between means and ends, and to make plans consciously. Unconscious occurrences, however, constraints, the 'pre-historical' nature of class societies, must also be taken into consideration. Sebastiano Timpanaro, an astute Italian Marxist philologist, has argued that 'the evolution of language is at a halfway point between biological evolution and the evolution of human "institutions", because of the major role played in it by non-finalistic and unconscious changes.'[30] Language, for MacDiarmid also, divides the continuum of experience, but it is not a system sufficient unto itself.

Perhaps the key word in MacDiarmid's definition of language quoted above is 'progressive'. MacDiarmid's belief in the potential inherent in mankind was encouraged by the growth of technological means of communication in the early decades of the century, and it was shared by Joyce. For MacDiarmid, these technological advances meant most significantly the possibility of intelligent communication on a global scale. In terms of any single person, the consequence of such historical development was a greater access to the literature of the world throughout history, and concomitantly a more rigorous selectivity in appreciating it. This accounts for the contradiction in Pound's *ABC of Reading*, where he claims that his guidelines will help the reader read better and read *less*, while his own reading (like MacDiarmid's) was voracious. In an article in *The Scottish Journal*,

MacDiarmid explained his earliest ambitions regarding 'The Key to World Literature':

> I determined long ago not to learn every language, but to acquire such a body of knowledge and understanding that I could see the poetical output of mankind as a whole and know what every sizeable poet 'stood for' and 'amounted to' in relation thereto, no matter in what language. There can be no absolute agreement on these things, since tastes differ, but what I proposed to myself was that with any such poet in any language I should be able at any moment to show (1) that I have a good appreciation of his (or her) achievement, i.e. know which of the six classes of writer as defined in Pound's *How to Read*[31] he or she falls into and precisely why, and (2) that I have, if not a consensus, at least an important and defensible body of critical opinion with me in regard thereto.[32]

Goethe had spoken frequently (and more frequently as he grew older) of 'world literature', and of how national characteristics would be prized increasingly for their individuality, distinctiveness, and difference. 'World literature', MacDiarmid claimed, was conceived in a similar way by Goethe, Maxim Gorky, and himself (*C.P.*, p.736). In *Lucky Poet* (pp.138–9), he referred to Gorky's essay on 'World Literature' of 1919, published in *International Literature* in April 1938, and he affirmed Gorky's intention of becoming acquainted with all the 'interacting influences in literature among nations, and, in general, with the entire sweep of literary evolution'. MacDiarmid quoted Gorky:

> The great merit of literature is the fact that by deepening our consciousness, amplifying our sense of life, and shaping our feelings, it reveals to us that all ideas and actions, that the whole world of the spirit, is made of human nerves and blood.
>
> *Lucky Poet*, p.139

So MacDiarmid understood the idea of world literature to be in alignment with the development of communism. Gorky again:

> The sphere of literary creation is the international of the spirit; and in our day, when the idea of brotherhood among peoples, the idea of a social international is being clothed with reality, in our day we are bound to make every effort to hasten the assimilation of the redeeming concept of all-human brotherhood by the mind and will of the masses.
>
> *Lucky Poet*, p.139

Even in Marx's time, as S.S. Prawer has shown, the possibility of considering an enormous range of literatures had already arrived. Marx himself was a storehouse of information and knowledge about the literature of a variety of different lands and cultures.[33] Despite his commitment to a comparative and historical approach to literature, however, 'world literature' for Marx meant essentially the literature of Western Europe. There is nothing to correspond with MacDiarmid's greeting (after Dylan Thomas) of the Nigerian writer Amos Tutuola ('Who has begun the structure of new African literature', *C.P.*, p.793), or of his opening out to include the literature of the East, and there is much of world literature of which Marx had no knowledge. Yet, for MacDiarmid, it is not simply a question of *possessing* the 'key' to world literature, or of having a secure body of knowledge of it. It is also a question of understanding and practising the dynamics that animate literature.

After quoting a letter from Engels to Franz Mehring, in which Engels admitted that both he and Marx neglected the way in which ideas arose for the sake of their content, MacDiarmid declared that it is at this point that Marxist critics must begin. Art, MacDiarmid wrote, must be shown to be 'something more than the "idealogical" [*sic*] representation of class forces in society.'[34]

At a time when he felt a strong need to explain his political commitment to his long-standing friend and mentor, the composer F.G. Scott, MacDiarmid wrote a letter expressing what he took to be the essential importance of Marx for his own purposes. He was moving away from writing those lyrics which Scott could have set to music and towards the modes of his epic poetry. Scott saw this poetic development as co-aligned with MacDiarmid's Marxism.

> Marx's social philosophy is an attempt to discover, and to help to bring into existence, the social, cultural, and educational conditions under which all men and women may develop significant human personalities. The belief of religious advocates, e.g. Jacques Maritain, in a 'personality' which can exist independently of physical, biological, historical and cultural conditions is a consequence of bad psychology and still worse metaphysics.

> It is in Marx's scientific critique of abstractions that his irreligion lies and not in the village atheism with which it is confused by many Marxists and most non-Marxists alike. This

critique of abstractions constitutes the gravest challenge to the philosophy and theology of Maritain and all his kind. For it cuts all dogmas at their root, especially those based on what is called analogical knowledge of proportionality, and reveals them as the conceptual instruments of systematically cultivated *obscurantism.*

. . . He is always asking: what is the earthly and empirical basis for unearthly and non-empirical dogmas? In the abstractions of theology he finds a fetishism of words which conceals specific historical and organizational needs. In the abstractions of economics he finds a fetishism of commodities which conceals the fact that men today are controlled by the very forces of production they themselves create. In the abstractions of jurisprudence he finds a fetishism of principles which conceals the genuine power distributions in society. Each set of abstractions is accompanied by a set of practices. Since these abstractions are non-empirical and non-historical, the only meaning that can be assigned to them is in terms of these very practices. Wherever abstractions are worshipped, whether it be in theology, politics or physics, the task of scientific (materialistic) method is to locate the concrete situation in which they were first introduced, to observe the practices (Praxis) which they set up, and their subsequent career in stopping more fruitful modes of procedure.[35]

We should emphasise MacDiarmid's concern here for 'more fruitful modes of procedure' and note that he is talking not only about Marx's social philosophy but also defending his own developing poetic procedure and ambitions to an old and trusted friend.

MacDiarmid and Joyce

It seems that MacDiarmid had read and responded to Joyce long before his great poetic tribute.[36] It has been claimed that Mac-Diarmid was reading *Ulysses* when it began to appear in Margaret Anderson's *Little Review* from 1918 on, and when Sylvia Beach published the book in 1922 in an edition of one thousand, Mac-Diarmid apparently obtained a copy of it.[37] The following year, in his journal the *Scottish Chapbook*, MacDiarmid remarked upon the noteworthy 'moral resemblance' between *Ulysses* and the *Dictionary of the Older Scottish Tongue*, from which he had begun to quarry the most striking and crystalline words and phrases for his early lyrics in Scots.

It is a startling conjunction: a dictionary and a novel. But if the comparison seems odd, it is also just. Both *Ulysses* and the *Dictionary* are great avalanches of language, wonderfully ample books. In the 'Oxen of the Sun' section of *Ulysses*, Joyce called the book a 'chaffering and all including most farraginous chronicle' — where 'farraginous' means 'farrago-like': a brazen display of wares and a compendium, very like a dictionary. The 'moral resemblance' MacDiarmid noted was linked to what he called a '*vis comica*' in both books: the refusal of either book to be limited by conventional moral constraints and prudery — and a fusion of that with a fresh and vivid humour. He discerned in both books something that would please the spirit of comedy. MacDiarmid's linking of morality and humour is a key aspect of many of his Scots lyrics — 'Scunner', for example, or 'Focherty' — and it emerges crucially in the passages surrounding the most famous section ('O Wha's been here afore me, Lass') of *A Drunk Man Looks at the Thistle*, which W.B. Yeats liked enough not only to anthologise[38] but to commit to memory.

However, MacDiarmid was to comment in 1934 that his use of Scots had barely touched the fringe of Joycean experimentation. He said it was 'practically confined to the revival of Scots words with no equivalents, or precise equivalents, in English, on the one hand, and a use of Gaelic and foreign phrases and allusions on the other'.[39] This opens up a linguistic question; but first a distinction must be made between Joyce and MacDiarmid. In *Lucky Poet*, MacDiarmid approvingly quoted an obituarist who said of Joyce's novels that 'even the strongest of his characters seems dwarfed by the great apparatus of learning he brings to bear on them. They are almost like atoms being smashed by a 250-ton cyclotron.'[40] The image is a nice one, but it reflects a very different kind of élitism from that presented by Joyce's so-called 'difficulty', and the sense behind the obituarist's comment is suspect. Leopold Bloom needs all the words Joyce gives him, and Joyce is never *merely* condescending or scornful to Bloom. Joyce likes Bloom and Stephen; he likes Molly even more. He criticises, satirises, and undercuts their levity; but they are not 'atoms' to be 'smashed' by the weight of *Ulysses*. If Joyce can be identified as the man who wrote the book Stephen would not write and neither Bloom nor Molly would read, he cannot be cut off absolutely from the creatural existence these characters seem to have, and *Ulysses* is also a recognition of that common creaturality. Moreover, Joyce is rarely as strident as MacDiarmid was, defending him in a review of some Joyce criticism in the *Daily Worker* of April 1957. (The context, it is true, goes some way to explain his stridency:

MacDiarmid would have wanted the readers of the *Daily Worker*, the Communist Party newspaper, to be also readers of Joyce.) He said there:

> The right to ignorance, the avoidance of the excruciatingly painful business of thinking, cannot be conceded by anyone concerned with the interests of the masses of mankind. Defective education, limited sensibilities and a restriction to rudimentary interests can never be permitted to establish themselves as criteria of literary criticism. The cultural issue is the crucial and all important one, and is the end, in the light of which everything else must be regarded simply as means.

'Joyce is hard', as MacDiarmid succinctly puts it: 'but so is life.'

Yet MacDiarmid's polemic is not entirely absent in Joyce. Joyce takes up a stance that seems to prefigure MacDiarmid in his essay of 1901, 'The Day of the Rabblement', where he writes: 'No man, said the Nolan, can be a lover of the true or good unless he abhors the multitude; and the artist, though he may employ the crowd, is very careful to isolate himself.'[41] There is also an affinity in that colloquial term 'the Nolan'. 'The Nolan' was Giordano Bruno of Nola, Joyce's favourite philosopher. Joyce's intention (according to his brother Stanislaus) in referring to Bruno as 'the Nolan' was to interest his readers by giving them the impression that the quotation was from a little-known Irish authority. 'Laymen', Joyce repeated, 'should be encouraged to think.'

Ellsworth Mason and Richard Ellman have commented that in Joyce's poem 'Dooleysprudence',[42] 'the artist is the common man, not the heroic stag', but Mr Dooley is referred to in the poem as 'the funny fellow' (in *In Memoriam James Joyce* MacDiarmid refers to himself: 'As one of the "funny ones," a race which includes / Any creature unlike his fellows / And sensitive of his unlikeness . . . '[43]), 'the meek philosopher', 'the cheerful imbecile', 'the tranquil gentleman who won't salute the State / Or serve Nabuchodonosor or proletariat . . . ' (which recalls MacDiarmid's phrase: 'I am *of* not *for* the working class'). Dooley's refusal of the options he is faced with is an act of political subversion, not merely an act of sage individualism. Joyce wrote the poem in Zurich in 1916, at a time when almost all of the socialist parties in Europe had failed to oppose the First World War even verbally. During the Second World War, Joyce refused to make any public pronouncements on Mussolini or Hitler but, in fact, he helped several Jews to escape from Nazi persecution to Ireland, the United States, and England. 'As an artist',

Joyce said to George Borach in 1918, 'I attach no importance to political conformity.'[44] That was not a mere renunciation; Mac-Diarmid might have said the same thing.

Joyce's position is difficult, then, to reconcile with orthodox political terms. MacDiarmid — who was certainly politically unorthodox, having been expelled (twice) from the Communist Party because of his nationalism, and having been rejected from the National Party of Scotland for communist deviation — was nevertheless also committed to the world of practical politics, the day-to-day business of being, for example, a socialist Justice of the Peace (in 1922), or the communist candidate who (in 1964) ran against the then Prime Minister Sir Alec Douglas-Home in Douglas-Home's home constituency. (MacDiarmid had rejoined the Communist Party in 1957 and remained a member for the rest of his life.) To step further back is to understand the politically unorthodox commitments of both Joyce and MacDiarmid in the context of Britain and the legacy of the British Empire. And this is also to understand their unorthodox attitudes to language: for the relation of political, literary, and linguistic identity was as intimate and imposing for MacDiarmid as it was for Joyce. For both men, the history of writing and rebellion was long and interwoven.

Joyce wrote in 1907: 'It will seem strange that an island as remote from the centre of culture could excel as a school for apostles, but even a superficial consideration will show us that the Irish nation's insistence on developing its own culture by itself is not so much the demand of a young nation that wants to make good in the European concert as the demand of a very old nation to renew under new forms the glories of a past civilization.'[45] Compare his lecture on 'The Centenary of Charles Dickens':

> To arrive at a just appreciation of Dickens, to estimate more accurately his place in what we may call the national gallery of English literture it would be well to read not only the eulogies of the London-born but also the opinions of representative writers of Scotland, or the Colonies or Ireland. It would be interesting to hear an appreciation of Dickens written, so to speak, at a proper focus from the original by writers of his own class and of a like (if somewhat lesser) stature, near enough to him in aim and in form and in speech to understand, far enough from him in spirit and blood to criticise. One is curious to know how the great Cockney would fare at the hands of R.L.S. or of Mr Kipling or of Mr George Moore.[46]

For Joyce *and* MacDiarmid, the status of the provincial intellectual was both literary *and* social, both a cultural matter and a
national one. Both men denied the very notion of the status of
the provincial intellectual as it was accorded by the anglocentric
establishment. Both were (and to some extent, MacDiarmid still is)
rejected and refused by English literary culture; and both, also,
rejected it.

The Irish literary movement Joyce turned his back on was very
different from the Scottish movement MacDiarmid began to bring
about in the 1920s, but both movements were similarly beleaguered
by the provincial status of their political contexts. Joyce's regret that
Yeats was too old to be influenced by him is indicative of the degree
to which an Anglo-Irish as well as an Irish nationalism was inimical
to the spirit Joyce was preparing to invoke. To Joyce, the politics
and language of nationalism seemed cripplingly insular. He held
very deep political beliefs about the dangers and the values, the
liability and privilege, of national identity, but the initial step of
exile and the eventual refusal to return shows the physical as well
as spiritual threat Ireland had come to represent for him. Its
nationalism was politically reactionary; its sexuality consummately
repressed.

When Joyce has Stephen declare that literature is 'the eternal
affirmation of the spirit of man' the word 'eternal' has as much
weight as the word 'affirmation'. Consequently, the stasis Joyce
sought in art is not to be understood as quiescence or neutrality.
That MacDiarmid saw the Irish literary movement as a *point de
départ* for the Scottish movement suggests that he understood both
the possibility of a continuity and the need for a change in the
production of such work as he, following Joyce, was capable. Mac-
Diarmid consistently refused to see in Scotland the Scotland that he
wanted; but he could live nowhere else for any length of time, and
his demand for political autonomy retained a dynamic importance
as an integral part of his life and work. Scotland, indeed, has not
been the same place since his death.

The contrast with Joyce is most strongly shown by MacDiarmid's
regret that — unlike Joyce's relation to Yeats — the younger figures
of the Scottish renaissance movement were too young to benefit
from the magnificent example of R.B. Cunninghame Graham. Cunninghame Graham's grandeur, his public personality, his radical
socialism, and the sober authority with which he actively advocated
militant demonstration were qualities MacDiarmid found to be sadly
lacking in almost all his political contemporaries. In Scotland, it was

not bigoted popular nationalism that had to be contended with but a middle-class, philistine indifference, a tendency to sentimentalise and dilute hard questions, and an ironical and self-belittling sense of critical humour. For MacDiarmid, Scotland was the site for his own demonstration: this is the political significance of his public persona, his celebrations, and his enthusiasms equally with his published venom. Political and spiritual oppressions were indissolubly mixed for him; while, for Joyce, the protest against the religious order led directly to socialist politics. As Dominic Manganiello has said, 'Joyce rejected all social ties manifested in the tyrannies of the Church, the family and the nation.'[47] When he revisited Dublin from Trieste in 1909, Joyce wrote to his wife Nora: 'I loathe Ireland and the Irish. They themselves stare at me in the street though I was born among them.'[48] Compare MacDiarmid's vitriolic outburst about 'all the drivel about "Home Sweet Home" four million cretins iterate'.[49]

The linguistic contradictions both men encountered in their cultures twist on the word 'English', with its ambivalent senses of linguistic pervasion, political dominance, and cultural ascendancy. In the establishment of bourgeois nation states the key factor of economic homogeneity has often been aligned with the establishment of linguistic homogeneity, and the appeal to linguistic 'purity' often functions with the appeal to other notions of purity — national and racial, for instance. This is relevant not only to Joyce and MacDiarmid but also to the situation which faces writers in many post-colonial or neo-colonial cultures in other parts of the earth. Consider the question in terms of Scots, however. In Chapter 1 of Volume I of the Aberdeen University Press *History of Scottish Literature*, a scholarly commentator discusses Middle Scots as a literary language:

> The claim that Middle Scots had its own standard, independent of the Southern Standard, raises the question of whether middle Scots should be regarded as a separate language from English or only as a separate dialect. The answer to this question depends ultimately on the definition of a language . . . If our definition of a language includes functional and social criteria, then there are good reasons for describing Middle Scots as a separate language: its use was not restricted to particular types of text or to particular situations, nor was its use restricted to a particular social group. It could even be used in diplomacy between countries (e.g. letters to English monarchs were frequently written in Scots although the replies

came in southern English). As a result of its official status and widespread use, Middle Scots developed a range of stylistic variation clearly illustrated in literary texts. On the other hand, dialects are usually restricted in their range of uses, e.g. they are not used for the records of parliament . . . In those terms, the situation of Middle Scots contrasts markedly with that of [e.g.] modern Austrian German which is not used for official purposes and does not display much stylistic variation; of course, it also contrasts with the position of Scots today.[50]

Scholarly caution is treading warily here on the slopes of a live volcano. Compare Norman MacCaig, whose own poetry is written in English:

Scots, it must be observed, is not English badly spelled; nor is it a dialect of English. To simplify, but not in a direction away from the truth: the Scots language was a development and by no means a degeneration of the Anglian branch of what is called Old English, and was originally spoken from the Forth to the Humber — that's to say, on both sides of the Border. The Saxon branch to the South flourished and became what we call English. With the establishment of the Border, the Anglian branch developed as Scots. Scots and English, therefore, are common languages with a common ancestor, and it is as absurd to call Scots a dialect of English as it would be to call English a dialect of Scots.

By our time, however, Scots had become weathered into dialects of itself, its vocabulary had become sadly impoverished. Hugh MacDiarmid set himself the enormous task of establishing 'a full cannon of Scots' — by enriching the vocabulary with whatever words suited his purpose, even if they had been obsolete for centuries. A queer marriage this, you might say, of the dying with the dead. The odd thing is, it worked, for himself if not for others, which only goes to show that you *can* strike water from the rock if your name is Moses. The importance of the language question for Scottish poets is under-estimated by many critics. Wilfulness and perversity have nothing to do with it. Sorley MacLean, a Scottish poet second only to MacDiarmid, writes in our third language (Gaelic) — and thereby restricts his intelligent audience to a mere handful. Nobody does that except for the deepest and most urgent reasons.[51]

As a vernacular language, Scots had been evolving quasi-independently from English (especially from the southern dialects) for over thirteen centuries. Its use in writing dates from the fourteenth century. The crucial development of the English language in Ireland was the Cromwellian settlement of the 1650s, and the result is a distinctively Irish speech — but not the equivalent of Scots. The English language in Ireland, like English in America, became so naturalised it seemed indigenous. But it is a very recent 'settler' and, as such, might be felt to be — to use a Joycean term — a usurper. Not that it could be replaced by a 'rightful heir' but it enforces a condition of estrangement by its presence alone. It is this condition which causes Stephen Dedalus to vent his anger in his diary at the end of *A Portrait of the Artist as a Young Man*, when he remembers his tense conversation with the English Dean of Studies about the words 'tundish' and 'funnel':

> April 13. That tundish has been on my mind for a long time. I looked it up and find it English and good blunt English too. Damn the Dean of Studies and his funnel! What did he come here for to teach us his own language or to learn it from us? Damn him one way or the other!

Seamus Heaney, in his poem 'Station Island', is recalling this when he conjures the spirit of Joyce:

> 'Who cares,'
> he jeered, 'any more? The English language
> belongs to us. You are raking at dead fires ... '

The critic Denis Donoghue's perceptive comment on this is that the English language may belong to us but it does not follow that we belong to it, or that Heaney dwells in it as comfortably as Philip Larkin or Charles Tomlinson. The problem lies in the imputation of bad faith towards the Irish (Gaelic) language, not the English, and towards the experience the Irish language alone takes responsibility for.[52] The Irish language, however, as the Irish poet and critic Tom Paulin has said, was never completely suppressed or rejected, and it became central to the new Irish national consciousness which formed late in the nineteenth century. This is the situation which Joyce parodies in the opening section of *Ulysses*, where the Englishman Haines addresses the Irishwoman who has brought in the morning's milk in Irish Gaelic, only to find that she cannot understand the language. The target of this is not only the pious conceit of the Englishman and the imperial condescension in his attitude but furthermore the expectations of the Irish revivalists themselves.

In Scotland in the 1920s it was Scots which was most often used as the language of nationalist poetry; Scottish Gaelic did not become important as a language of the Scottish literary renaissance until the late 1930s and the 1940s.[53] MacDiarmid once commented that Scots — vernacular Scots — *included* English. But that, too, begs the question. For Scots was a flourishing vernacular language when MacDiarmid was a boy and inherently different from — indeed, defined against — English. Scots was for the playground; English for the classroom. Tom Paulin also noted:

> The history of a language is often a story of possession and dispossession, territorial struggle and the establishment or imposition of a culture. Arguments about the 'evolution' or the 'purity' of a language can be based on a simplistic notion of progress or on a doctrine of racial stereotypes. Thus a Spenserian phrase which Samuel Johnson employs in the famous preface to his dictionary — 'the wells of English undefiled' — is instinct with a mystic and exclusive idea of nationhood. It defines a language and a culture in terms of a chimerical idea of racial purity.[54]

The position of Dictionary Johnson is ultimately one of xenophobia, exclusivity, and (as such) sentimentalism (any claim for exemption is sentimental). It is a privileging of English that was echoed down to I.A. Richards and beyond. Joyce exorcises this notion by subsuming it in the larger question of how adequate any language can be. If this is a theoretical question, it is also a profoundly political one. Joyce rejected the Irish nationalist argument because it could not accommodate what *he* could accommodate. A homogeneous image of Ireland was proposed by the Celtic Revival and the Anglo-Irish Yeats. Such an image was forcefully enacted during the Easter Rising. But to Joyce, the image seemed fatally limited. Throughout Joyce's work, with increasing complexity and thoroughness, the notion of a 'pure' racial, national, or linguistic identity is shown to be not simply reactionary but an aboriginal impossibility.

The idea itself is constantly undermined by shifting understanding, plurality, and variousness.[55] As Lloyd Fernando has written in 'Joyce and the Artist's Quest for a Universal Language' in a book published in 1986 in Singapore (that is to say, at some distance from the Anglo-American critical establishment), if there are at least forty languages working in *Finnegans Wake*, none of them can claim total aptitude. 'It is not surprising at all that before leaving Ireland the only thing [Stephen] finds himself "armed" with besides exile and cunning is — silence.'[56]

Perhaps one of the reasons for Joyce's going abroad into a European exile was the English language itself. If English once seemed to augur well as the 'basic' world language, we should also understand the significance of that as part of the imperial legacy; how its presence in colonial or post-colonial societies is due to the imperial histories of Britain and America; and, consequently, how much that notion of 'basic' (or 'pure') English makes the English language everywhere a foreigner.

Joyce is a master of English in *Dubliners*, the *Portrait*, and *Ulysses*, but it is the multilingual Joyce of *Finnegans Wake* MacDiarmid especially celebrates, praising him for 'vastly outrunning present needs / But providing for the developments to come'.[57] MacDiarmid claims Joyce as part of the Celtic world — that is, a world conspicuously without an imperial history of its own in national or linguistic terms but whose people were always *both* the exploited and oppressed *as well as* the exploiters and oppressors. MacDiarmid referred in 1934 to the recording Joyce made, saying that 'In *Work in Progress*, Joyce, using about a score of languages [*sic*], becomes not less, but more, Irish. "Annia Livia Plurabelle" may look incomprehensible on the printed page; but on the gramophone record, in Joyce's own voice, it gets right over to every hearer . . . '[58] This is the Joyce MacDiarmid celebrates and eulogises in his *In Memoriam* poem, for, despite the very actual differences between them (the overtly didactic element in MacDiarmid, his explicit political commitments, Joyce's careful disengagement from any public demonstrations of enthusiasm, and the enormous personal restraint with which he balanced his literary generosity), they do share an effortless compulsion to enter fully into the present century, and they understand fully the implications this has for language.

MacDiarmid, like Joyce, willingly and irreversibly enters a world of global consequence and linguistic variety all but incommensurate with a single person's experience.[59] If Joyce and MacDiarmid anticipate more contemporary writers like Wilson Harris and Derek Walcott who exploit the condition of post-imperial collapse to create great writing from a wonderfully unstable language, then Joyce and MacDiarmid were indeed 'providing for the developments to come'. For both men, like these Caribbean writers, understood that one's native language is (like one's native land) in a constant condition of

crumbling and reformation, and, more instructively, that for the
artist (if not for the society) this is a source of energy and a creative
potential, a potentially liberating force rather than a restrictive,
debilitating, or coercive one.

'The World of Words' and Language

Millennial Poetics

'The World of Words', like all of MacDiarmid's epic poetry, is
millennial, and MacDiarmid's attitude to language is that of a millennial poet. In the Introduction to his anthology *The American
Long Poem*, Stephen Fender characterises as central to his selection
the idea of 'millennial poetics' and refers to Emerson's essay 'The
Poet'. There, he argues, Emerson is adapting to the sphere of aesthetics an old English and American tradition of millennial prophecy,
which included apocalyptic sermons adducing contemporary signs
portending the end of history.

> These signs may be natural disasters, recent disorders in the
> state, or something else noteworthy to which the preacher can
> refer knowing the audience will follow his references. History
> is thought to be drawing to a close because it has grown too
> 'old' in accretions of habit and formality; church law and
> polity have grown too complex for their original function; the
> hierarchy has lost touch with ordinary people and can be
> influenced by powerful interests; forms of worship — physical
> and verbal — have grown too stylized to mean anything to
> ordinary parishioners; images and paraphernalia clutter the
> churches themselves. The same disorder is mirrored in the
> state: the king's advisors insulate him from the people; civil
> service posts are bought and sold; the wealth unevenly distri-
> buted. After the cataclysm that brings an end to historical
> time, the millennium itself, the thousand years of peace, will
> begin. Conditions in the millennium will be the exact opposite
> of those prevailing before the cataclysm: all the elaborations
> of law, polity, formula and image will have been stripped
> away; so will civil servants and priests — the ordinary man
> will no longer need intermediaries between himself and his
> God and king; worship and government will become plain
> things, directly expressed.[60]

For the apocalyptic poets in Fender's anthology — Whitman, Hart

Crane, Pound, Stevens, Williams — the characteristic paradox of millennial poetry arises: how to present in a pre-apocalyptic world both a version of the post-apocalyptic poem and information about the poem and about the decadence it might replace; how to present simultaneously the inevitability *and* the desirability of that change. Fender allows some of Emerson's descriptions of what the ideal poet should be to characterise Whitman and Pound, who, in Emerson's words, present as poetry the simple acts of announcing and affirming. 'Bare lists of words are found suggestive . . . The vocabulary of an omniscient man would embrace words and images excluded from polite conversation.' And he says that much of these poets' work seems the product of a 'grotesque apprenticeship to chance event' — they incorporate scraps of 'factual' material found in the actual world about them. These themselves can be ephemeral or historically significant, but the poem's context confers an urgency and coherence upon them by including them in a kind of vision. As a result, the long poem might arouse certain expectations in the reader of formal structure, of the relevance of individual titles, of ultimate illumination, which are encouraged only to be denied.

When 'The World of Words' begins with something called an 'Idea and Word Chart' by which a world vocabulary is made accessible and a 'vision of world language' is invoked, we have to deal with the text as we have it and also consider the millennium to which it refers. MacDiarmid's millennium differs from that of the American poets, moreover, in that it is Marxist; his vision of world language is a communist one. It is exactly in keeping with the formula proposed by Stalin (or Stalin's writers) in *Marxism and the Problem of Linguistics*, where we read that in 'the epoch *after the victory of socialism* on a world scale' the imperialist policy of suppressing and assimilating languages will no longer exist.

> Here we shall have not two languages, one of which is to suffer defeat, while the other is to emerge from the struggle victorious, but hundreds of national languages, out of which, as a result of a prolonged economic, political and cultural co-operation of nations, there will first appear most enriched unified zonal languages, and subsequently the zonal languages will merge into a single international language, which, of course, will be neither German, nor Russian, nor English, but a new language that has absorbed the best elements of the national and zonal languages.[61]

This is the situation implied in the original Author's Note to *In*

Memoriam James Joyce, where MacDiarmid claims that the only situation in which such a unification of diversities as that he envisages can be achieved is 'a society which I naturally visualize as Marxist'.

The social vision of the American poets derives from puritan tradition, and Fender's answer to the question 'how to work the poetics to present the reformed state as perfect and unachieved?' is the open-ended poem which prompts readers to construct their own closure. This is very much in the spirit of individualism that puritan tradition has underwritten, and it is something MacDiarmid, despite his claim to be free of any supernatural faith, could not completely escape. Indeed, he had already celebrated fanatic puritanism in 'The Covenanters' (in *Second Hymn to Lenin and Other Poems*, published in 1935):

> The waves of their purposefulness go flooding through me.
> This religion is simple, naked. Its values stand out
> In black and white. It is the wind of God;
> Like standing on a mountain top in a gale
> Binding, compelling, yet gloriously freeing.
> It contains nothing tawdry or trivial.
> Its very ugliness is compelling,
> Its bleakness uplifting.
> It holds me in a fastness of security.

> > *C.P.*, p.551

The certainty that runs through this is directly inherited from puritan tradition, and it is problematic. The last great poet to confront its difficulty was Milton, in *De Doctrine Christiana*, taking Protestantism to its logical conclusion, and admitting that a church can be composed of a single person. For Protestantism rejects any mediation between the individual, honest Christian and the vernacular Bible he or she can read. But a number of individual readings will inevitably produce a number of different understandings, and a number of different meanings. To accept and endorse one over any other would be to accept the social mediation of such meanings — which is the way of Catholicism. For MacDiarmid, the attempt to graft this puritan 'purposefulness' onto communist ideology resulted in his sometimes stormy relationship with the Communist Party of Great Britain, as well as the complexities and contradictions in the poetry itself.[62]

These complexities and contradictions cannot be simply explained away. MacDiarmid's loyalty to his political beliefs can look very like dogmatic adherence in some lights, and his Stalinism has drawn a range of antipathetic responses, from sheer incredulity to violent hostility. In the terms of the present discussion, the revolutionary millennium the poetry invokes should be understood as neither purely literary nor purely political, but rather as something that partakes of both the literary and political spheres. Perhaps the point at which the problems can be most clearly located in the poetry is where the notion of millennial transformation (the shift through revolution into a future state, where 'mature art' is possible and the repressions of state control have withered away) coincides with the practice of the text. If the former is thought of as something which happens through a course of sequential events in time, the latter can be seen existing in the poetry as a quality or technical characteristic. This means that the poetry itself is 'millennial' but the society in which it is published and circulated remains on this side of the transition. We shall return to this question when we come to the final section of the poem, 'Plaited Like the Generations of Men'.

'The World of Words'

The second section of *In Memoriam James Joyce*, to quote Edwin Morgan, 'moves in roughly the same territory as the first, but is directed more towards the psychology of readers' reception and perception of words, letters, metres, syntax, symbols, spelling, calligraphy, shibboleths, secret languages — everything involved in the complex relations between writing, speech, and thought.'[63]

'The World of Words' has two epigraphs. The first is from Yeats's 'The Song of the Happy Shepherd' from *Crossways* (1889): 'Words alone are certain good.' The second is from the essay 'God-Makers' by J.B.S. Haldane, in *The Inequality of Man and other essays* (1932):

> The philosophy of the Middle Ages was the work of men who were ignorant of nature, but learned the Latin grammar. Neglecting the verbs, they tried to describe the universe in terms of substantives and adjectives, to which they attributed an independent existence under the name of substances and accidents or attributes. Modern physicists are engaged in a somewhat similar attempt to describe it in terms of verbs only, their favourite verb at the moment to undulate, or wiggle.

Haldane was a physiologist, biochemist, and geneticist, who came from a distinguished Scottish family and spent his working life mainly in England and India. He was a member of the Communist Party and contributed over three hundred articles to the *Daily*

Worker, motivated by his sense of the responsibility of the scientist to the non-specialist. He would appear to belong to another world than Yeats's, yet the epigraphs complement each other by suggesting the contiguity of object-based and relational ways of understanding language. Implicit in the Yeats quotation is the certainty allowed by specific things in an age of chaos and dissolution. 'The Song of the Happy Shepherd' begins:

> The woods of Arcady are dead,
> And over is their antique joy;
> Of old the world on dreaming fed;
> Grey Truth is now her painted toy;
> Yet still she turns her restless head:
> But O, sick children of the world,
> Of all the many changing things
> In dreary dancing past us whirled,
> To the cracked tune that Chronos sings,
> Words alone are certain good.[64]

To Yeats, the physical presence of the word on the page or the mental apprehension of certain words in particular formal relations to each other sets words off as distinct, singularly reliable *things* in a world of confusion and discord. For Haldane, however, language is a metaphor for natural philosophy, and the volatility of verbal functions in grammar corresponds to modern physicists' understanding of the universe. Haldane's essay is about the creation of the founding religions and is a warning against idealism as something that may lead towards unproductive and dogmatic forms of sacralising worship.[65]

'The World of Words' opens with a semi-abstract vision of something like a universal word processor, which will put both words and ideas 'at your fingertips'. A felicitous apprehension of formerly elusive meanings and words is now or will soon become possible, MacDiarmid claims. The tone and syntax of the verse combine to effect a spontaneity of announcement and affirmation, starting in the present tense, exclaiming: 'Easy — Quick — Sure — The exact word / You want — when you want it . . . ' (*C.P.*, p.805). But if the opening announcement is immediate, there is none the less the implication that this 'Idea and Word Chart' is not yet actually in existence and the tense changes from present to future:

> It puts words and ideas at your finger tips,
> It will enable you to open the flood-gates of the mind

And let the torrent of drama and tragedy —
Human strife, flaming love, raging passion,
Fiendish onslaught, splendid heroism —
Flow from your pen, leap into type
And fly to your readers, to grip them and hold them
Enthralled by the fascinating spell of your power.

C.P., p.805

While the poem partly exemplifies the process it describes, the process described seems also to be an objective or goal. Then Mac-Diarmid changes tack. We are quite suddenly off on a rapid tour through a series of lists of writers upon the relation of words to psychology, perceptiveness, aesthetics, temperament, physiognomy, upon the relation of sound to meaning (with reference to criticism that takes account of acoustic terms, optical-kinaesthetic reactions and the tactical imagery of, for example, Keats). MacDiarmid's lists here have an accumulative power. He balances in juxtaposition the need 'for the capture of objects complete / By the assimilative imagination' and the 'gap in Athena's speech' — the silence neither Aeschylus nor Dante could fill. The plentitude of language forms is set against the silence language cannot enter. Against this he sets Goethe's ' . . . although men be stricken dumb in woe / A God did grant me words to tell my sorrow'. And against *this* he puts the *Rubaiyat*'s mysterious line: 'U danad u danad u danad u—'. He affirms both the value and usefulness of language, for expression as well as designation, and returns to what transcends expression and acknowledges what cannot be accurately pointed to. Aware and insistent that detailed observation, proper focus, balanced allocation are desirable, and that the linguists he names — Alspach, English, Downey, Bullough, Roblee, Washburn, and others — offer the most helpful insights and analyses, MacDiarmid also bears in mind that they are all finally of no help in dealing with the ineffable bases of language. This insistence on the ineffable, that which remains beyond our expressive or analytic abilities, is typical, and it maintains a sense of secular wonder. It is an indication of a kind of wilful submission that leaves itself open and receptive to everything that remains undefined. It is a refusal to offer a closed, secure explanation, and is to that extent in keeping with the procedure of the poem, which, instead of presenting accurate or reliable summaries of contemporary developments in linguistic studies, races with breathtaking speed through lists and names.

However, even the bare titles of the books and the small quotations, paraphrases, or distillations from them are sufficient to indicate the vastness of the field. We are 'familiar with' (MacDiarmid asserts) the unknown tongues that follow derangement of the senses, the sudden fluent speech of mutes, Korzybski, Richards, and the ideas that are mentioned in passing, which often alert the reader to any tendency to gloss or skip over the passages:

> . . . the longer most people live
> The less they are inclined to examine objects in all their parts,
> Hence if they look at them from a new point of view
> They often see something in old familiar things
> They had not noticed before —

C.P., p.813

The spontaneous, energetic play of names and ideas, one suggesting the next, multiplying out of all proportion, each ready to be dropped for the next with no notice given, suggests that every new name or idea occupies a potential facet of the vision as a whole. There are also guests not yet arrived whose places await them.

A little later in the poem, MacDiarmid addresses Joyce directly: 'Ah, Joyce, this is our task': making a single creation 'of all these oppositions'.

> With natures like ours in which a magnetic fluidity
> That is neither 'good' nor 'bad' is forever
> Taking new shapes under the pressure of circumstances,
> Taking new shapes, and then again,
> As Kwang makes Confucius complain of Laotze,   5
> 'Shooting up like a dragon.'
> But, taking my life as a whole,
> And hovering with the flight of the hawk
> Over its variegated landscape,
> I believe I detect certain quite definite 'streams of tendency'   10
> In that unrolling map,
> Moving towards the unknown future.
> For one thing I fancy the manner I have allowed
> My natural impulses towards romance and mysticism
> To dominate me has led to the formation   15
> Of a curious gap or 'lacuna'
> Between the innate and almost savage realism,
> Which is a major element in my nature,
> And the imaginative, poetical cult
> Whereby I have romanticised and idealized my life.   20

In this realistic mood I recognise
With a grim animal acceptance
That it is indeed likely enough that the 'soul'
Perishes everlastingly with the death of the body,
But what this realistic mood, into which   25
My mind falls like a plummet
Through the neutral zone of its balanced doubt,
Never for one single beat of time can shake or disturb
Is my certain knowledge,
Derived from the complex vision of everything in me,   30
That the whole astronomical universe, however illimitable,
Is only one part and parcel of the mystery of Life;
Of this I am as certain as I am certain that I am I.
The astronomical universe is *not* all there is.

So this is what our lives have been given to find,   35
A language that can serve our purposes . . .

                                                        C.P., pp.821–2

The call to Joyce at this point in the poem restores its focus and underscores the impression of personal involvement. The duality of 'the innate and almost savage realism' and 'the imaginative, poetical cult' which romanticises and idealises is a peculiar disclosure. It opens up the possibility of rhetorical self-hypnosis to which Mac-Diarmid returns in 'Plaited Like the Generations of Men', and it also suggests the contempt MacDiarmid feels for others which is also registered in the last section of the Joyce poem.

The shifts over the three parts of the passage quoted (ll. 1–6, 7–20, 21–34) are abrupt, but in the last part at least an immediacy is achieved. There is a sensible awareness of the abstract words evoking space, the 'mind' falling 'like a plummet' through zones of uncertainty, of the discernible, astronomical universe, and the mystery which imbues our apprehension of it.

The vocabulary of the passage is strikingly similar to that used by John Cowper Powys in an essay on Walt Whitman, and Mac-Diarmid's argument is close to the assertive optimism Powys praises in the American.

> Without *mind* of some sort — though not necessarily without the particular multifarious human minds that people our earth — this visible world of the senses would simply cease to exist; for to *be* there, and to have no consciousness, would be identical with not being there at all. It would leave the universe a complete blank.

Now since the adherents of the astronomical world *as all there is* are constantly referring to immensities of time — these sacred 'immensities' with which they would overawe a mind that can travel through eternity a billion times faster than the fastest light-wave — when nothing but blind forces and the possibility of blind mathematical symbols existed, we are forced to assume that for unthinkable periods of time there was simply *nothing anywhere.*[66]

Powys goes on to argue against these 'adherents' and to celebrate the awareness of 'teeming Reservoirs, Levels, Regions and Dimensions of Life' which is evident in Whitman.

MacDiarmid was not merely inspired by Powys's prose, however. He has, in fact, made a direct transcription — not from Powys's essay on Whitman but from three paragraphs in the final pages of the last chapter of Powys's *Autobiography*.

With a nature like mine in which a magnetic fluidity, that is neither 'good' nor 'bad,' is forever taking new shapes under the pressure of circumstances — taking new shapes and then again, as Kwang makes Confucius complain of Laotze, 'shooting up like a dragon' — it is not easy to weigh or measure any change in the core of character.

But taking my life as a whole and hovering with the flight of a hawk over its variegated landscape, I believe that I detect certain quite definite 'streams of tendency' in that unrolled map, moving towards the unknown future. For one thing, I fancy that the manner in which I have allowed my natural impulses towards romance and mysticism to dominate me has led to the formation of a curious gap or 'lacuna', between the innate and almost savage realism, which after all is an element in my nature, and the imaginative, poetical cult, whereby I have romanticized and idealized my life.

In this realistic mood I recognize with a grim animal acceptance that it is indeed likely enough that the 'soul' perishes everlastingly with the death of the body. But what this realistic mood, into which my mind falls like a plummet through the neutral zone of its balanced doubt, never for one single beat of time can shake or disturb is my *certain knowledge*, derived from the 'Complex Vision' of everything in me, that the whole astronomical universe, however illimitable, is only one part and parcel of the Mystery of Life. Of this I am *as certain as I am certain that I am I.* The astronomical universe is *not* all there is; but whether this certainty implies the survival of any portion or any degree of my own consciousness after death is a very different matter; and of this, I confess, I am *not* certain.[67]

It is worth noting how MacDiarmid drops that last part of that final sentence, which would have altered the mood of the poem completely. His appropriation is by no means indiscriminate. But it is, obviously, extensive. And there is clearly something outrageous about taking a passage from a major autobiography and presenting a personal statement in it as his own. Yet is this all that MacDiarmid does? He makes no acknowledgement to the *Autobiography*, but Powys is quoted in an epigraph to *In Memoriam James Joyce* and it is known that MacDiarmid thought highly of him. Moreover, although MacDiarmid keeps the words 'My' ('My natural impulses', 'My mind') and 'I' ('I recognize . . . '), he does begin the passage by changing Powys's 'with a nature like mine . . . ' to 'with natures like ours'. And by that he seems to mean Joyce and himself. By implication, too, he might mean, or invite, the reader to be part of this confluence. Is he not, then, including Powys also? Ending the verse-paragraph with a climactic assertion, MacDiarmid throws the certainty of authorial intention into serious doubt. What are we to make of 'Of this I am as certain as I am certain that I am I'? Who are we to imagine is speaking here? And how does that alter the statement which follows this assertion of certainty? To judge from the paucity of commentary on these texts, conventional criticism is helplessly inhibited before them.

The metaphorical juxtaposition of polar exploration and journeying through dictionaries, which we have already discussed, leads on to a rejection of the kind of textual compilation MacDiarmid does *not* want: the monstrous, sterile work which Flaubert satirised so thoroughly in *Bouvard and Pécuchet* and which formed the subject of his two immense studies, the *Dictionnaire des Idées Reçues* and the *Sottisier*. MacDiarmid is here adapting a passage from G.W. Stonier's Introduction to the translation of *Bouvard and Pécuchet* which he made with T.W. Earp.[68] MacDiarmid says he has all mankind 'like a few friends at the fireside':

> . . . without recourse to the *Dictionnaire des Idées*
>
> *Reçues*
> And the *Sottisier*, that Siberia of the human spirit,
> The ghastly miles stretching endlessly on every side . . .
>
> C.P., p.824

He goes on:

> My muse 'needeth no simple man' — no 'review of all the
>   sciences
> As they appear to two lucid enough minds
> Of a mediocre, simple order' . . . or a few million such minds
> '*Pas de monstres et pas de héros,*'
> Not overhung with the 'weight of all the world'
> But only with a vast panoply of knowledge
> That seems more and more fantastic,
> Tired Jobs, agèd eagles, Bouvard and Pécuchet,
> Coping with the immense florilegium of nonsense they have
>   compiled
> As a result of their search, i.e. with Flaubert's *Sottisier*
> Brought up to date by H.L. Mencken and Gerald Barry
>
> > C.P., pp.824–5

In Stonier's introduction we find not only the source of this passage
but also the source for the quotation from Maupassant within it;
MacDiarmid takes both without acknowledgement beyond the hint
in the reference to the two petit-bourgeois heroes. *Bouvard and
Pécuchet* is, we are told,

> . . . a satire on self-education, an epic of the commonplace,
> with a *bourgeois* Mister Everyman in place of the hero of a
> Morality Play and a Correspondence College in the back-
> ground. (Flaubert's vision is prophetic.) It is a satire, too, on
> the futility of wrong methods. But is that all? Maupassant's
> description, 'a review of all the sciences as they appear to two
> lucid enough minds of a mediocre, simple order,' is so far
> accurate. But as the book advances, the characters of Bouvard
> and Pécuchet change; they themselves become less ridiculous,
> however helpless in small things, the vast panoply of knowl-
> edge seems more and more fantastic; and when at the end of
> their adventures, like tired Jobs, they sit down to copy again,
> what they are going to copy is the florilegium of nonsense
> which they have compiled in the course of their search, i.e. the
> *Sottisier* elaborately collected by Flaubert himself. They have
> grown aware (we are told) of stupidity, and no longer tolerate
> it; indeed, they are imbued, though to a limited degree, with
> the critical spirit of their author, and over them, as over him,
> there hangs 'the weight of all the world.'[69]

Further on we read: '*Pas de monstres et pas de héros!* — the comic pair are neither.' And again:

> Stupidity — that more than anything — excited, and depressed Flaubert in life, and as an artist he returned to it again and again with exasperated success. In *Bouvard and Pécuchet* he discovers a whole continent, a Siberia of the human spirit, the ghastly miles stretching endlessly on every side. All of us, except the brutishly stupid, are aware of these regions in ourselves, but, frightened by their extent, we tolerate or ignore them.[70]

MacDiarmid makes the comparison between Flaubert's *Dictionnaire* and *Sottisier* and his own rag-bag poem only to reject it. He is no Bouvard or Pécuchet. Some lines earlier MacDiarmid had referred to Mozart:

> — The sense of pure delight and spiritual deportment,
> One's element running pure,
> Precision, crispness, and grace . . .
>
> C.P., p.826

To illustrate this 'element' or 'spiritual deportment' MacDiarmid graphically, and largely parenthetically, describes the poise, balance, and swiftness of a master swordsman. Then he moves to archery to illustrate the same point:

> So too archery in the traditional Japanese sense
> Is not a sport, not even an art.
> It is a spiritual discipline with the aim
> Of hitting not a material but a spiritual goal,
> 'So that fundamentally the marksman aims at himself
> And may even succeed in hitting himself.'
> The bow and arrow are merely the means
> Of achieving a state of spiritual enlightenment,
> Wherein the bow, arrow, marksman, and target
> As well as everything else in the universe,
> Become one. The problem of hitting the target
> Thus becomes entirely secondary.
> It is merely something which invariably happens
> Once the correct spiritual state has been reached.
>
> C.P., p.828

MacDiarmid refers us to Eugen Herrigel's *Zen in the Art of Archery* and the passage is, in fact, adapted from Herrigel's book:

By archery in the traditional sense, which he esteems as an art and honours as a national heritage, the Japanese does not understand a sport but, strange as this may sound at first, a religious ritual. And consequently, by the 'art' of archery he does not mean the ability of the sportsman, which can be controlled, more or less, by bodily exercises, but an ability whose origin is to be sought in spiritual exercises and whose aim consists in hitting a spiritual goal, so that fundamentally the marksman aims at himself and may even succeed in hitting himself.[71]

MacDiarmid quite radically simplifies. He cuts out Herrigel's assessment of archery as an art, as a national heritage, and even as a religious ritual. Instead, as MacDiarmid has it, it is a 'spiritual discipline'. He thus concentrates human activity into spiritual sensibility without reference to any particular religious dogma. Compare MacDiarmid's verse with Herrigel:

Do 'I' hit the goal, or does the goal hit me? Is 'It' spiritual when seen by the eyes of the body, and corporeal when seen by the eyes of the spirit —or both or neither? Bow, arrow, goal and ego, all melt into one another, so that I can no longer separate them. And even the need to separate them has gone.[72]

There is greater fortitude in the verse, where 'Bow, arrow, marksman and target / [. . .] Become one', than in Herrigel's fluid imagery and his rhetorical questions. In the poem, the imagery is set in the context of references to Ulysses' bow, the arrow from the Indian classic *Ramayana*, with its magical properties, and the martial arts of the master swordsman in the preceding passage.

The passage transcribed from Herrigel, together with the following narrative passage transcibed from T.H. White, occupy a central place in this section of the poem. What relevance do they have to the question of language?

One clue is the Nietzsche quotation which bridges the transcription from Herrigel and the transcription from White. It is an inversion of the final sentence of the Funeral Song from *Thus Spoke Zarathustra*: 'And only where there are graves are there resurrections.'[73] We are suddenly reminded that *In Memoriam James Joyce* is in a sense a 'Funeral Song', too. We are, we have been told, living in days of enforced linguistic uniformity, and consequently mental, physical, and spiritual oppression; but also in 'days nevertheless of the revival and extension of Tual, Faroese, Irish Gaelic, and a thousand more'. One of the poem's main concerns is the death and revival, limitation and extension, loss and recovery of languages. This is the dramatic epicentre which is formed by MacDiarmid's transcription from T.H. White's *The Sword in the Stone*.

> I rejoiced when from Wales once again
> Came the fff-putt of a triple-feathered arrow
> Which looked as if it had never moved.

This first quotation from White is given a footnote which refers us to Dylan Thomas, implying a sense of resurrection and, at the same time, a sense of continuity. That is, while this arrow from Wales — Thomas — comes 'once again' and is a reason for rejoicing, it looks 'as if it had never moved': it occupies its rightful place, which was never really occupied before by anything other than itself. It is no revelation. Yet it is a return.

Here is T.H. White:

> . . . Every Thursday afternoon, after the last serious arrow had been shot, they were allowed to fit one more nock to their strings and to shoot the arrow straight up into the air. It was partly a gesture of farewell, partly of triumph, and it was beautiful. They did it now as salute to their first prey.
>
> The Wart watched his arrow go up. The sun was already westing toward evening, and the trees where they were had plunged them into a partial shade. So, as the arrow topped the trees and climbed into the sunlight, it began to burn against the evening like the sun itself. Up and up it went, not weaving as it would have done with a snatching loose, but soaring, swimming, aspiring to heaven, steady, golden and superb. Just as it had spent its force, just as its ambition had been dimmed by destiny and it was preparing to faint, to turn over, to pour back into the bosom of its mother earth, a portent happened. A gore-crow came flapping wearily before the approaching night. It came, it did not waver, it took the arrow. It flew away, heavy and hoisting with the arrow in its beak.
>
> Kay was frightened but the Wart was furious. He had loved his arrow's movement, its burning ambition in the sunlight, and, besides, it was his best one. It was the only one which was perfectly balanced, sharp, tight-feathered, clean-nocked, and neither warped nor scraped.
>
> 'It was a witch', said Kay.[74]

MacDiarmid collates the characters of the Wart and Kay into a single 'I'. His transcription emphasises the moment of triumph and farewell, the conjunction of sunset, closure, ending, and the burning, golden and superb light, the sense that although this is his best arrow, it is also his last shot.

> But now the bowman has fitted one more nock
> To his string, and discharged the arrow straight up into the
>   air
> Partly as a gesture of farewell, partly of triumph,
> And beautiful! — I watched the arrow go up.
> The sun was already westing towards evening
> So, as the arrow topped the trees
> And climbed into sunlight,
> It began to burn against the evening like the sun itself.
> Up and up it went, not weaving as it would have done
> With a snatching loose, but soaring, swimming,
> Aspiring towards heaven, steady, golden and superb.
>
> Just as it had spent its force,
> Just as its ambition had been dimmed by destiny
> And it was preparing to faint, to turn over,
> To pour back into the bosom of its mother earth [,]
> A terrible portent happened.
> A gore crow came flapping wearily
> Before the approaching night.
> It came, it did not waver, it took the arrow,
> It flew away, heavy and hoisting,
> With the arrow in its beak. I was furious.
> I had loved the arrow's movement,
> Its burning ambition in the sunlight,
> And it was such a splendid arrow,
> Perfectly-balanced, sharp, tight-feathered,
> Clean-nocked, and neither warped nor scraped.
>
> I was furious but I was frightened.

C.P., pp.828–9

At the theft of the arrow 'Kay was frightened but the Wart was furious'. MacDiarmid's first response is 'I was furious', then he lists examples of crows acting as portents elsewhere in history: Valerius Corvus (a Roman hero of the fourth century BC, who did battle with a giant Gaul and was victorious owing to a raven flapping its wings in the giant's face), and the ancient Irish epic *The Tain* (in which the evil crow the 'Morrigu' appears), for example. These two distinct passages are bridged by a tonal shift, moving across Kay's wary response to the lead-in to the list:

> I was furious but I was frightened.
> It is a very old and recurring portent in our history.

C.P., p.829

This conflation of the different responses of the Wart and Kay and the movement through the list that follows on: all this shows the protean, accommodative nature of MacDiarmid's first person. Moreover, the transcription from prose to verse itself is a fascinating study. All the minor changes, the substitutions of 'the' for 'his', the minor omissions (White's 'the trees where they were had plunged them into a partial shade'), and additions ('A terrible portent' for 'a portent'), the bridge-passages in MacDiarmid ('But now the bowman . . . '): all these contribute to the alteration of the movement of the passage, and effect a contextual relevance and continuity. We read the different passages in different ways. For example, where White continues his description of the rising arrow through a single paragraph, MacDiarmid takes us up with the arrow, and pauses. Trepidation is implicit as the next lines in their 'falling' sound enact descent:

> Just as it had spent its force,
> Just as its ambition had been dimmed . . .

C.P., p.829

The tension is already there in the syntax, but the line arrangement heightens this tension by returning the eye to the word 'Just' at the start of each line, and so adds a kind of suspense to the narrative. It is a commonplace that we read poetry more slowly, more carefully, than we read prose, yet there is a distinctive impetus in MacDiarmid's text. He moves then in a series of 'leaps' from White's narrative to the various instances in which the crow has figured as an image of imminent disaster.

Not having done with the image, and remembering the concerns of loss and retrieval, MacDiarmid changes tone to return with affirmation and asseveration, saying that the crow shall not have the arrow for ever: 'We shall get it back' and 'rejoice when the War is over', and the triple-feathered arrow comes once again from Wales, repeating the verse in reference to Dylan Thomas.

The effect of the whole passage is a dramatic re-enactment of the implicit strains of continuity (symbolised by the perfection and beauty of the arrow) and the historical, physical event of its theft. It is a narrative presentation of concerns otherwise expressed elsewhere in the poem, whose hitherto explicit terms have been linguistic.

Now the lists begin again. Prompted by the archery imagery, we are given examples of verse forms which are said to represent a bow, a sword, and the *go-mutika*, 'shaped like a stream of cow's urine'. We are informed what wood is best to make bows from, what string, what steel, what feathers go into the making of the arrow. A steep transition follows: these are examples of the kind of information the half-illiterate, dull-eyed, vacant-faced talesmen (or jurors) at the Scottsboro trial are incapable of taking in. This reference is worth elucidating. In 1931, in Scottsboro, Alabama, nine black youths were charged with rape and convicted by an all-white jury, although doctors testified that no rape had occurred. In 1932 the United States Supreme Court overturned the convictions but two of the youths were later retried and reconvicted. The four youngest were freed after six years in jail. The Scottsboro trial was a *cause célèbre* for many North American radical groups, and is commemorated in John Dos Passos's epic novel *U.S.A.* MacDiarmid asserts that 'All the most vital evidence for the defence [was] debarred, / Human nature apparently constitutionally incapable of hearing it' (*C.P.*, p.832).

'*Bien (dit M. Teste). L'essentiel est contre la vie*' (*C.P.*, p.833). This quotation from Paul Valéry which follows is an epigram on the title page of the book to which MacDiarmid refers us, Norman Suckling's *Paul Valéry and the Civilized Mind*. And the next passage is also transcribed from this book. Earlier on, we noted how MacDiarmid defined language as the instrument for the progressive articulation of the world in spatial and temporal terms, since the space–time network is 'the distinctive character of human consciousness'. When MacDiarmid quotes Suckling here, it is to affirm values that are 'Invulnerable to the decay of time / Or the disappointment of imperfection': for only by means of such 'values' may we 'become "changed into ourselves by eternity"'. This last phrase is from Mallarmé, quoted first by Valéry, then by Suckling, and then by MacDiarmid. But it is also an echo of the third-century neo-Platonic philosopher Plotinus: 'Many times it has happened: lifted out of the body into myself; becoming external to all other things and self-encentred; beholding a marvellous beauty; then, more than ever, assured of community with the loftiest order; enacting the noblest life, acquiring identity with the divine.' Here is the threshold across which, MacDiarmid implies, the millennial transformation will occur.

> Out of the intensity of consciousness of individuality
> The individuality itself seems to dissolve
> And fade away into boundless being . . .
> The loss of personality seemingly no extinction
> But the only true life.

C.P., p.834

(This threshold of revelation foreshadows the epiphanic moments described near the beginning of the last section of *In Memoriam*, and the relation between individuality and the masses of humankind which is also suggested here is something to which we shall return in the next part of this chapter.) Suckling's book is important as literal source-material, but it also contributes to the alteration in the tone and pace of the remainder of the poem.

> For it is death that most of all reveals love in its aspect of *résistance à la durée* — liberation from devouring time, the true durability in the domain of the timeless — because the function of death is, more than all else, to mark off that which is timeless from that which is merely living. That which merely lives must also die; eternity is a quality quite different from life, and it is not by aligning itself with the factors making for living, as such, that the love of Tristan and Iseult has made itself immortal. Especially is it those who are aware that there is no hope for us in the illusion of an ultimate union with a universe brought to perfection by a process of evolution (according to the modern fashion) or of an expiation (according to the ancient one) — those who 'n'ont point de perception intime de cette *substance des choses que nous devons espérer*' as Valéry put it in his ironic italics; those for whom 'la mort ne représente qu'une des propriétés essentielles à la vie: celle de perdre toutes les autres' (Stendhal in Var. II, p.131) — who will best understand that the things least conditioned by life are also least frustrated by death, and will therefore best understand love, since love is indeed one of these, finding (as it does) a sort of crown in death because it needs no realization in a cycle of renewal.[75]

MacDiarmid transcribes this passage and then adds: 'Here or anywhere else', and comments in passing '(Out of the mouths of babes — and Sucklings!)'. MacDiarmid adds such wryly humorous divagations. He says also that 'as a Scottish Borderer / I still take an unholy delight / . . . / In occasional ascoholic invasions / Of the autotelic . . . ' (*C.P.*, p.835). 'Ascoholic' and 'autotelic' are Suckling's words. Ascoholic, Suckling says, means that which is 'inevitable but insignificant in our lives'. ('I am here under the necessity of inventing a new word', he admits, and MacDiarmid uses it as if it were a common figure of speech.) While there is a humour in this, the verse remains animated, yet it is an attempt to escape from this kind of animation MacDiarmid is trying to describe when he goes on to refer to his vision as one of understanding, not creation, 'in no sense dynamic or prophetic'. We are then presented with 'the atmosphere of a pagan burial' and returned at last to the poem's most frequently central, recurring 'location', the *aonach* (a Scottish Gaelic word MacDiarmid glosses as a solitary place and a place of union) of Joyce's death chamber, and another address to Joyce. There then follows the climax of the argument of 'The World of Words' in the revelation of proposed millennial linguistic evolutionary developments:

> . . . five hundred to a thousand generations ago
> Through some overcoming of inertia,
> A loosening of connections in the nervous centre,
> There was a general development
> Of the power of conscious reflection.
> A true step of evolution took place.
> The new species of man was marked among other things
> By the loss or degeneration
> Of many important instincts
> Such as nutrition and reproduction.
> These now require intelligent guidance.
> The power of conscious reflection
> Is still only at an early and comparatively rudimentary stage,
> But we are committed to it;
> It is an irreversible specialization,
> And, judging by the incredible number of our nerve cells,
> There is already ample room for its development.
> We are literally at the opening of a new era

C.P., p.837

The way in which tense is modulated from past through present to a sort of 'future imperative' is noteworthy here, as the quietly assertive tone is evenly sustained. It is also important to consider the reality being discussed. It does, in fact, seem provable that consciousness is socially determined. The elaboration of the tool-making capacity of the australopithecine required an expansion of the frontal area of the cerebral cortex, and the hominid brain consequently grew from 500 cubic centimetres 1.5 million years ago, to 1100 cubic centimetres 350 000 years ago, and eventually to the modern 1400 cubic centimetres. Innate cognitive capacity is indeed a mode of production of material life. But one might accuse Mac-Diarmid of a rather gross application of this complex fact. Perhaps this derives from the idea that human 'nature' can be altered in quite short periods of time, which is a questionable reading of Marx.

> We must aim at producing
> The most intensely organized individual
> In proper balance with a society
> Itself in proper ecological balance;
> The recognition of our responsibility
> In promoting these values
> Is the first essential;
> We must put all our reliance in the intellect
> And develop it in everybody;
> The demand for intellectual leadership to-day
> Far exceeds the supply.
> Variation must be encouraged
> Rather than suppressed.
>
> *C.P.*, pp.837–8

The last two verse-paragraphs are hymns to 'Speech. All men's whore. My beloved!' MacDiarmid has moved from the 'Idea and Word Chart' with which 'The World of Words' began to language in its functional capacities and uses in the daily lives of men and women. He has moved from abstract notions of language to intimate uses of language in enunciation. 'The World of Words' ends by evoking 'Some idea of what the process of literature could be', and the word 'process' should be noted. Rather than denote a finished product or commodity, MacDiarmid is referring to an aspect of behaviour impossible to isolate from humanity:

> Something far more closely related
> To the whole life of mankind
> Than the science of stringing words together
> In desirable sequences.
>
> *C.P.*, p.840

It is worth pausing here to draw some conclusions from our

reading of this section of *In Memoriam James Joyce*, for we have already encountered the most important aspects of the poem's procedure (lists, transcribed passages of narrative, philosophy or scientific or biological speculation, and a mixture of assertion and prediction). Also, we are by now well acquainted with the way the poem deals with its 'subject': language. It would be helpful to stand back from the subject for a moment and consider it in relation to the poem's procedure so far. We cannot step back and out of it entirely, of course: language is just as much our medium as the poem's. But to the extent that our discourse is formally different from that of *In Memoriam*, we might attempt a brief description of its peculiarities.

We mentioned in Chapter 1 that Picasso and Georges Braque introduced collage as a revolutionary form into the world of 'high art' in the early decades of the twentieth century. It is not necessary here to discuss the history of collage in modern art, but it is worth pointing out its significance as a formal principle. The procedure of collage is to take a variety of different objects already in existence and to relocate them in a new pattern which will present in its entirety both startling connections and alarming disruptions. The object is to present not continuity but rupture. 'Collage' is usually taken to mean the transfer of the materials to the new context (the procedure), and 'montage' usually refers to the way the borrowed or stolen materials present their new meaning (the object, the 'work of art').

It is appropriate to think of *In Memoriam* in these terms. The closest approximations to the 'stolen materials' are the units of prose MacDiarmid has transcribed into verse. And to a degree that changes from one example to another, these are isolable units. But they are not single 'elements'. For they are all constructed from the medium which pervades the poetry as its subject: language. To the extent that we see them as fragments, the poem is collage; and to the extent that we see them as all part of a transformative flow, the poetry is defiant of such a definition.

It is possible to explain this historically, to some extent. For MacDiarmid comes across the division which critics have described as lying between 'modernism' and 'post-modernism'. Most of the great works of modernism, while they foregrounded their own methods of construction, were predicated on idiosyncratic styles. In conventional terms, post-modernism can be generally characterised as the surrender of such individuality into the anonymous world of total incorporation. People are now perceived politically in the mass, and not as individuals or personalities. The demise of the individual was, it has been argued, the social equivalent of the 'death of the author' in literary terms. We are already familiar with the questionable nature of 'authorship' from Foucault, whose ideas we introduced in Chapter 1. A more radical version of the thesis is that not only did the individual die, but she or he never really existed anyway. A unique personal identity is a myth. Now, MacDiarmid began writing as a modernist, in that his early Scots lyrics and *A Drunk Man* are clearly related to the international literary movement known as symbolism, which formed the basis of modernist poetics. But he continued to write and, crucially, altered the modes of his writing at least until the 1950s (and, indeed, later). Whether or not he subscribed to such 'movements' as modernism and postmodernism, there can be no doubt that the shift across MacDiarmid's work chronologically reflects the major shift in twentieth-century literary culture. And it is an accurate reflection. One of the main reasons for devoting attention to MacDiarmid's later poetry is that it brings us so much further towards the contemporary, and reveals just how far MacDiarmid was able to come *through*.

For it must be allowed at once that although his work spans the century, he does not entirely relinquish the securities of certain modernist strategies. He maintains his claim to a Marxist world view; he asserts his belief in the cultural identity of Scotland and his own individual qualifications. In a note at the beginning of the *Disjecta Membra* manuscripts of the never published or completed *Impavidi Progrediamur* (at present held in a private collection), he wrote:

> Write this poem as things are today
> is like cornering a car at high speed
> on a mountainous road and
> suddenly seeing
> an obstacle offering only
> one chance in a million of clearance
> Write this poem — but it could never have been
> thought of, possible at any other time
> since the world began
> or by and to any other
> man.

But, as we have seen, in the course of *In Memoriam James Joyce*, such claims to identity are complicated, if not completely undermined, by their being produced through the words of others.

The most revealing account of the complexity at work here, especially as it pertains to language, has been given by the French psychoanalyst Jacques Lacan (1901–81), and, since I will be referring to some of the ideas and concepts he formulated in Chapter 3, it would be wise to introduce them at this stage. For our purposes, it will suffice to describe the importance of Lacan's contribution in these ways: he considered schizophrenia to be a *language disorder*, and he suggested that it was not only the features of context or thematic qualities which revealed psychical conflicts but also, and in interconnected ways, the formal procedures of expression. Consider for a moment how these ideas might apply. For Lacan, the experience of time, the human understanding of passage through time, is an effect of language. Because the sentence articulates experience through time, the experience a sentence articulates can be *ordered*. If, however, we abandon the laws of temporal continuity which allow sentences to function in that way, we are forced to live in a perpetual present where experience is lost. Order redeems experience from oblivion. Thankfully, it is difficult to do away with order. The language-forming habits of our minds are very quick to draw meaning from complex structures. Instantaneous images and juxtaposed phrases — the very forms we associate with symbolist and modernist poetry — are by now part of the poet's stock-in-trade. But such procedures, when they are used in poetry, are allowed certain sanctions. No-one talks in everyday speech the way a symbolist poet writes. And yet, as soon as we say that, we are reminded of the way the language of *The Waste Land*, for example, actually makes very poignant use of the speech of its author's wife, and the broken phrases of the poem echo and impose an emotional order upon the broken speech of the schizophrenic.

But *The Waste Land* is a wonderful example of order being recovered, in a particular sense. It has become by now thoroughly encrusted by commentary and criticism. It exists as the paradigmatic 'modernist' poem in a way that MacDiarmid's poems do not. Perhaps this accounts, to some extent, for the reluctance of many important critics to engage with MacDiarmid's work. MacDiarmid is far more threatening than Eliot because his identity in the critical pantheon is not so securely established. Certainly, the problems that we have looked at in *In Memoriam James Joyce* so far are deeply related to the problems diagnosed by Lacan. For if, as Lacan has it, schizophrenia is a language disorder, it follows that the ordering offered by language is exactly what constructs and confers identity. MacDiarmid, in focusing so determinedly upon language as a *politi-*

cal question has come straight to the heart of the political struggle. He is perfectly accurate when he says that 'linguistic imperialism' sums up all other forms of imperialism. Furthermore, if the identity constructed and conferred by language (or its lack) is not only a matter of content but also of form, then MacDiarmid has produced, in *In Memoriam James Joyce*, a work whose formal properties lock it into the struggle for the identity it is seeking to construct.

Let me turn this another way. The schizoid combination of Mac-Diarmid's communism and his Scottish nationalism has often been remarked. If one considers this in the light of what we have just discussed, in Lacanian terms, these two political drives can be understood to be not in conflict with each other but aspects of the same dynamic. Instead of two drives towards opposing ends — the one craving exemption (Scotland as a distinct and singular thing) and the other demanding global economic co-operation — we have two desires identical in being continually unrequited. The frustrations of daily reality which left those desires, for all of C.M. Grieve's lifetime, unrequited, should not be understood as merely debilitating. For those frustrations were tokens of a culture of reaction and repression, in the face of which a practice of resistance will always be needed. This is what MacDiarmid's epic poetry is.

The Opposition

The 'English Ethos' and the East

Everyone who loves birds, though he cannot deny the sparrow many virtues, shrinks at the thought of his capacity for mere multiplication and is haunted by a nightmare vision of a world from which the more fastidious species have been banished, leaving all one sparrowdom. A similar horror fills the mind of the humanist when it occurs to him that English may be destined to be the language of the human race.

Basil de Sélincourt[76]

'The Snares of Varuna' and 'The Meeting of the East and the West' introduce oriental (particularly Indian) literature and philosophy. The importance of orientalism for MacDiarmid is that it urges the necessity of moving beyond a Eurocentric cultural hegemony by presenting as value an understanding of cultural significance in global terms. If MacDiarmid adopts and accommodates oriental literature (as Edward Said has argued is the inevitable practice of Western authors[77]), he is doing so in a deliberately confrontational manner, to oppose what he has called the 'English ethos'. What that phrase means is brought out in the fifth section of the book, 'England is our Enemy', where the insularity of English literature and English literary criticism is linked to an imperial history and its furthest legacies. In noting how English literary criticism has erected 'a stone-heap, a dead load of moral qualities', it should be remembered that MacDiarmid is aligning himself once again with Joyce.

'The Snares of Varuna' begins in anger and rage. The first five verse-paragraphs lead easily from the opening image. 'The world is fast bound in the snares of Varuna' to concrete instances of evils at work in the world. In Hindu mythology, Varuna is one of the Adityas, the divine sons of Aditi, the 'great earth mother', and constant companion of Vishnu. Varuna is associated with the moon, for he shines at night and is represented as a white man riding on the back of a sea monster. He witnesses everything and controls the seasons and the rains. His brother Mitra is associated with the sun, and shines (or sees) by day. MacDiarmid seems to imply that Varuna's stranglehold is inimical and in evidence everywhere. However, the examples given of sadistic authoritarianism — concentration camps, the cat o' nine tails, policemen assaulting their prisoners — are set against the outlawed claims of avowed freedom-fighters. Then, taking his indignation further still, MacDiarmid comments that even if the masses of mankind were freed from their current condition of enforced slavery of body and mind, they would be incapable of using their new wealth and freedom. Like animals who in the course of evolution have regressed, not developed, humankind will lose its humanity and return to barbarism. And most people remain ignorant or indifferent to the increasing intensity of this trend.

> The ancestors of oysters and barnacles had heads.
> Snakes have lost their limbs
> And ostriches and penguins their power of flight.
> Man may just as easily lose his intelligence.
> Most of our people already have.
> It is unlikely that man will develop into anything higher
> Unless he desires to and is prepared to pay the cost.
> Otherwise we shall go the way of the dodo and the kiwi.
> Already that process seems far advanced.
> Genius is becoming rarer,

Our bodies a little weaker in each generation,
Culture is slowly declining,
Mankind is returning to barbarism
And will finally become extinct.

C.P., p.842

Note how the syntax and punctuation here contribute to the gloom. The full stops (there are seven sentences in the first half of the verse-paragraph) keep the voice and the eye from running on. The commas in the eighth sentence drop you, from the end of each line, to one more funereal statement.

> I think that it is quite as likely as not that scientific research may ultimately be strangled ... before mankind has learnt to control its own evolution.

> If so, evolution will take its course. And that course has generally been downwards. The majority of species have degenerated and become extinct, or, what is perhaps worse, gradually lost many of their functions. The ancestors of oysters and barnacles had heads. Snakes have lost their limbs and ostriches and penguins their power of flight. Man may just as easily lose his intelligence.

> It is only a very few species that have developed into something higher. It is unlikely that man will do so unless he desires to and is prepared to pay the cost. If, as appears to be the case at present in Europe and North America, the less intelligent of our species continue to breed more rapidly than the able, we shall go the way of the dodo and the kiwi. We do not as yet know enough to avert this fate. If research continues for another two centuries it is probable that we shall. But if, as is likely enough, the welfare of our descendants in the remote future can only be realised at a very considerable sacrifice of present happiness and liberty, it does not follow that such a sacrifice will be made.

> It is quite likely that, after a golden age of happiness and peace, during which all the immediately available benefits of science will be realised, mankind will very gradually deteriorate.

> Genius is becoming rarer, our bodies a little weaker in each generation, culture is slowly declining, and in a few hundred or thousand years — it does not much matter which — mankind will return to barbarism, and finally become extinct.[78]

This is from another essay by J.B.S. Haldane entitled 'Man's Destiny'. I quote Haldane in full partly to show just how much MacDiarmid left out. The first four lines in the MacDiarmid passage are only half of Haldane's first paragraph, and it is worth noticing the simplicity of the line divisions MacDiarmid has made. What in Haldane is speculative prose becomes didactic verse in MacDiarmid, and the rhythm of MacDiarmid's lines is, above all, what enforces that didacticism and gives it novelty. The first two sentences of Haldane's second paragraph are conflated and rearranged in Mac-Diarmid, and a line is taken from the middle of this paragraph. The rest is omitted until the final paragraph, whose first and last lines are brought together, and – crucially – whose tense is changed.

The change of tense is perhaps the most important change Mac-Diarmid makes, and to emphasise this he adds two other lines: 'Most of our people already have' (lost their intelligence) and 'Already the process (of evolutionary regression) seems far advanced.' The result of this is to change the meaning of the passage. MacDiarmid insists on the contemporaneity of these events, while Haldane points to them as probable future developments. However, MacDiarmid himself states categorically, later on in *In Memoriam James Joyce*, 'pessimism is false', and although his reworking darkens and toughens Haldane's tone, it will lead on to equally intense affirmations of possible alternative developments.

It is the lesson of Sophocles's play *Philoctetes* that the spurned and outcast member of society holds a critical and essential place within it, and MacDiarmid finds in the perennial existence of such outcasts a kind of consolation. An element of thankfulness enters the poetry when the poet switches from denunciation to delight, celebrating the fact that even manic depressives, schizophrenics, and melancholics retain something essential to humanity, despite all constraint to equalise idiosyncrasies. That sense of the idiosyncratic, the sense of variety and of perpetuating variety, sustains the dynamic force of all MacDiarmid's work. It was explicitly formulated in his overtly anti-Fascist writing, in 'England's Double Knavery':

> The effort of culture is towards greater differentiation
> Of perceptions and desires and values and ends,
> Holding them from moment to moment
> In a perpetually changing but stable equilibrium . . .

C.P., p.1138

'The Snares of Varuna' ends with a parenthetical assertion of delight in the poet's potential capacity, picking up from a series of angling metaphors and leading on past Melville to the monsters of the deep, catalogued, lifted up and thrown back in. It ends with a joky semantic convulsion when the poet's friend laughs and says:

'Let me see you catch anything yet
Big enough not to throw in again.'

C.P., p.851

'The Meeting of the East and the West', like 'The Snares of Varuna', opens with a rhetorical invocation of an oriental context and plunges straight into specific detail. Confronted with the possibility of unification, one is also confronted with 'a gigantic maze / Of faulty knowledge . . . '. And the first verse-paragraph goes on to cite examples of the influence of Indian literature and philosophy on the West, and in particular in Germany. Freidrich Schlegel, A.W. Schlegel, and Franz Bopp prompt further lists of names: 'Lassen, Webber, Roth, Boehtlingk, Max Muller, / Buehler, Keelhorn, Oldenberg, and countless others' (*C.P.*, p.853). A comparison of Hegel and Kant with Indian philosophy concludes only that any parallels that may exist are no more than coincidences of results arrived at from totally differing starting points. MacDiarmid assembles various instances of German appropriation of Indian thought to form a chronological development, an example of a particular (and particular kind of) meeting of the East and the West. From Schopenhauer we move to Nietzsche, and then to Wagner, who, in 1855, sketched a drama using a story from the Buddhist text *Divyâvadâna* as a source. From there to Yeats advising young poets to read the *Upanishads* (Hindu religious writings of *c*.800–500 BC) is but a short step. Then follows what MacDiarmid calls 'a Sanskrit verse of extreme beauty'.

The concluding three verse-paragraphs of this section are on a different subject: the point of contact between Chinese and Western music, with a few passing references to the Chinese language. There is no overt connection between the Sanskrit and the 'Chinese' passages, except the umbrella of 'the East' MacDiarmid has put up over this section of *In Memoriam*. The final verse-paragraph takes us back from the specific instances of individual responses to Chinese literature to the idiosyncrasies of Chinese music.

'England is Our Enemy' begins in quite a different world from the preceding sections. This section follows an argument, proceeding by question and highly reasonable answer; but the rational tone is undercut by the outrageous humour and ironic disdain of English literature. MacDiarmid argues that great art is, in a sense, axiomatic; that is, it must reveal particular qualities of humanity. Though you may not like a certain quality, you must accept its existence to appreciate the full picture. For example, he says, no Frenchman can afford to ignore Racine or Villon; no human being can afford to ignore say, Heine:

> To know all the writings of Heine
> Is not necessary, but not to know
> How Heine mixed, alternated, or employed
> Flippancies and sentiment is to have a blind spot
> In your knowledge of how
> A part of humanity may be appealed to:
>
> Who among English writers is thus axiomatic?
>
> C.P., pp.859–60

And without much generosity, he answers, 'None!'

This argument itself is not exactly watertight, but MacDiarmid presses on, asking why the British government never thinks of publicly broadcasting English literature to encourage patriotism, implying both that it is because the government is incapable of thinking that literature has a patriotic value at all, and also that, as far as English literature is concerned, it has not. He sees this in contradistinction to the art of France, and the possession of that art by the French people. The arts, in particular the written arts, of Great Britain, have been forced away from the masses by the 'highly refined imaginations of the more select classes'. This means that the best writer in English can expect or hope for an infinitesimal audience: in 100 000 souls, MacDiarmid says, quoting Ford Madox Hueffer, five are 'reasonably civilised'. Our literature can hardly be called national, then: unlike the literature or culture of Periclean Athens, whose every inhabitant knew at least something of Sophocles, Euripides, Pheidias. None the less, MacDiarmid says, between the stormy blasts of political hypocrisies and commercial pressures, there has been produced 'a great body of beautiful and humane work'.

There then follows a comic interlude with a British Cabinet Minister trying to make a claim for his civilisation's place in the sun. In parenthesis, MacDiarmid comments that all of even Scotland's public men 'are as nothing' to the little-known, unfamiliar name of Father Iain of Barra, or R.B. Cunninghame Graham, or, indeed, even himself. He concludes by saying that such people make Europe into nations; are, separately, the glories of Europe, their works going together, each one contributing to a grand, imperishable fabric. As for England, it is possible, he concedes, a change may come. We must evaluate and shun any commercial consideration coming between us and the general revaluation of literature. And these considerations (like professors of literature and Honours examinations) should be left to die out, isolated, but not forgotten, lest they should creep quietly back again.

Man and the Masses
Brecht:

> Man does not become man again by stepping out of the masses but by stepping back into them. The masses shed their dehumanization and thereby become man again – but not the same men as before.[79]

What Brecht is referring to here (the passage is from an essay criticising George Lukács) is the hope that a dehumanised notion of 'the masses' might recover a sense of human consequence by virtue of the politicisation of the individual. And it is a hope MacDiarmid shares; not, it must be admitted, a hope that he shares consistently throughout his career. We have also to take into account those fervid rejections of mass culture and mankind-in-the-mass in which MacDiarmid indulged. But MacDiarmid was not an élitist in the sense of Yeats: he did not consistently hold up aristocratic ideals, or settle for the essences of selfhood and *Zeitgeist*. He also insisted upon questions of class, the linguistic variety of the peoples of the earth, and a solidarity of human worth. In the three central sections of *In Memoriam James Joyce*, that variety and solidarity are given expression as a kind of reconciliation is attempted between Eastern and Western thought, in order to effect a visionary triumph over what MacDiarmid calls the 'English ethos'.

I do not intend here to criticise the shortcomings of MacDiarmid's understanding of Eastern philosophy and religious thought. It is clear that MacDiarmid comes at the end of a well-defined tradition of Western appropriators of Eastern writing and, indeed, he locates himself in such a position. It seems to me more important to establish the kind of use to which he is putting the weighty bulk of cultural matter that is evoked by the code-phrase 'Eastern thought'.

MacDiarmid says in the poem that there are two kinds of knowledge: knowing about things and knowing things. This distinction in kinds of knowledge is richly suggestive. We mentioned in Chapter 1 the distinction made by Roland Barthes between *work* and *text*. This in some ways parallels MacDiarmid here, for knowledge of *works* (say, the knowledge held by a librarian, publisher, or bookseller) is distinct from knowledge of *texts* (say, that of a critic, teacher, or poet). But they are not completely opposed. Further, such distinctions recall that proposed by Jacques Lacan between 'reality' and the 'real': one is displayed, the other demonstrated. Similarly, MacDiarmid's 'two kinds of knowledge' are not mutually exclusive. Rather, they represent in an immediate way both a cultural division of global scale and the broadest division in the masses of the world. When he goes on to say that he seeks 'their perfect fusion in my work', he is announcing a desire he knows will continue to be unappeased.

The idea of the masses is the single greatest consideration underlying all modern epic work, from its beginning in Doughty, to Charles Olson. Olson made exactly this point when he visited Ezra Pound in St Elizabeth's Hospital in the 1940s.

> Pound can talk all he likes about the *cultural lag* in America . . . but he's got a 200 year *political lag* in himself. It comes down to this: a rejection of the single most important fact of the last 100 years, the most important human fact between Newton and the Atomic Bomb — the sudden multiple increase of the earth's population, the coming into existence of the *MASSES*. Pound and his kind want to ignore them. They try to lock them out. But they swarm at the windows in such numbers they black out the light and the air. And in their little place Pound and his kind suffocate, their fear turns to hate. And their hate breeds death. They want to kill. And, organized by Hitler and Mussolini, they do kill — millions. But the breeding goes on. And with it such social and political change as they shall not understand.
>
> It is *economics* that finally confronts them, this science of the *masses*. And it is economic necessities which underlie the revolution in society and politics.
>
> In Pound I am confronted by the tragic Double of our day. He is the demonstration of our duality. In language and form he is as forward, as much the revolutionist as Lenin. But in social, economic and political action he is as retrogressive as the Czar.[80]

MacDiarmid, as might be expected, never wrote anything as intimately critical of Pound (and never was as close to him as Olson). Pound, in *The Cantos*, seemed to MacDiarmid to have had a political sense of various civilisations, of culture as the practice as well as the possession of people, whether in the African pre-historic societies Frobenius claimed to have distinguished or in Chinese history. Olson's criticism of Pound raises questions MacDiarmid himself never addressed to Pound directly. Yet it is a recurring aspect of MacDiarmid's own poetry and a vivid one: the conflict that exists between the individual intellectual and the masses of mankind; the unitary consciousness of the poet's self and the peoples of the world as a whole. This is what provides the suspenseful balance of *The Eemis Stane*; it is one of the essential questions grappled with in *On a Raised Beach*; and it figures explicitly in the 'Author's Note' to the MacLellan edition of *In Memoriam James Joyce*. There MacDiarmid quotes Thornton Wilder, who wrote:

> For better or worse, world literature is at hand. Our consciousness is beginning to be planetary. A new tension has been set up between the individual and the universe. It is not new because poets and entire literatures have been lacking in the sense of the vastness of Creation, but new in the response provoked in the writer in relation to his own language and his own environment. Where in literature do we find signs of one or other aspect of this planetary consciousness? For all its Xenophobia, the Old Testament abounds in the consciousness of the human as multitude and of time as incommensurable. The *Iliad* precisely states its rosters in the thousands but conveys them in the millions. I do not find this sense in the *Aeneid*. Reading the *Divine Comedy* the head reels and the heart shrinks before it. Over and over one has felt it before Dante himself exclaims: 'I had not known that death had undone so many' (a phrase which T.S. Eliot calls upon the *The Waste Land*; an emotion scarcely to be found elsewhere in all European literature, for all its Dances of Death, its *Oraisons Funèbres*, and its Urn-Burials). I find it in Don Quixote, on that road which seems to have no beginning and no end. I do not find it in Shakespeare — diversity of souls is not the same thing as multiplicity of souls. I do not find it in English literature. I do not find it in French literature, not even in Pascal. Occasionally Victor Hugo seems to be blowing himself up to achieve it, but the efforts end in rhetoric. All Oriental literature is filled with it; it is the predominant note in the Sanskrit. Though the consciousness of the multiplicity of souls is not the only ingredient in world literature, it is an essential one. It is often present without being accompanied by its temporal compon-

ent: the realisation of the deep abyss of time. Nor does the presence of these realisations in itself constitute a superiority. For the present all we can say is that once a mind is aware of it, it is not possible to *unknow* it. And it is the character of the modern mind that it knows this thing. The literature that it writes must express it: that every man and woman born is felt to be in a new relation to the whole.[81]

Despite this 'consciousness of the multiplicity of souls' being found in Homer, Dante, and oriental and Old Testament literature, masses are a new historical phenomenon and the significance of these literatures — especially oriental literature — is that they can help us come to terms with it. I have heard it said there are now more people alive than have ever died.

These concerns relate to *In Memoriam James Joyce* as a whole. MacDiarmid discussed the similarities of Scotland and China at length in *Lucky Poet*. He said there that the attitudes of the English resemble those of the Japanese in the deification of the sovereign, while in China (according to Mencius) a 'monarch whose rule is injurious to the people should be dethroned':

> As Professor McNair lists them, on the one side (Japanese) some of the outstanding features are will-to-power, tenacity of purpose, and decisiveness of action, 'direct or devious, the latter at times to the point of what the Westerner is inclined to term treachery'; on the other side (Chinese) — passive resistance, tendency to compromise and procrastination, and in addition, having been pacifically inclined for ages, the Chinese in contrast to what their aggressive neighbour was doing, tended to ignore 'realities'. The parallel is very close.[82]

MacDiarmid is saying that Scotland is to England as China is to Japan. If we accept this as something for the most part implicitly present in the poetry, the connection between MacDiarmid's concern with an East–West synthesis and his denunciation of the English ethos is clear. What seems an elliptical juxtaposition of Sanskrit and Chinese is a conflation of the oriental ethos with the Scottish one of the author made in an attempt to effect an implicit rejection of the English one. That the English ethos is made explicit in the third poem serves more than one function, for when MacDiarmid is able to say what he means by 'the English ethos', he defines the terms of the whole argument. The way he does this is not entirely without ambiguity, however. I am not sure, for instance, whether he *would* have regarded Trollope, Jane Austen, and the Mrs Gaskell of *Mary Barton* as 'English authors / Authentic in their methods'. And, more troublingly, I am not entirely clear about what 'Authentic in their methods' really means, or that writers should necessarily be 'axiomatic'. (Or, indeed, exactly what 'axiomatic' means. It is possible to see MacDiarmid's praise of Heine quoted above as merely self-congratulatory.) This may well be caused by MacDiarmid's source-material, for there seems sufficient internal evidence in 'England is Our Enemy' to suggest the extensive use of source-text(s).

None the less, the poem does clarify what the phrase 'the English ethos' means to MacDiarmid. It represents a refusal to engage actively in the inheritance of a people's property. It represents the sick élitism which attempts to maintain a status quo injurious to the health not only of the masses but also of those intent on maintaining it. It represents blockage and thwarted progress, a denial of 'more fruitful modes of procedure'. It represents the very evils described at length in the first five verse-paragraphs of 'The Snares of Varuna'. The evils embodied by 'the English ethos' are the reasons why 'England is Our Enemy', but it would be wrong to limit them to England (as MacDiarmid makes clear in his parallel with Japan). The wrongs may be 'as one with England's name' but they are also working everywhere.

Why MacDiarmid focused his account of the influence of Indian thought on Germany is explained in these lines:

> Heine's words remain true: 'Portuguese, Dutchmen, and
>   Englishmen
> Have brought home from India the treasures in their big ships.
> We were only lookers-on. But the spiritual treasures of India
> Shall not escape us.'
>
> C.P., p.856

In *Widening Horizons in English Verse*, a short book of formidable range and power, John Holloway has discussed and sketched the process of the migration of Indian literature and thought to Britain in the nineteenth century. In England there had been translations of the Indian classic texts the *Mahabharata* and the *Ramayana* in 1835, by a certain Dean Millman, but they were in effect intended as an attempt to fill a gap. Because only specialist scholars came into contact with Sanskrit, the translations, it was thought, might begin to effect contact stimulating to poets.

In 1852 Ralph Griffith published a collection of translations not only from the great epics (including the *Baghavad Gita*, which is a selection of the *Mahabharata*) from *Sakontala*, and from the *Gita Govinda*, all of which had been translated before; but also from the great early masterpieces of Sanskrit, the *Laws of Manu* and the *Vedic Hymns*. But Griffith too, in his *Preface*, hints at neglect of Sanskrit verse on the part of the English public, and a shortage of available translations; in particular, he notes that Wilson's *Cloud Messenger* is readily available only to scholars, and that Dean Milman's book is out of print.[83]

Griffith also says that not many will be willing to master Sanskrit for the sake of its poetry – 'in these utilitarian times'. The times *were* utilitarian, and this led inescapably to effect something of a recession of interest in the Hindu world in the second quarter of the nineteenth century. But, generally speaking, enthusiasm for Indian culture flourished better in Germany, because it had no consular side; it could take the ideal and ignore the real which embodied it. Many reasons conspired against an English enthusiasm for Indian life: missionary pressure towards conversion; the developing clan of Westernised Indians; the discovery of more debased forms of Hinduism as more backward areas of the country were opened up — all these worked against a recognition of the qualities of Indian culture. In short, the colonial effort itself worked against the discovery and dissemination of these qualities.

If we continue the comparison of MacDiarmid's Germany in 'The Meeting of the East and the West' with nineteenth-century England, the values MacDiarmid is affirming become increasingly clear. In Tennyson's last collection of poems, *The Death of Oenone* (1892), there is one poem set in the Orient: *Akbar's Dream*. This refers to the great mogul emperor who was an almost exact contemporary of Queen Elizabeth I, and the poem closes in a hymn in a typically Persian or Arabic metre or stanza form. But even in so far as Tennyson does represent the East in his poem, he repudiates it at the end. The true salvation of India comes:

> From out the sunset poured an alien race,
> Who fitted stone to stone again, and Truth,
> Peace, Love and Justice came to dwell therein.

John Holloway's comment on this is: 'Tennyson adds that the aliens from the west abolished suttee, child-marriage and perpetual widowhood into the bargain. It only remained for him to add a reference to clubs, tennis, milky tea, and not being able to speak foreign languages, to complete the picture as we have it in E.M. Forster's novel.[84]

The English in India in the nineteenth century, then,

> . . . having once been cosmopolites of *power* if one may so put it, in the process of ceasing to be *that*, we had also, in part at least, to cease to be cosmopolites of culture. . . . '[W]herever we direct our attention to Hindu literature, the notion of infinity presents itself' . . . this same sense of metaphysical profundity, even obscurity, of the Hindu tradition may be found more easily in the work of those who belonged to other national cultures . . . [I]n Yeats, taking his work generally, we can find a considered and pondered sense of traditional Indian culture, and its importance, such as could not well be matched in the work of any other major English poet of Yeats's own time . . . [85]

. . . for Eliot, when he wrote *The Waste Land*, 'was not an English poet, and was not drawing on anything that English culture had given him'.[86]

John Holloway's description of specifically *English* responses to Indian culture tells a story within definite limits. When MacDiarmid traces Indian influences through the Schlegels, Goethe, Muller, and on to Schopenhauer, Nietzsche, Yeats, and by implication himself, he is presenting a much more devious and affirming narrative. As recounted history alone it is an exciting and revealing sequence of events. Its positive charge contrasts with the story Holloway tells, of a progress towards milky tea, and the contrast reveals something of the oppositional nature of MacDiarmid's texts.

What MacDiarmid was opposing is clear from a review of I.A. Richards's *Basic English and Its Uses* from the *Times Literary Supplement*, 22 January 1944, which it is likely MacDiarmid had read, since (as we shall see) so much source-material comes from this journal throughout the decade:

> Mr Richards foresees, English with or without Basic bids fair to become the future second language of the world, the supranational language which is by now overdue as the means of man's expressing his supranational needs. While the national languages will naturally continue and will deserve all encouragement, a supranational language has now become a necessity. What is that supranational language to be? Not Esperanto

or Ido or any of the made up languages, which are stillborn. It must be a living speech. Possible competitors, since they are spoken by large populations, with English, are Spanish, Chinese, Russian, German, French, Italian. But on examination, none of these meets the standard exacted of the desired supranational language, which must be easy to learn (no elaborate verb systems), contains the most universally useful literature, is now used by the most people, is most generally taught, is likely to serve as the best bridge, lends itself best to films, radio and recording. In these six respects everything points to English.

This gives some idea of the literary scene contemporary with the composition of *In Memoriam James Joyce*, and into which MacDiarmid's poems were intended to be launched. *The Battle Continues*, MacDiarmid's four-thousand-line 'reply' to the South African poet Roy Campbell, who supported Franco during the Spanish Civil War, was written in the 1930s but not published until 1957. In a similar way, the immediate historical relevance of *In Memoriam James Joyce* may have been vitiated to some extent by the time-lapses between composition, publication, and circulation. However, 'England is Our Enemy' retains a usefully agitational quality. The kind of intervention MacDiarmid is willing to attempt here is prompted by an awareness of reality outwith the poem. For the meeting of the East and the West is not only a meeting of cultures but a meeting of peoples. It is a recognition of the masses who shed their dehumanisation whenever they are stepped back into, and 'become man again — but not the same men'.

'Plaited Like the Generations of Men' and the Problem of Metaphysics

In his essay 'The Task of the Translator', Walter Benjamin writes:

Fragments of a vessel which are to be glued together must match one another in the smallest details, although they need not be like one another. In the same way a translation, instead of resembling the meaning of the original, must lovingly and in detail incorporate the original's mode of signification, thus making both the original and the translation recognizable as fragments of a greater language, just as fragments are part of a vessel. For this very reason translation must in large measure refrain from wanting to communicate something, from rendering the sense, and in this the original is important to it only insofar as it has already relieved the translator and his translation of the effect of assembling and expressing what is to be conveyed. In the realm of translation, too, the words ξω δοχπ πω σ λyos [in the beginning was the word] apply. On the other hand, as regards the meaning, the language of a translation can — in fact, must — let itself go, so that it gives voice to the *intentio* of the original not as reproduction but as harmony, as a supplement to the language in which it expresses itself, as its own kind of *intentio*. Therefore it is not the highest praise of a translation, particularly in the age of its origin, to say that it reads as if it had originally been written in that language. Rather, the significance of fidelity as ensured by literalness is that the work reflects the great longing for linguistic complementation. A real translation is transparent; it does not cover the original, does not block its light, but allows the pure language, as though reinforced by its own medium, to shine upon the original all the more fully. This may be achieved, above all, by a literal rendering of the syntax which proves words rather than sentences to be the primary element of the translator. For if the sentence is the wall before the language of the original, literalness is the arcade.[87]

What Benjamin characterises as the translator's technical translinguistic method is parallel to MacDiarmid's method of rewriting, rearranging, and refashioning 'originals' to effect a secondary assembling, one whose novelty likewise signifies a 'longing for linguistic complementation'. The translator must produce a transparent translation, which does not block out the light shining from the original, but which allows the 'pure language' to shine more clearly on the original, 'as though reinforced by its own medium'. The full significance of these illuminations only becomes apparent when we understand what Benjamin means by 'pure language'. Earlier in the same essay he had written:

If there is such a thing as a language of truth, the tensionless and even silent depository of the ultimate truth which all thought strives for, then this language of truth is — the true language.[88]

Benjamin quotes Mallarmé:

'Les langues imparfaites en cela plusieurs, manque la suprême: penser étant écrire sans accessoires, ni chuchotement mais tacite encore l'immortelle parole, la diversité, sur terre, des idiomes empêche personne de proférer les mots qui, sinon se trouveraient, par une frappe unique, elle-même matériellement la vérité.' ['The imperfection of languages consists in their plurality, the supreme one is lacking: thinking is writing without accessories or even whispering, the immortal word still remains silent; the diversity of idioms on earth prevents everybody from uttering the words which otherwise, at one single stroke, would materialize as truth.'] If what Mallarmé evokes here is fully fathomable to a philosopher, translation, with its rudiments of such a language, is midway between poetry and doctrine. Its products are less sharply defined, but it leaves no less of a mark on history.[89]

This is troublesome. Benjamin reads Mallarmé in order to endorse 'the immortal word', to approve his notion of 'the true language' or 'the pure language' — a notion which definitely smacks of idealism. Yet Mallarmé himself seems to be saying rather that such a thing *cannot* exist. He is not seriously suggesting that the problem can be solved by a single language. For Mallarmé, what 'is lacking' is very much the point, and it is not about to make an appearance. The problem arises in the tension between Benjamin's idealist yearning for a material demonstration of 'linguistic complementation' and Mallarmé's denial of that as a possibility. And this problem lies at the heart of MacDiarmid's difficulty in 'Plaited Like the Generations of Men'. For while he recognises the plurality of languages he also longs for a metaphysical complementation, something that will not compensate for pluralities and fragmentations so much as confer upon them a more coherent significance and therefore transform them into something that might be understood as unitary. This might be clarified by a quotation from elsewhere in MacDiarmid's work:

> One loves the temporal, some unique manifestation,
> Something irreplaceable that dies.
>
> But one is loyal to an ideal limit
> Involved in all specific objects of love
> And in all cooperating wills.
>
> Shall the lonely griefs and joys of men
> Forever remain a pluralistic universe?
> Need they, if thought and will are bent in common interest
> In making this universe *one*?

C.P., p.958

In 'Plaited Like the Generations of Men' more than in any other part of *In Memoriam James Joyce,* he attempts to bend 'thought and will' in 'common interest'. And, to use Benjamin's description of the problem he has set himself, one might say that MacDiarmid's task here is the task of the translator, because he has chosen to stand in this section of *In Memoriam James Joyce* 'outside, facing the wooded ridge', instead of 'in the centre of the language forest'. In Benjamin's distinction:

> The intention of the poet is spontaneous, primary, graphic; that of the translator is derivative, ultimate, ideational. For the great motif of integrating many tongues into one true language is at work. This language is one which the independent sentences, works of literature, critical judgements, will never communicate — for they remain dependent on translation; but in it the languages themselves, supplemented and reconciled in their mode of signification, harmonize.[90]

'Plaited Like the Generations of Men' begins where the spontaneous, primary, graphic intention of the poet leaves off. It is not concerned with naming things, but with becoming aware of the greatest harmonies. It begins:

> Come, follow me into the realm of music. Here is the gate
> Which separates the earthly from the eternal.
> It is not like stepping into a strange country
> As we once did. We soon learn to know everything there
> And nothing surprises us any more. Here
> Our wonderment will have no end, and yet
> From the very beginning we feel at home.
>
> C.P., p.871

What was the 'strange country' we once stepped into? We are only told of it that, while there, we soon learned how to understand everything about it and nothing about it surprised us after that. From this, Margery McCulloch[91] has suggested that MacDiarmid is referring to a short sentence further back in *In Memoriam James Joyce,* where, in 'The Snares of Varuna', we are enjoined to 'look at the harebell as if we had never seen it before' and follow MacDiarmid's voice as it uses a tone very similar to that at the beginning of 'Plaited Like the Generations of Men':

> Come. Climb with me. Even the sheep are different
> And of new importance.

The coarse-fleeced, hardy Herdwick,
The Hampshire Down, artificially fed almost from birth,
And butcher-fat from the day it is weaned,
The Lincoln-Longwool, the biggest breed in England,
With the longest fleece, and the Southdown
Almost the smallest —

C.P., pp.844–5

This passage continues listing sheep, then goes on to list flowers. The wonder in the tone is tempered by a reductive sense of humour. (The rapt vision of English sheep prompts the reflection that in England the men and the women are almost as interesting as the sheep.) Then this part of the poem shifts, via a long parenthesis, and addresses the influence of Plato's and Aristotle's metaphysics over scholastic and modern logic: an unfortunate influence, Mac-Diarmid says (although he has not entirely escaped it himself).

Nowhere in its inception or development does this passage correspond with the 'strange country' at the opening of 'Plaited Like the Generations of Men'. It is not a country in which we soon 'know everything': all we learn of it is the interesting variousness of its sheep and flowers. Things cease to surprise only because they cease to be mentioned. I share with Margery McCulloch the belief that the opening of 'Plaited Like the Generations of Men' is a reference to an earlier poem; however, I think that it refers much further back in MacDiarmid's poetry, and reflects back upon itself the weight and consequence of the allusion.

This 'strange country' we once stepped into is described as an earthly place, in contrast to the eternal realm we have now entered. It is a strange place, unfamiliar, perhaps hostile, certainly curious. Also, an effort to learn all about it results in a grasp or understanding in which no surprises remain for us. It is not like this eternal realm, where we are unending in wonder yet always feel at home.

These qualities suggest one place more than any other in all MacDiarmid's *œuvre*: the stark, terrestrial reality of the raised beach from *Stony Limits and Other Poems* (1934). There is a sense in which 'Plaited Like the Generations of Men' is a 'translation' of 'On a Raised Beach'. Knowledge of the earlier poem certainly complements our reading of the later one. The scene of 'On a Raised Beach' is the most naked and located of MacDiarmid's major poems, and, in its involvement of landscape and quest, leads on implicitly from the three elegies which directly precede it in that volume. The landscape becomes more and more extreme, from the Highland pastoral of 'In Memoriam: Liam Mac'Ille Iosa', to the lonely island of 'Vestigia Nulla Retrorsum' (in memory of Rilke), to the hallucinatory desert of 'Stony Limits', where the whole scene seems to be encompassed in Doughty's giant skull. While these poems stand independent of each other, they seem to lead inexorably to the definitive achievement of 'On a Raised Beach'. The recurring struggle to 'get into this stone world', grappling with specialised vocabulary, the concentration on the question of material reality and spiritual presence: all these are efforts towards a self-realisation akin to, but not the same as, the mystic's experience of oneness. As T.J. Cribb has pointed out, it is dissimilar though related to Christ's injunction 'Seek, and ye shall find' (Matthew 7: 7); and, if idealist, it is different from Plato's syllogistic subversion of all desire as unappeaseable in this 'illusory and less real' world of shadows (*Republic* IX, 584–6).[92] We are not given an overflow of mind and will such as we find in Renaissance copiousness, nor is it the intense identification with an object we find in Romantic epiphany. The whole man is engaged, not just his mind: we are aware of his body, his actions, his feelings. Yet, while he rejects mystical intervention, insisting constantly on remaining with the demonstrative and the deictic, he is none the less closely pressed by a sort of metaphysics. The point is that he wants bread from stones in any case, for the stones are not left as indifferent matter: they are the source of our knowledge of reality. They are, to put it another way, the material things which perhaps can supply metaphysical meaning.

MacDiarmid's view of matter, owing something to Nietzsche, something to Marx, and much to modern physics, gives him the ability to assert the simultaneity of spirit and matter in the late but revealing interview with Walter Perrie. The austerity with which he chose to end 'On a Raised Beach' (justifiably revised from an earlier, more reassuring, ending in a first draft), suggests that he has not been entranced by his concentration on spiritual realities, but has remained aware throughout of the mundane world, his body, a bird's movement, the stones. Eternity is a given dimension of matter, for him; thus he can twin it to the moment of the poem. And the poem effects in its course the realisation of that for which it is striving. Those stony words in the last paragraph are set against those of the first paragraph, but, after the progress of the poem, they do not come as a surprise but as an assured certainty. They are still difficult, but they are now familiar.

Since 'On a Raised Beach' is, I think, referred to at the beginning of this final section of *In Memoriam James Joyce*, it might help to bring in the most penetrating guide to that poem — Donald Mackinnon's *The Problem of Metaphysics*. MacDiarmid himself was keen to point out the value of this book, and while its importance has a stronger bearing to the earlier poem, it is not without relevance to MacDiarmid's renewed commitment here. In Chapter 5, 'Ethics and Metaphysics', Mackinnon says that our separation of the world of nature from that of freedom is an equivocal one.

> If we go further, and say we belong to both realms, we are in danger, by our intellectual indulgence in use even of that rarefied metaphor, of supposing that in however vague and elusive a way, the patterns of the natural realm and the moral realm correspond. Yet the matter cannot rest there; for we know that we ourselves belong to both realms, and this quite simply because we are ourselves agents whose actions are also objects for our understanding, in whose biographies causal continuities can clearly be traced, whose behaviour is a measure not only predictable in principle, but predictable in practice. It is only, therefore, when we recognize the inherent limitations of that understanding's operation that we can school ourselves to the acknowledgement of that which lies outside its scope. Yet, in the end we face the question how we are ready to say anything of that which lies outside those limits, without using those concepts which we have restricted to use within the limits of experience, *partly to establish room for the claim upon us of that which we say lies altogether outside that experience.* The contradiction there is inescapable . . . Primal causality has been wrenched apart from the causality of nature by the extravagance of speaking of the former as timeless. But what, if anything, does that achieve except to advertise that what is most fundamental is beyond the reach of representation? Yet without representation, what is left but aphasia?[93]

It is clear that the problem Mackinnon sets himself to confront is all but identical to that which MacDiarmid poses. Mackinnon's book, in fact, is a bold and powerful explication of many of the ideas of 'On a Raised Beach', as if it had been written backwards from the poem, a discussion of which concludes the book. Behind Kant, for both men, there is Hume. Of Kant's advances on Hume in fundamental questions in the philosophy of psychology, Mackinnon says that they

> provide the foundation of his relentless criticism (in the 'Paral-

ogisms of Rational Psychology') of traditional metaphysical argument for the immortality of the soul which finds its alleged point of departure in a failure to grasp the limited and relative character of the irreducible uniqueness of status we have to concede to the unitary subject in experience. [p.4]

What consequence has this for 'Plaited Like the Generations of Men'? If MacDiarmid's allusion at the opening of the later poem is indeed referring us to 'On a Raised Beach', as I believe, then the consequences are of major importance. He is making a distinction between two locations from which poetry is written, and if 'On a Raised Beach' has a profound and seminal importance to his whole career then we should accord the latter poem equally serious consideration. The realm of music is of equal if not greater viability than the raised beach, to excite and arouse the poetic sensibility he presents to us. The first line, in fact, asserts that he is writing *from* 'the realm of music' itself, and that we must read as if, in the words of Christian Morgenstern that will be quoted later in the poem, this text comes 'from beyond'.

There is a further consideration to take into account, which the Scottish composer Ronald Stevenson has pointed out: the entire passage (verse-paragraphs 1–3 and 5–8) relies on and draws heavily from the writing of the Italian-Austrian composer Ferruccio Busoni (1866–1924). MacDiarmid does, in fact, refer us to Busoni. The passage in question is from a letter Busoni wrote to his wife, from Dayton, USA, dated 3 March 1910, headed:

The Realm of Music
An Epilogue to the New Aesthetic

Come, follow me into the realm of music. Here is the iron fence which separates the earthly from the eternal. Have you undone the fetters and thrown them away? Now come. It is not as it was before when we stepped into a strange country; we soon learnt to know everything there and nothing surprised us any longer. Here there is no end to the astonishment, and yet from the beginning we feel it is homelike.

You still hear nothing, because *everything sounds*. Now, already you begin to differentiate. Listen, every star has its rhythm, and every world its measure. And on each of the stars and on each of the worlds, the heart of every separate living being is beating in its own individual way. And all the beats agree and are separate and yet are a whole.

Your inner ear becomes sharper. Do you hear the depths and the heights? They are as immeasurable as space and endless as numbers.

Unthought-of scales extend like bands from one world to another, *stationary*, and yet *eternally in motion*. Every tone is the centre of immeasurable circles. And now *sound* is revealed to you!

Innumerable are its voices; compared with them, the murmuring of the harp is a din; the blare of a thousand trombones a chirrup. All, all melodies, heard before or never heard, resound completely and simultaneously, carry you, hang over you, or skim lightly past you — of love and passion, of spring and of winter, of melancholy and of hilarity; they are themselves the souls of millions of beings in millions of epochs. If you focus your attention on one of them, you perceive how it is connected with all the others, how it is combined with all the rhythms, coloured by all kinds of sounds, accompanied by all harmonies, down to unfathomable depths and up to the vaulted roof of heaven.

Now you realize how planets and hearts are one, that nowhere can there be an end or an obstacle; that infinity lives in the spirit of all beings; that each being is illimitably great and illimitably small: the greatest expansion is like a point: and that light, sound, movement and power are identical, and each separate and all united, they are life.[94]

MacDiarmid's use of Busoni is, in Benjamin's words, a 'real translation' — it is 'transparent'. His reference to 'On a Raised Beach' is not an imposition on Busoni's text but arises easily from both its words and their meaning. The realm of music described by Busoni might itself have been suggestive of 'On a Raised Beach'. The similarities are immediately striking. When Busoni talks of the simultaneous separateness and unity of all things, and of the music of planets and hearts being one with each other, we may recall MacDiarmid on that beach, shedding the encumbrances that muffle contact with elemental things, and going apart

> Into a simple and sterner, more beautiful and more oppressive
>   world,
> Austerely intoxicating; the first draught is overpowering;
> Few survive it. It fills me with a sense of perfect form,
> The end seen from the beginning, as in a song.

It is no song that conveys the feeling
That there is no reason why it should ever stop,
But the kindred form I am conscious of here
Is the beginning and end of the world.
The unsearchable masterpiece, the music of the spheres,
Alpha and Omega, the Omnific Word.
These stones have the silence of supreme creative power . . .

C.P., pp.428–9

The difference lies in the oppressiveness. For in *In Memoriam James Joyce* the oppressiveness of reality has been greatly alleviated. Having encountered that reality in 'On a Raised Beach', a freedom from the fetters of logocentricism and anthropocentricism has been won. The abyss has given him wings. The music carries him.

Not only does the earlier poem prefigure developments in the later work, it transforms our responsiveness both to Busoni's and to MacDiarmid's work. It should become clear that MacDiarmid's context is wholly realised as his own. Together these factors reveal the validity of MacDiarmid's method. The extensive quotation comes from a realm of music which is as much a part of Mac-Diarmid's vision as it is of Busoni's. And, as we proceed, I hope to show MacDiarmid's development of source-material in 'Plaited Like the Generations of Men' supports the contention that the poem is a 'translation' of this kind *almost in its entirety*.

The poem begins, then, by enjoining the reader to follow the poet's voice, see, feel, and hear with him, and be guided by him. We are not given a self identified in a place as we were in 'On a Raised Beach'. Instead, the ribbons of music and the 'plaited' generations suggest the underlying motif of weaving, or braid-binding of self, language, and place.[95] Edwin Morgan has noted that, in this final section of the poem, MacDiarmid attempts to draw all the strands together, achieving only a partial success, but establishing the main, positive theme of belief in human evolution with the evolution of language.

MacDiarmid lists a number of examples of revelation: Buddha by the Bo-Tree, Socrates dreaming of the Sybil, Descartes dreaming of the Dictionary, and, above all, the revelation of St Paul, where all is changed 'in the twinkling of an eye'.

Because in that moment the individual chooses himself
And thereby all may be changed.
The moment partakes of eternity:
It is then eternity penetrating time.   C.P., p.873

The final illustration of the moment of revelation comes from the French novelist who was President de Gaulle's Minister for the Arts, André Malraux. Not from *Days of Wrath*, however, as MacDiarmid tells us — there is no such book — but from *Days of Contempt*, in the Left Book Club edition of 1936 in the translation by Haakon M. Chevalier. MacDiarmid here changes the significance of the original while literally quoting word for word. He changes the context of the event to suit his own purpose in a prefatory paragraph:

> Or like that moment in which Kassner assembles
> The scattered fragments of his personality
> By identifying a strain of music
> Heard through the walls of his cell
> With the struggle of his comrades throughout the world
> In the same cause.

C.P., p.874

Then he quotes:

> 'Kassner, shaken by the song,
> Felt himself reeling like a broken skeleton.
> These voices called forth relentlessly
> The memory of revolutionary songs
> Rising from a hundred thousand throats,
> Their tunes scattered and then picked up again by the crowds
> Like the rippling gusts of wind over fields of wheat
> Stretched out to the far horizon.
> But already the imperious gravity of a new song
> Seemed once more to absorb everything into an immense
>   slumber;
> And in this calm, the music at last rose above its own heroic
>   call
> As it rises above everything
> With its intertwined flames that soothe as they consume,
> Night fell on the universe,
> Night in which men feel their kinship on the march
> Or in the vast silence,
> The drifting night, full of stars and friendship.'

C.P., pp.874–5

In Malraux's novel, Kassner does not identify a strain of music outside the walls of his cell. In Chapter 2, he is described trying to retain his sanity in solitary confinement by remembering an occasion of solidarity in his past. He has been prompted to do so by a guard who passes the cell, humming. The tune his thoughts return to him is the 'Internationale' and he recalls a time when it was sung, thus imaginatively freeing himself from the terror of solitary confinement. The occasion he remembers is when the workers of Essen had been beaten down by SA-men, who then demanded that they should sing their song. They sang 'with such fierce hope ringing in their voices that the non-commissioned officer had drawn his revolver and fired'.[96] MacDiarmid's quoted sequence then begins, with two changes. He drops a parenthesis of Malraux's. Malraux writes of the voices evoking the memory of revolutionary songs from many other throats, and then writes, in brackets, 'and no music is more exalting than a refrain pealed forth by a multitude'. MacDiarmid cuts this. The second change is simply a mistake. Where Mac-Diarmid has a comma afer 'consume', Chevalier's translation has the correct semi-colon. (This is a mistake in both the MacLellan edition of the poem and *The Complete Poems*.)

Malraux's text is quoted, not absorbed, because it serves as one of a number of instances of self-realisation. It is of no consequence that the character involved is fictional, since the reason for its inclusion is the truth of the revelation not the verifiability of whether it happened to a historical person.

It is on a note of quiet harmony that this first part of 'Plaited Like the Generations of Men' ends: 'The drifting night, full of stars and friendship'.

The second 'movement' introduces doubt. MacDiarmid asks whether this positive vision has not led the poem to the point where it is subject to all the charges commonly laid against rhetoric, and admits that the poem is, in some sense, merely evidence of ideas and values not yet wholly assimilated by the sensibility. He realises he is communicating an enthusiasm for 'a certain use of language' rather than ordering his materials. What prompts this realisation is the suspicion that he will be led to repeat himself so much that he will forget to mention the underlying and 'ultimate metaphysical scheme' he *does* want to affirm. He asks, 'Have I failed in my braid-binding / At this great crisis':

> At this moment when braidbinding as never before,
> The creation of the seamless garment,
> Is the poet's task?

C.P., p.876

MacDiarmid's uneasiness in the parentheses which follow (on pp.876–7) springs from a sense of the limits to which an ideal of 'civilisation' can be fulfilled; and also from the possibility that an ultimate aesthetic ideal may evolve that would be little less exclusive than Platonic intellectualism. He fears the temptation of vanity and the exclusiveness leading to vanity, while he proclaims and celebrates self-universal participation. This problem he resolves by asserting that contempt of the simple-minded is a necessary factor in further evolution from a state of simple-mindedness. A reference to two specific people and the introduction of colloquial terms helps balance the difficulty of the more abstract speculations. He condemns Horace Tograth ('the Australian chemist / Who led the world-wide pogrom against poets'), Mr Furber ('the Canadian dilettante'), 'And all yahoos and *intellectuels-flics*'. And he comes to rest on the only verifiable fact he says he has: that even if Kant believed it was immoral to suppose one's self at all metaphysically distinguishable from another, there are no means by which he can decide categorically that there are other *selves* at all; and, if there are, whether or not they exist in the self-universal 'We' of the poem.

This is, in some ways, the crux of the matter: any attempt to come to grips with MacDiarmid's work necessarily involves a struggle to come to a satisfactory understanding of the meaning of his 'first person' — whether singular or plural. We shall return to this question and explore its significance in detail in the final chapter.

In the next lines of the poem, MacDiarmid seems to affirm his selfhood and identity. But the affirmation is taken from a passage of Thomas de Quincey's *Suspiria De Profundis*. At least, that's what we are referred to. MacDiarmid gives no reference to the second part of the de Quincey quotation, which is separated from the passage from *Suspiria* by the lines

> It is with me now, surveying all life
> From the heights of Literature and the Arts, as it was
> With Thomas de Quincey when he made
> A symbology of the view he commanded
> From the eminence of Everton.

> *C.P.*, pp.878–9

What follows is clearly also a quotation from de Quincey. But it is not from *Suspiria De Profundis* (and not even directly from de Quincey) but an article in the *Times Literary Supplement*.

> He saw life as warfare and harmony, a conflict of opposites and a balance of opposites, and that vision was his from childhood. 'The horror of life mixed itself already in earliest youth with the heavenly sweetness of life.' And, again, in

'Suspiria', that tumult of images, 'Everlasting layers of ideas, feelings, have fallen upon your brain softly as light. Each succession has seemed to bury all that went before. And yet, in reality, not one has been extinguished . . . the fleeting accidents of man's life, and its external shows, may indeed be irrelate and incongruous; but the organizing principles which fuse into harmony, and gather about fixed or pre-determined centres, whatever heterogeneous elements life may have accumulated from without, will not permit the grandeur of human unity to be greatly violated, or its ultimate repose to be troubled, in the retrospect from dying moments, or from other great convulsions.'[97]

And from the second and third columns:

He speaks somewhere of his natural inclination for a solitary life. He makes a symbology of the view he commanded from Everton. Liverpool represented the earth, with its graves and its sorrows left behind, 'yet not out of sight nor wholly forgotten'. The moving sea typified the mind. He seems to be standing aloof from the uproar of life; here was a respite, the tumult in suspense:- 'Here were the hopes which blossom in the paths of life, reconciled with the peace which is in the grave; motions of the intellect as unwearied as the heavens, yet for all anxieties a halcyon calm: tranquillity that seemed no product of inertia, but as if resulting from mighty and equal antagonisms; infinite activities and infinite repose.'[98]

MacDiarmid's use of de Quincey here is particularly interesting, for it is the hypnotic, opiate quality of the writing which he first draws on. He puts the first quotation from the *Times Literary Supplement* in short, light, limpid lines which themselves fall 'softly as light'.

Everlasting layers
Of ideas, images, feelings
Have fallen upon my brain
Softly as light.
Each succession has seemed to bury
All that went before.
And yet, in reality,
Not one has been extinguished . . .

C.P., p.878

He then builds on the conviction and assurance of his avowal of inextinguishable 'ideas, images, feelings', and associates his different, more purely cerebral, non-geographical location with de Quincey's specific one. He returns to this distinction in the parenthesis which follows and, taking his sceptical questioning further and further, becomes embroiled in a dilemma of faith and doubt. What follows is a series of long, convoluted, multiple parentheses filled to over-flowing with tortured diction and broken syntax. The single major problem here (*C.P.*, pp.879–81) is how or if the syntax and punctuation are working. Contradictory possibilities open up so that the operation of reading the passage and trying to make sense of it is like keeping your finger on the knot while trying to tie it up with the same hand. The difficulties are such that a sustained attempt to come to terms with the passage demands some patience.[99]

In effect, the logic of the parentheses is flaunted by the way they are arranged. Seen in this way, MacDiarmid's alogical parenthesising is a potentially creative breakdown of the rules of 'grammar', not just in a self-indulgent, glibly self-posturing, or dramatising way, but as a fiat, something inevitable thrown up in the poem's enormous wake. It is patently *not* 'artfully contrived'. Rather, it might be called 'an error'. But I also think MacDiarmid himself did exactly the kind of puzzling you and I might do whenever we read and try to make sense of this passage as he was putting the poem together, shifting it from here to there and this way and that, but at some point simply stopping, knowing that it said what needed to be said as well as it would, and believing that further struggling would be irrelevant.

The verse is liberated from this clottedness and density with a call to Joyce, and the cautionary exclamation 'not a word, not a word!' MacDiarmid imagines he is looking at Joyce's grave and contemplating the fact that we are beginning more and more to see behind, or through, things to something they hide:

> For the most part cunningly,
> With their outward appearance,
> Hoodwinking man with a façade
> Quite different from what it actually covers.
> – An old story from the point of view of physics.
> We know to-day what heat, sound, and weight are,
> Or at least we have a second interpretation,
> The scientific one. But I know now
> Behind this there is another and many more.

C.P., p.882

These further 'interpretations' provide a sense of the world of 'Plaited Like the Generations of Men'. The exactitude and splendour of Joyce's language reveal him as the trail-blazer for literary developments akin to the development by which we have been able to break up and reassemble the erstwhile chaste 'phenomena of nature'. Later MacDiarmid mentions the pattern cards of dye-stuffs, which display syntheses of colours not occurring in, but transcending, nature, to appease the aesthetic sense of colour. Technology has enabled man to improve on nature, by inventing supernormal versions of normal stimuli. He likes brightly-coloured flowers, so he breeds extra-bright ones. He likes a soft bed to sleep on, so he develops a whole range of supersoft surfaces on which to rest and relax.

In MacDiarmid's poem, however, the technique of using sources to constitute a movement in verse suggests itself as a further, equivalent method of 'interpreting'. If an unnaturally coloured flower (that is, a flower whose colour has been produced by the intervention of man in its reproduction) may be called a 'translation' of its duller, less aesthetically pleasing, former self, likewise MacDiarmid's use of sources is a process of translation. We read these passages *through* the 'transparency' of the linguistic medium of Benjamin's translator.

> And I know with Christian Morgenstern
> That the time will come soon when we will write
> 'From beyond'. I mean about much the same things
> As always. But whose peculiar fascination now
> Will be made transparent.
> They will be characterised with entire belief
> In their reality. Yet they will have
> The effect of hallucinations. They will hold us
> Spell-bound like some of the themes of poetry
> As we have known it hitherto
> But the awe experienced by him
> For whom the old world has collapsed
> (The change which takes place is not, in fact
> An abandonment of belief seriously held
> And firmly planted in the mind,
> But a gradual recognition of the truth
> That you never really held it.
> The old husk drops off
> Because it has long been withered
> And you discover that beneath it
> Is a sound and vigorous growth —)
> Will be expressed in their portrayal too,
> So they will at once entertain

And excite a profound uncanny wonder,
Falling athwart
The tideless certainty of our disinterestedness.

                                                          C.P., p.883

   It will come as no surprise by now that although we are referred
to 'Christian Morgenstern: *Stufen, Eine Entwicklung in Aphorismen
und Tagenbuchnotizen* (Munich: Piper Verlag, 1951)', in fact, the
relevant source is not Morgernstern's book itself but yet another
Times Literary Supplement review. This is a full page review of the
book MacDiarmid mentions, and one by Michael Bauer, *Christian
Morgenstern: Leben und Werk*. In it we find:

> The parable (*Stufen*, page 222) on originality, dated 1913, so
> oddly like Kafka's parable *Der Angruf*, which in its turn seems
> a descendant of Kleist's *Fabel ohne Moral* — three brief pieces
> of astonishingly revelatory writing, by three men apparently so
> very unlike to each other, yet all akin in their vital, consuming
> preoccupation with the Absolute, as in their early death —
> gives a faint hint of what Morgenstern might have done if he
> had felt impelled to write narrative prose. That he did not
> seems cause for regret when one reads his analytical comments
> on Dostoevsky, or that disturbingly intuitive note (1906): 'A
> time will come when stories will be written "from beyond". I
> mean stories about much the same things as those of to-day,
> but whose peculiar fascination will be that the people por-
> trayed will be made transparent — held up against the mystery.
> They will be characterized with entire belief in their reality,
> yet they will have the effect of hallucinations, they will hold
> us spellbound like some of the themes of poetry as we have
> known it hitherto, but the awe experienced by him for whom
> the old world has collapsed will be communicated in their
> portrayal too, so that they will at once entertain and excite an
> uncanny wonderment.' There speaks the same sense of the
> dual nature of reality that in another, more frivolous, mood
> made Morgernstern, amid the typical public celebrations of
> the centenary of Schiller's death, privately replace 'that once
> dear name' by re-christening Schiller — Max Zottuck. It is the
> dual vision of the seer who sees the shape of things to come,
> perhaps of things eternal, superimposed on his everyday world.
> Christian Morgenstern, who was never able to write this narra-
> tive prose that he foresaw, the imaginative prose of our
> immediate future — perhaps already in existence, though

unknown, unprinted — anticipated it potentially in the transparency of his essential verses, which float upward, lightly,
luminously outlined 'against the mystery'.[100]

MacDiarmid makes some specific changes, asserting not 'A' but
'The' time will come and adding 'soon'. He changes Morgenstern's
passage from referring to narrative prose to writing in general. He
takes a longer view, saying instead of 'the same things as those of
to-day', 'the same things as usual'. He repunctuates the passage
(which is all one sentence). He drops one phrase (an important one:
' — held up against the mystery'). He changes 'communicated' to
'expressed'. He makes 'wonderment' simply 'wonder' and then adds
two further lines, qualifying the wonder with disinterestedness. The
most important of these changes is the transformation of the subject,
narrative prose, to writing in general. It is not 'the people portrayed'
who will be 'made transparent' but the 'peculiar fascination' of the
writing itself. MacDiarmid interposes in parenthesis two analogies,
the first relating to an evolution of ideas held in the mind, the second
to physical reality. The analogies thus bolster the evolutionary ideas
he attaches to creative writing. The 'old world' for MacDiarmid,
transcribing this passage in 1951, must have been very different in
some senses from Morgenstern's, in 1906. Yet perhaps the 'new'
ones they both invoke have certain affinities.

It is with the central idea of transparent, hallucinatory fascination
that they both come together. And, while acknowledging Mac-
Diarmid's debt both to Morgenstern and to the *Times Literary
Supplement* reviewer, it is to MacDiarmid's sense of this fascination
I wish to return. This writing 'from beyond' refers to the millennium.
Yet it also represents a kind of writing which might not wait for
events to catch up with it, but which has appeared here before the
general evolution has occurred. Certainly, if 'All but an infinitesimal
percentage of mankind / Have no use for versatility and myriad
mindedness; / Evolution means nothing to them' — then there is no
reason to expect this writing 'from beyond' to wait for any change
in them. MacDiarmid refers to them in parenthesis and quotation
marks:

('Larvae, hallucinated automata, bobbins,
Savage robots, appropriate dummies,
The fascinating imbecility of the creaking men-machines,
Set in a pattern as circumscribed and complete
As a theory of Euclid — essays in a new human mathematic.')

C.P., pp.883–4

These phrases are cogged together out of Wyndham Lewis's collection of stories and essays *The Wild Body*, first published in London in 1927, where we find, for example:

> The fascinating imbecility of these creaking men-machines, that some little restaurant or fishing-boat works, was the original subject of these studies, though in fact the nautical set never materialized. [p.232]

And again:

> Yet we have in most lives the spectacle of a pattern as circumscribed and complete as a theorem of Euclid. So these are essays in a human mathematic. [p.223][101]

In a post-Nietszchean fashion, Lewis's intention in the book is to set over against these 'automata' the subject of the title of his book — The Wild Body — and condemn their ideas as in this chapter's title: 'Inferior Religions'. Lewis's 'automata' are reminiscent of the 'atoms' smashed by the 250-ton cyclotron, to quote once again the obituarist of Joyce whom MacDiarmid approved. But the contrast with Joyce makes the difference clear. Lewis is contemptuous of his 'circumscribed' characters in a way Joyce never is. And MacDiarmid, for all that he distances himself from 'characters', engages his readers with a different mode of address. *In Memoriam James Joyce* is one of those works which has passed beyond the matrix which the oppressive, opaque literalness of ' On a Raised Beach' was a struggle to understand. It is written as if 'from beyond' — from the further side of a transition. In political terms, this situation was described by Brecht:

> The practical methods of the revolution are not revolutionary, they are dictated by the class struggle. It is for this reason that great writers find themselves ill at ease in the class struggle, they behave as though the struggle was already finished, and they deal with the new situation, conceived as collectivist, which is the aim of the revolution. The revolution of the great writers is permanent.[102]

It is permanent as such a thing can be, but permanently requiring complementation, equally. The 'linguistic complementation' Walter Benjamin saw the translation requiring finds an equivalent in the visionary complementation (and the reader's participation) in 'Plaited Like the Generations of Men'. We can assume that Benjamin's language of truth, his 'true language', is to be seen shining beyond the transparent assemblage of source-material in the 'poetry' itself. This is the 'mystic materialism' of Guadapada's bed, 'for another's use, not for its own'. And of ' . . . this world / Of words, thoughts, memories, scientific facts, literary arts' which has several component parts rendering no mutual service. MacDiarmid's humour and his political commitment fuse here in optimistic assurance:

> Ah Joyce, enough said, enough said!
> Mum's the word now! Mum's the word!
> Responsibility for the present state of the world
> And for its development for better or worse
> Lies with every single individual;
> Freedom is only really possible
> In proportion as all are free.
> Knowledge and, indeed, adoption (*Aneignung*)
> Of the rich Western tradition
> And all the wisdom of the East as well
> Is the indispensible condition for any progress;
> World-history and world-philosophy
> Are only now beginning to dawn . . .
>
> C.P., p.884

MacDiarmid's faith in the inevitability of this evolutionary process, in full recognition that only a tiny number of people are 'aware of it yet', commands some respect. Sir Charles Sherrington is quoted to confirm the belief that the complex, not the simple 'is nature's climax of rightness', and this has a strangely humbling effect. Sherrington actually provides the source for the next passage, about the development of the embryo in the womb and its uncanny preparations for life in the world outside. The humility which comes into the tone of the poetry at this point is moving, and conspicuously lacking in stridency. It is at the furthest remove from Pound's more famous dictum in Canto LXXXI: 'Pull down thy vanity'. The passage has been extensively commented on by Edwin Morgan in the 1978 essay 'MacDiarmid's Later Poetry Against an International Background'. Morgan concludes, 'by looking at quoted contexts, [we] can certainly reveal more of the inner life of the poem than we might suspect from a surface reading.'[103] His analysis of MacDiarmid's use of Sherrington conveys enthusiasm for Sherrington as well as MacDiarmid, but there are one or two further points. In the context of the poem, the continuity of the transcribed material with what has gone before and comes after is important. The repeatedly italicised confident future tense 'will' extends and enforces the sense of provision and store for the future while exemplifying the physical development at work in a biological context. If the embryo described on p.886 is a metaphor, it has a physical tangibility. Morgan notes the multiple recession occurring when MacDiarmid quotes Sherrington, who is quoting Cajal, who in turn is quoting Virgil (or, rather, misquoting Virgil). There is a similar recession when MacDiarmid quotes Sherrington and writes:

> All is provided. As Aristotle says,
> 'To know the end of a thing is to know the why of it.'
>
> > *C.P.*, pp.886–7

For Sherrington, in fact, wrote more extensively:

> All is remembered; no detail is forgotten . . . Fernel's Preface (1542) wrote 'as Aristotle says to know the end of a thing is to know the why of it'. And similarly today the biologist writes, 'we can only understand an organism if we regard it *as though* produced under the guidance of thought for an end', as a final clause at work.[104]

Here, MacDiarmid is quoting Sherrington, who is quoting Fernel, who is quoting Aristotle. But MacDiarmid chooses to telescope the whole thing, and allow the Aristotle quotation to appear in the poem directly (produced under the guidance of thought for an end, as a final cause at work). The distractions he might have included by a fuller quotation are indeed, as Edwin Morgan says, 'unerringly deleted'. The immediacy thus effected allows the jump from biological instance to philosophical idea, to literary analogy, and back (in the next paragraph, still dealing with the foetus in the womb) to a further biological example. Unseen gestation is effectively represented as a principal concern of the poem, and also by the method the poem employs. The idea of invisible actions suddenly emerging in the context of the poem as appropriated and apposite ideas (as, for example, with this very paragraph) is constantly maintained.

What is registered in this part of 'Plaited Like the Generations of Men' is the need for contact with the natural sciences and also for 'polemics against all idealistic and biological elements in the philosophies which have arisen from reflection on the natural sciences alone'. Here, MacDiarmid's Marxism does indeed provide a 'dynamic *Weltanschauung*' and his materialism is at last exactly that described by Sebastiano Timpanaro:

> When Lenin presses his opponents on the question of the

relationship between thought and the brain, when he states that 'sensation depends on the brain, nerves, retina, etc., i.e. on matter organized in a definite way' and that 'sensation, thought, consciousness are the supreme-product of matter organized in a particular way', when he exposes the religious and obscurantist elements which exist in even the most up-dated 'immanentism', he demonstrates an awareness that materialism is much more than a gnoseological theory. Materialism entails also the recognition of man's animality (superseded *only in part* by his species-specific sociality); it is also the radical negation of anthropocentrism and providentialism of any kind, and it is absolute atheism.[105]

The depiction follows of Joyce's death-chamber, and of those 'on the other side' when Joyce 'passed over' who found not 'another queer bird gone' or even a 'Metaphysical Buzzard' — but a beautiful, magnificent peacock, its transitional movement representative of 'the Creative Act'. The image of the peacock's flight through the open window symbolises the moment of '*ek-stasis*' itself, a term from Heidegger which signifies a position apart from ontological relativity — and invokes the moment of revelation referred to earlier in the poem in connection with Descartes, Buddha, St Paul, and Malraux's Kassner. With Joyce here, that 'supreme faction' is allowed a 'supreme' complementation.

The ending of the poem is delightful in its naiveté and overt digressiveness. 'Chau for now', he says to Joyce. 'And so I come to the end of this poem . . . '. But the naiveté has an important effect, and the digression is purposeful.

The transcendent, the concept of 'beyond' has been a factor contributing to the philosophical dilemma in the central part of the poem, yet the emphasis and directness with which MacDiarmid uses the idea of a metaphysical hinterland are continually subjected to penetrating criticism — not the criticism of the philosopher but of the ironist. The close of the poem invites laughter and release, relief from a concentrated and exacting demand, and release into an inviting and participatory comedy. The final line ('*Sab thik chha*' — common sailors' and dockers' bazaar-bat round all the ports of India, meaning, 'Everything's really perfectly okay') — may well be taken as in some sense reflecting the inclusive, vulgar, and pacific 'Yes' which closes *Ulysses*, but it is also an answer to the sombre sonority of the last line of *The Waste Land*.

The space in which the poem moves, from which MacDiarmid

has rejected anthropocentrism and with it any specific location of landscape, has plenty of room for variation in tone, and the value of ironic humour is put to some use. That — in contrast to 'On a Raised Beach' — alleviates the oppressiveness of the fundamental problems posed in the poem, and allows MacDiarmid to make a world of the play of his imaginings.

Like Benjamin's 'translation', MacDiarmid's text demands complementation. But to carry the analogy further, the complementation any individual reader is liable to provide will never be enough. As well as the complementation any reader may bring to the text, there is also what Benjamin referred to as a 'pure' or 'true' language which will complement any actual language of the text itself. Indeed, this is the *only* complementation Benjamin allows for. And this can be discerned in 'Plaited Like the Generations of Men' not only as an implicit aspect of textual practice but as an explicit component of the poem's argument.

For all the syntactic convolution of the central part of the poem, the problem facing MacDiarmid is fundamentally related to that Donald Mackinnon sets out to deal with when he says:

> No one would deny the extent to which parabolic discourse may illuminate human life by renewing simplicity, etc. Yet, the crucial question remains whether, by means of parable, myth, saga, etc., we are enabled to make significant statements about that which lies beyond the frontiers of conceivable experience.[106]

I do not think there would be a problem if it ceased to be posited that we *are* enabled to. And I think that, in the world Mackinnon writes of as lying 'beyond the frontiers of conceivable experience', we have an analogy for the world Benjamin designates as 'the tensionless and even silent depository' of the 'true language'. MacDiarmid's problem in the last major section of *In Memoriam James Joyce* was to bring the serenity he had achieved out of that hinterland of silent potential and onto the page *while maintaining a Marxist ethic*. Only by confronting this problem in a way that allowed the poetry itself to be engaged and battle-scarred in the process could a possible resolution be achieved. A complex, provisional but pragmatic notion of the unitary is therefore sustained by the possibility of the purposive development of all the discrete parts which go into its formation.

Notes

1. Hugh MacDiarmid, 'Author's Note', in *In Memoriam James Joyce* (Glasgow: William MacLellan, 1955; repr. 1956), pp.11–18 (p.11).
2. Ruth McQuillan, 'The Complete MacDiarmid', in G. Ross Roy (ed.), *Studies in Scottish Literature*, XVIII (Columbia, SC: 1983), pp.177–209 (p.199).
3. *The Letters*, p.161.
4. *C.P.*, pp.704–12.
5. *The Letters*, p.447.
6. Alan Bold, *MacDiarmid. Christopher Murray Grieve. A Critical Biography* (London: John Murray, 1988), pp.378–9.
7. *The Letters*, p.470.
8. Ibid., p.453.
9. Ibid., p.454.
10. Ibid., p.455.
11. W.N. Herbert, 'MacDiarmid: Mature Art', in Kenneth Buthlay (ed.), *Scottish Literary Journal*, 15(2), November 1988, pp.24–38, (p.27).
12. McQuillan, op cit., p.202.
13. *C.P.*, p.1462.
14. *The Letters*, p.656.
15. In conversation with Michael Grieve, 17 January 1989.
16. Michael Grieve and Alexander Scott (eds), *The Hugh MacDiarmid Anthology* (London: Routledge & Kegan Paul, 1972). See also Alan Bold, *MacDiarmid. Christopher Murray Grieve. A Critical Biography* (London: John Murray, 1988).
17. TSS in private collection.
18. In conversation with Norman MacCaig, 17 January 1989.
19. In conversation with William MacLellan, 16 December 1988.
20. *C.P.*, pp.767–76.
21. Fergussons's proleptic acuities show up in it, for example, on p.57: 'In the windows of the motor shops we see engines wonderfully lit, compared with which *most* sculpture, especially the not modern, is merely stupid and boring.'
22. Edwin Morgan, 'James Joyce and Hugh MacDiarmid', in *James Joyce and Modern Literature*, ed. W.J. MacCormack and Alistair Stead (London: Routledge & Kegan Paul, 1982), pp. 202–17 (pp.211–12).
23. Marcel Raymond, *From Baudelaire to Surrealism* (London: Peter Owen, 1947), pp.355–6.
24. Evgeny Zamyatin, 'Literature, Revolution and Entropy', in *Dissonant Voices in Soviet Literature*, ed. Patricia Blake and Max Hayward (London: George Allen and Unwin, 1964), pp.12–19 (pp.15–16).
25. For the meanings of *schablone* and *bordatini* I am grateful to Edwin Morgan.
26. Cf. Daniel Cory, 'Ezra Pound: A Memoir', *Encounter*, 30(5) (1968), p.38. And Catherine Seelye (ed.), *Charles Olson and Ezra Pound: An*

Encounter at St. Elizabeths by Charles Olson (New York: Grossman/-Viking, 1975), p.136.

27. Shakespeare, *Macbeth*, II. iii. 12–21 (Arden edn), ed. Kenneth Muir (London and New York: Methuen, 1986), pp.59–60.

28. Maud Ellmann, *The Poetics of Impersonality: T.S. Eliot and Ezra Pound* (Brighton: The Harvester Press, 1987), p.25.

29. MacDiarmid also wrote in on the 17th humbly to submit that 'A poem of over 6,000 lines should not be subjected to this sort of stricture on the strength of two alleged faults in the last few lines.' It is also worth noting that in *Finnegans Wake*, Joyce addresses Walt Whitman, whom MacDiarmid claimed as one of his favourite poets, saying: 'Chau, Camerade!'

30. Sebastiano Timpanaro, *On Materialism* (London: NLB, 1975), p.212.

31. Pound's six types of great writer were first described in the *New York Herald Tribune* in January 1929 and first published in *How to Read, or Why* in London in 1931. They are:
    (1) The inventors, writers who had discovered a process or processes.
    (2) The masters, who had been able to assimilate and co-ordinate a large number of previous inventions and bring the whole to fullness.
    (3) The diluters, who had followed inventors or masters, producing something of lower intensity.
    (4) The writers who had done more or less good work in the more or less good style of a period (he suggested Wyatt, Donne, Herrick).
    (5) The masters of *Belles Letters* (like Prévost), who had not invented a form but had brought some mode to a very high development.
    (6) The starters of crazes, writers who had launched a wave of fashion which had subsided and left things as they were.

32. Hugh MacDiarmid, 'The Key to World Literature', *The Scottish Journal*, 4 (1954), pp.12–13.

33. Marx's thoughts on the impossibility of epic poetry in an age of mass communication are important in this regard. He argued that Greek art and the Greek epic are bound up with certain forms of social development, certain shared beliefs and mythologies determined, at a primal stage, by socio-economic considerations. Consequently, the conditions under which the Homeric epics could flourish have gone forever; no modern epic could match the Greek standard, for it would seem childish by comparison. But Marx's views here are, of course, the product of his own time and conditions. See S.S. Prawer, *Karl Marx and World Literature* (Oxford: Oxford University Press, 1976).

34. 'The Politics and Poetry of Hugh MacDiarmid', in *Selected Essays of Hugh MacDiarmid*, ed. Duncan Glen (London: Jonathan Cape, 1969), pp.19–37 (p.31).

35. Edinburgh University Library, Special Collections Department, C.M. Grieve Collection, Gen. 887, ff.65–9, E67/9, Letter to F.G. Scott, pp.7–16 only, n.d.

36. Cf. Edwin Morgan's valuable account 'James Joyce and Hugh MacDiarmid', which discusses not only Joyce's influence on MacDiarmid but also suggests how MacDiarmid may have influenced Joyce (see note 22).

37. Alan Bold, *MacDiarmid. Christopher Murray Grieve. A Critical Biography* (London: John Murray, 1988), p.130. But see also the caution advised by Patrick Crotty, in a review of Bold's biography, in the *Scottish Literary Journal Supplement*, 30 (Spring 1989), pp.16–19 (p.17).

38. In *The Oxford Book of Modern Verse 1892–1935* (Oxford: Oxford University Press, 1936), pp.324–5.

39. 'The Case for Synthetic Scots', in *At the Sign of the Thistle* (London: Stanley Nott, 1934), pp. 177–96 (p.184).

40. *Lucky Poet*, p.407.

41. Ellsworth Mason and Richard Ellmann (eds), *The Critical Writings of James Joyce* (London: Faber & Faber, 1959), pp.68–72 (p.69).

42. Ibid., pp.246–8.

43. *C.P.*, p.741.

44. Dominic Manganiello, *Joyce's Politics* (London: Routledge & Kegan Paul, 1980), p.231.

45. 'Ireland, Island of Saints and Sages' (1907), in Mason and Ellmann (eds), *The Critical Writings of James Joyce*, pp.153–74 (p.157).

46. 'The Centenary of Charles Dickens', in Louis Berrone (ed. and transl.), *James Joyce in Padua* (New York: Random House, 1977), pp.33–7 (pp.35–6).

47. Manganiello, op. cit., p.218.

48. Quoted in Edwin Morgan, 'James Joyce and Hugh MacDiarmid' (see note 36).

49. 'Poetry and Science', in *Selected Essays of Hugh MacDiarmid*, ed. Duncan Glen (London: Jonathan Cape, 1969), pp.233–47 (p.235). The comment is repeated elsewhere.

50. Alex Agutter, 'Middle Scots as a Literary Language', in R.D.S. Jack (ed.), *The History of Scottish Literature: Volume I, Origins to 1660 (Mediaeval and Renaissance)*, (Aberdeen: Aberdeen University Press, 1988), gen. ed. Cairns Craig, pp.13–25 (pp.23–4).

51. Norman MacCaig, 'A Note on the Author', in Hugh MacDiarmid, *Scottish Eccentrics* (New York: Johnson Reprint Corporation, 1972).

52. Denis Donoghue, 'We Irish', in *We Irish: Essays on Irish Literature and Society* (New York: Alfred A. Knopf, 1986), pp.3–18 (pp.12–13).

53. The publication in 1943 of Sorley MacLean's *Dàin do Eimhir agus Dàin Eile* (by William MacLellan, who also published *In Memoriam James Joyce* twelve years later) has been called an event after which poetry in Gaelic could never be the same. Seamus Heaney has said also that for a younger generation of writers the poetry of Sorley MacLean has had 'the force of a revelation'. See Raymond J. Ross

and Joy Hendry (eds), *Sorley MacLean: Critical Essays* (Edinburgh: Scottish Academic Press, 1986).

54. Tom Paulin, 'A New Look at the Language Question', in *Ireland and the English Crisis* (Newcastle: Bloodaxe Books, 1984, repr. 1987), pp.178–93 (p.178).

55. It is exactly this plurality and variousness in Joyce that MacDiarmid celebrates. In *Aesthetics in Scotland* (written in 1950 but not published until 1984) MacDiarmid assessed Joyce's work as being a *summa* of its age. He takes into account Joyce's interest in the cinema ('both a science and an art, and therefore the most characteristic expression of our time'), his recognition of the work of impressionist painting, defining the object through the eyes of the beholder, his understanding of the Wagnerian school of composition, blending music and ideas thematically, his awareness of the international psychoanalytic movement, and of Bergson, Whitehead, and other philosophers who were positing relational theories of existence. See Alan Bold (ed.), *Aesthetics in Scotland* by Hugh MacDiarmid (Edinburgh: Mainstream, 1984).

56. Lloyd Fernando, 'Joyce and the Artist's Quest for a Universal Language', in *Cultures in Conflict: Essays on Literature and the English Language in South East Asia* (Singapore: Graham Brasch, 1986), pp.67–82 (p.80).

57. *C.P.*, p.887.

58. Hugh MacDiarmid, *At the Sign of the Thistle* (London: Stanley Nott, 1934), p.118. It would be interesting to know just how MacDiarmid came by this recording.

59. The danger that exists here, and the criticism one might make of both the Joyce of *Finnegans Wake* and the later MacDiarmid, is that in their work there is a collapse of narrative particularity. Joyce telescopes characters from world myths, religions, and literatures into protean types or dream-figures whose semblance to 'characters' (such as Stephen or Molly or Bloom) is distant. To go beyond the association of, say, Billy Budd and Christ, and to identify them as merely aspects of a larger human quality diminishes their particularity and the particular qualities they have in their own 'narratives' and in their own right. Similarly, MacDiarmid, in 'Cornish Heroic Song for Valda Trevlyn', for example, following the rather wild speculations of E.A. Waddell, collapses together King Arthur, Thor, Her-Thor, Thor Eindri, and Indra in a synthesis of Celtic, Norse, and Indian mythologies which supports his own poetic practice and his pan-Celtic mythic vision. By attempting to cover all the ground, accommodate all the variations, they are both, perhaps, constrained by the patterns of their own imaginations.

60. Stephen Fender (ed.), *The American Long Poem: An Annotated Selection*, (London: Edward Arnold, 1977), pp.2–3.

61. J.V. Stalin, *Marxism and the Problem of Linguistics* (Peking: Foreign Languages Press, 1972), pp.51–2. But I acknowledge the caution of

Peter McCarey, the voice of experience, who writes: 'Working as a translator in a number of United Nations agencies I have seen what happens to languages after prolonged economic, political and cultural co-operation of nations, NGOs, and multinationals. The working languages (they are, of course, and by Stalin's consent, English, Russian and not German but French) are used largely by people who have learned them in adulthood. They converge and become more abstract because when a specific term has no equivalent in another language, it is either borrowed or translated with a generic term. They are sanitized to avoid giving unintended offence (e.g. one place insists on lexical equivalents of 'endogenous' because—'native' has colonial connotations for English speakers, 'autochthonous' has similar problems in Spanish, as 'indigenous' has in French). Denotation is simplified and connotation, the communal aspect of language, is regarded as interference; no community — no epic. What results is not a world language, but an international chewing-gum, desperanto, and if it is allowed to slash and burn its way through the linguistic rainforests of the world, a lot of people will lose their tongues.' Peter McCarey, 'Mungo's Hat and Maxwell's Demon: On *The History of Scottish Literature*, vols. I–IV, general editor Cairns Craig, Aberdeen: Aberdeen University Press, 1987–8', *Edinburgh Review* 84 (1990), pp. 93–112, p. 112.

62. See Colin MacCabe, '"So truth be in the field": Milton's Use of Language', in Susanne Kappeler and Norman Bryson (eds), *Teaching the Text* (London: Routledge & Kegan Paul, 1983), pp.18–34 (p.32).

63. Edwin Morgan, 'James Joyce and Hugh MacDiarmid' (see note 22), p.212.

64. W.B. Yeats, 'The Song of the Happy Shepherd', in *Selected Poetry*, ed. A. Norman Jeffares (London: Macmillan, 1971), pp.1–2 (p.1).

65. J.B.S. Haldane, 'God-Makers', in *The Inequality of Man and Other Essays* (Harmondsworth: Penguin/Pelican, 1932, repr. 1937), pp.170–86 (the epigraph is taken from p.177).

66. John Cowper Powys, 'Walt Whitman', in *The Pleasures of Literature* (London: Cassell, 1938; repr. London: Village Press, 1975), p.455.

67. John Cowper Powys, *Autobiography* (London: John Lane, the Bodley Head, 1934; repr. London: Pan/Picador, 1982), pp.648–50. It is worth noting that when I asked MacDiarmid where he had come across the word 'Esplumeoir' (which entitles a poem that offers a series of metaphors for eternity), he told me that it came from Powys.

68. Gustave Flaubert, *Bouvard and Pécuchet*, transl. T.W. Earp and G.W. Stonier (London: Jonathan Cape, 1936).

69. Ibid., p.9.

70. Ibid., p.10.

71. Eugen Herrigel, *Zen in the Art of Archery* transl. from the German by R.F.C. Hall, Foreword by Dr D.T. Suzuki (London: Routledge & Kegan Paul, 1953), p.14.

72. Ibid., p.86.
73. Friedrich Nietzsche, *Thus Spoke Zarathustra*, transl. R.J. Hollingdale (Harmondsworth: Penguin, 1972), p.136.
74. T.H. White, *The Sword in the Stone*, in *The Once and Future King* (London and Glasgow: Fontana/Collins, 1973), p.53.
75. Norman Suckling, *Paul Valéry and the Civilized Mind* (London: Oxford University Press, 1954), p.250.
76. Basil de Sélincourt, *Pomona: or, the Future of English* (London: Kegan Paul, Trench, Trubner, undated but pre-1927), p.29. For more contemporary reference, see 'Flower of English Yanked into a Computer', *The Sunday Times*, 5 February 1984, p.5. In this article by Veronica Horweth and Simon Winchester we were told that the Oxford English Dictionary was being computerised, the idea being to ensure that 'English becomes the base definition language for the whole world — the language by which all others are judged'.
77. Edward W. Said, *Orientalism* (Harmondsworth: Penguin/Peregrine, 1985).
78. Haldane, op. cit., pp.140–5 (pp.142–3).
79. Bertolt Brecht, 'Against Georg Lukács', in Ernst Bloch, Georg Lucács, Bertolt Brecht, Walter Benjamin, Theodor Adorno, *Aesthetics and Politics* (London: NLB, 1977), pp.68–85 (p.69).
80. Catherine Seelye (ed.), *Charles Olson & Ezra Pound: An Encounter at St. Elizabeths* (New York: Grossman Publishers/Viking, 1975), p.531.
81. *In Memoriam James Joyce* (Glasgow: MacLellan, 1955; repr. 1956), pp.14–15.
82. *Lucky Poet*, p.369.
83. John Holloway, *Widening Horizons in English Verse* (London: Routledge & Kegan Paul, 1966), p.73.
84. Ibid., p.81.
85. Ibid., pp.81–2.
86. Ibid., p.83.
87. Walter Benjamin, 'The Task of the Translator', in *Illuminations*, pp.69–82 (pp.78–9).
88. Ibid., p.77.
89. Ibid., p.77.
90. Ibid., pp.76–7.
91. Margery G. McCulloch, 'Hugh MacDiarmid: A Study of Three Poems' (M. Litt. thesis, 1977, Glasgow University Library).
92. T.J. Cribb, 'The Cheka's Horrors and "On a Raised Beach" ', *Studies in Scottish Literature*, XX, ed. G. Ross Roy (Columbia, SC: 1985) pp.88–100. I have paraphrased some of Cribb's essay in this paragraph because it seems to me one of the most sustained and insightful readings of the poem.

93. D.M. Mackinnon, *The Problem of Metaphysics* (Cambridge: Cambridge University Press, 1974), pp.63–4.
94. Ferruccio Busoni, *The Essence of Music and Other Papers*, transl. from the German by Rosamond Ley (London: Rockcliff, 1957), pp.188–9. (It is not certain that this is the translation MacDiarmid used.)
95. Nevertheless, it is surprising to discover that the braid-binding effected by the poem itself extends even to footnotes. At the word 'woven', we are referred to Professor R.B. Onians's book *The Origin of European Thought* (London, 1952). The extensive footnote we are given is lifted, with some deletions and compressions, from a review in the *Times Literary Supplement*. Here the anonymous reviewer tell us,

> The third section is concerned chiefly with words connected with fate which can be interpreted as terms connected with spinning and weaving and the use of their product. Thus the well-known phrase 'on the knees of the gods' refers to the gods sitting down to spin men's fates. The word *peirar*, often translated 'end', means a bond or cord (consisting of good or bad fortune) which the gods can put on a person or an army (and Ocean is the bond round the Earth, although here the bond is slipping over into the meaning of boundary and so end); the image of binding is often used to express the power of fate or the gods over men, and if we ask what these cords are with which fate binds men, Professor Onians answers that they are the threads which fate or the gods have spun, and that in certain phrases fate itself is thought of as a thread or bond which is put upon men. He also interprets two well-known Homeric passages by these means: the 'jars of Zeus' in the twenty-fourth book of the *Iliad* are jars from which he selects wool for spinning fates, and the 'scales of Zeus' in the twenty-second book are the scales in which the spun wool of two fates is weighed one against the other. A further very important chapter deals with *telos*. *Telos* (which means 'end' in later Greek) in Homer 'covers a man's eyes and nostrils' and so seems also to be some sort of bond, and from the original meaning the later and more abstract meanings can be developed.

And three columns on:

> *Peirar* even in Homer already has the abstract meaning of boundary, but the boundary is doubtless still felt as a physical rope: the words associated with it — binding, fettering, crowning — become the normal verbs to use when men's fortunes, good or bad, are to be described.

The article also discusses Onians's remarks on the words *thymos*, *psyche*, *moirais*, *phren*, and *noos*. Noos may have informed 'Noösphere' from the first section of *In Memoriam*, where MacDiarmid locates his poem in a place where nothing matters 'save Implex and Noösphere'. 'Implex' is from Valéry's *Idée Fixe*, and signifies a person's capacity for potential development. But 'Noösphere' is not Valéry's term. The word comes in *The Phenomenon of Man* by Teilhard de Chardin, where it signifies the invisible sphere of the mind, world-consciousness and its relations to 'nous' (pronounced 'noos', meaning 'intellect') and 'noose' (which is literally a bond or snare) are obvious. (D.M. Mackinnon, the author of *The Problem of Metaphysics*, also had a hand in the translation of *The Phenomenon of Man*.) Onians, says the *Times Literary Supplement* reviewer, calls 'nous' Homer's one psychological term. It 'cannot be identified with anything physical, but seems to have been an abstract term from its origin', and it 'expresses either the particular movement, purpose, or, relatively permanent, that which moves, the purposing consciousness'. The 'purposing consciousness' is a term very much to the point, and the Homeric reference is doubly appropriate in a work intended to stand as a modern epic and as an elegy for the author of *Ulysses*.

96. André Malraux, *Days of Contempt*, transl. Haakon M. Chevalier (London: Victor Gollancz, 1936), p.54 (the full passage quoted is from pp.54–5).

97. 'De Quincey's Retreat: The Uncharted Lands of Dream', *The Times Liteary Supplement*, 10 June 1939, p.340.

98. Ibid.

99. The first parenthesis opens (on p.879) with 'Even so am I now transformed . . . ' and ends with the question ' . . . of religious perceptions?' on the next page. This raises difficulties. Where does the main verb arrive? Having read these pages more times than I care to remember, I still cannot answer this question. Also, the full stop between 'nature' and 'Yet discovering the secret of thought' (on p.880) has to be a comma, or else nonsense is made of the question mark at the end of this parenthesis. The parenthesis closes and on the next line another immediately begins, the bracket opening on: 'But it conflicts with our felt love . . . ' and closing after ' . . . they would wish to be.' (pp.880–1). This must be read as a further development of the preceding question. It is syntactically continuous with it, effectively part of the same question. Normally, what is outside a parenthesis cannot take its cue from what is inside. But here it does. The following section, from 'Being in short as where literary art . . . ' to ' . . . the universe as a whole?' (p.881) must be extra-parenthetical, because it has to flow immediately up to the beginning of the next section, which reacts directly against it ('Ah! no, no! Intolerable end'). Otherwise, the closing of the brackets after 'radical of religious perceptions' would

occur at the end of the whole following section, on p.882 or indeed somewhere after. To what position can that closing bracket be postponed? Wherever it occurs it will break the flow, and immediately after these multiple parentheses, 'Plaited Like the Generations of Men' resumes a relatively fluent movement, continuing to the end of the book.

100. 'Christian Morgenstern', *The Times Literary Supplement*, 6 July 1951, p.420.
101. The book also provides the source for the line 'Laughter is the representative of tragedy when tragedy is away' *C.P.*, p.771; *The Wild Body*, p.237.
102. Quoted in Colin MacCabe, *James Joyce and the Revolution of the Word* (London: Macmillan, 1978), p.171.
103. Edwin Morgan, 'MacDiarmid's Later Poetry Against an International Background', *Scottish Literary Journal*, 5(2) (December 1978), pp.20–35 (pp.29–30).
104. Charles Sherrington, *Man on His Nature* (Harmondsworth: Penguin 1955), pp.106–7.
105. Timpanaro, op. cit., pp.248–9.
106. Mackinnon, op. cit., p.94.

3.

The First Person

What is perhaps most surprising (and in some ways, confusing) about MacDiarmid's use of the first person singular is the distance at which it stands from a consistently identifiable persona, or personae. MacDiarmid's poems are not precisely 'dramatic monologues' and do not entirely belong in the tradition of dramatic monologue which runs into modernism through Browning to Pound and Eliot, and has been a major strain in English poetry at least since John Donne. MacDiarmid's 'I' extends beyond the provenance of particular poems to signify a function which is as much political as literary and has to do not only with 'the poem as artifice' but also with a real and alterable political condition. Therefore, the speaker of many of MacDiarmid's poems is not specified as a particular person but is an amalgamation of C.M. Grieve, his construct 'MacDiarmid', and a mass of different source-texts. What this amounts to in effect is the creator and inhabitant of a fictitious world, a world whose semblance to identifiable actuality might sometimes seem rather stretched, but whose purpose might be described as the presentation of the actual world in the light of what it is possible to make of it. Unless we accept the political dynamic running through MacDiarmid's work in this way, we shall misjudge his place among his peers. He does not provide us with poetry as aesthetically *comprehensible* as Pound's 'Mauberley' or Eliot's 'J. Alfred Prufrock', but is inevitably concerned to break down the aesthetic constraints which delimit those characters and those poems. One might argue, in his defence, that it is high time such an attack was mounted. The aesthetic accomplishment of 'J. Alfred Prufrock' is, arguably, something that makes the reprehensibility and cowardice of the actions described in that poem all the more easy to empathise with uncritically, for it directs attention to itself as accomplishment rather than to those actions as, in some senses, frankly contemptible.[1]

Harvey Oxenhorn commented in 1984 that 'MacDiarmid's singularity among modern poets lay in his insistent effort to integrate personal and representative voices.'[2] That integration results in the kind of poetry we have been studying, which is not entirely the product of a 'fire-eater in his kilt' nor that of a merely 'gentle, vital, visionary man'; nor yet someone who is somewhere 'between' those two extremes, but rather someone larger than either, someone in whom they come together. Having seen the extent to which *In Memoriam* is a *constructed* object, an artifice, it is impossible to forget that MacDiarmid's poetry generally is to an exceptional degree, a 'made thing', an integration of voices. The practice of criticism which often (dealing with Pound or Eliot, for example) seeks to reconfirm authorial identity through the fragments of the text seems inapplicable here. And this is because the 'self' which has produced this 'made thing' is not interested in being accepted in the same way. Indeed, the self as it is presented through MacDiarmid's work makes a progress through forms in which autonomous identity might be inferred, towards forms which deny the validity of that autonomy. One of the things this final chapter is intended to do is to give some idea of that progression by looking at a number of instances from various points throughout MacDiarmid's career where he has been, or might be, accused of plagiarism.

Of course I am not concerned with plagiarism as a simple means of dismissing a text, and we have dealt at some length with transcribed material already and seen how it can be understood operating in highly sophisticated ways in MacDiarmid's poetry. Here, however, I wish to keep the argument straightforward, and begin with a discussion of the term 'plagiarism' itself and Kenneth Buthlay's persuasive exposition of the three principal ways in which instances of MacDiarmid's 'plagiarism' are of interest in terms of traditional literary criticism. These modes of interpreting MacDiarmid's 'plagiarisms' are dependent on the certain and fixed identities of MacDiarmid, the authors he has plagiarised, and the works of each. Buthlay never raises the question of intertextuality, and thereby sidesteps the theoretical problems and pleasures raised by MacDiarmid's texts. This is the area to which we shall return in the final sections of this chapter, and at the end of the book we shall reintroduce the idea of modern epic poetry and the subject of language, and attempt to consolidate the main arguments which have been running through the book.

Plagiarism

'Plagiarism' is a term that suggests the law courts, and it might simply be left at that. But the assumptions that lie unquestioned in the mind when the word is used are quite complex. The accusation is often not that the 'plagiarist' has done another writer damage (if it were, the fact of the plagiarism being identified itself immediately redresses the situation in a literary if not financial sense). It is rather that a pretence has been connived, the power of the accusation residing in the fact not that someone else wrote something but that this one did *not* write it — a wholly different emphasis. It suggests a deceit and testifies to the investment of faith we make in the notion of the writer as 'original' creator. But, clearly, it is not that we always specifically demand of writers that their work, in this obvious sense, be 'original'. The case of 'found poetry' shows that, and would suggest that it is rather a case of knowing where one stands. It has to do with our insistence on the right to know the meaning of the text, and then be sure that our knowledge is given assent from somewhere. A problem arises if the defining assumption is made of the text having to mean in terms of its origin in the mind of the poet. The matter of what we are led to expect is very important here. Eliot sanctions his plagiarising by setting it up very carefully (the notes to *The Waste Land* are the perfect example); though, of course, he is fooling us, and does not reveal the half of it (for example, that 'Death by Water' is a pretty exact translation from the French). Nevertheless, the rules for reading have been laid down and given an acceptable authority. With MacDiarmid, however, there is not that clear certainty of 'how to read'. What many readers take from the aura surrounding MacDiarmid's omniscient manner gives rise to assumptions that are thrown into confusion by the discovery of 'plagiarism'. It is precisely because his tone is often so resoundingly assertive or self-affirming that it can be very unsettling to discover that that 'self' is not there at all.

Beyond that, since lots of people detest MacDiarmid for various reasons (especially political), the charge of plagiarism comes as a handy brick to throw, despite the facts that (1) everybody does it; (2) it is not what you do but the way that you do it; (3) as far as poetry is concerned, MacDiarmid can do almost anything he likes; and (4) property is theft, and vice versa. In the end, 'plagiarism' is a smoke-screen and the debate is really not about property but about sincerity, which is impossible to define, except (1) for the self, from the self, and within the self; and (2) as a socially constructed set of terms, mediated through custom and form — which brings us back to the law courts. The force of the charge of plagiarism lies in the sense that it is a duplicitous and dishonest activity. It may be possible, however, to reverse my argument and say that it is 'sincerity' which is the smoke-screen, that the argument *is* fundamentally about property, and that the motive behind the theft is concealed. And, of course, such an argument is politically volatile: it assumes a different character depending on what one's attitude to property is. What determines that attitude, I would suggest, is a political question precisely because it is a question of position within a structure of power. For power creates the function of position; and position creates the function of identity.

Plagiarism is also a different thing from quotation, but which is which is then powerfully implicated in the meaning of the poetry. In this whole area, MacDiarmid causes multiple difficulties, because in some cases he himself appears not to be certain of what he is doing, so that the questions raised are never answered, and the anarchy remains forever valid. The wish-fulfilment that 'sincerity' would sanction is *not* vouchsafed. And by denying themselves such 'certainty' MacDiarmid's texts insist that their primary function lies in their appropriation by the reader; their help in his or her production of reality. Even the ultimate wish-fulfilment of being able to place his works on the shelf reserved for 'classics' is itself permanently shelved. If our inheritance of the classical categories has been all too purged of its bitter riddles, its madness, and its life, MacDiarmid helps reclaim these things, for he knows as surely as Nietzsche did that one must have chaos within one's self 'to give birth to a dancing star'.

'Old' and 'New' Plagiarism

Kenneth Buthlay has suggested that any given instance of MacDiarmid's 'quotations' or 'appropriations' might be worth the reader's attention on at least three counts.

> Firstly, the passage he has lifted from another writer may be of interest in itself, for any number of reasons. Secondly, he may see in what was written something quite different from that which the author saw, and this may prove to be illuminating in a different way. And thirdly, he may use the 'found' material skilfully and interestingly for his own purposes in the writing of a poem — and clearly there may be considerable artistic value in this activity itself, aside from any credit that

may be due for the ability to spot such material and how it might be used.[3]

Bearing these points in mind, I wish to turn now to a number of instances of MacDiarmid's 'appropriations'. They range from early Scots lyrics to 'Dìreadh III', effectively spanning MacDiarmid's poetic career. Apart from the different kinds of 'appropriation' to be examined, a more complex consideration arises: the protean nature of the first person in the poems. This consideration complicates the security of identity which Buthlay attaches to the poet, the poems, and the work, and the authors of the 'found' materials. MacDiarmid's practice in these poems undermines the lyrical construction of the ego which runs through much post-Romantic understanding of literature. The individual human subject has been the single most essential assumption in literature at least since the Romantics, and the most famous example of it is the individual consciousness of the poet. Fundamentally, this is what the text of any lyric poem represents and Palgrave's *Golden Treasury* is the exemplary refinement of that kind of treatment of poetry. Individuality, as we have seen, is broken down in MacDiarmid's epic work, as it foregrounds the methods of its own construction. The text reveals itself as a construction, and not the unmediated outflowing of a Romantic sensibility. It works to deny the traditional bourgeois sense that the author is the exclusive owner of what he or she produces, yet at the same time the authorial function of the name 'MacDiarmid' is not relinquished.

There is evidence that MacDiarmid was engaged in this activity in full knowledge of its subversive character. On 14 January 1938 he wrote to William Soutar to thank him for a copy of a letter by Alan Hodge which had just appeared in the *Times Literary Supplement*. Hodge was asking for assistance in a study he was doing of 'the synthetic elements in modern poetry' from readers acquainted with 'the theory that "poetry is common property" ' and aware of examples of synthetic poetry 'especially in the works of poets of Communistic sympathies'.[4] MacDiarmid told Soutar that he was hard at work 'with an enormous poem in MSS on huge unmanageable pages of grocery-paper . . . (not only is it multi-linguistic but it is in praise of multilingualism in literature and all its practitioners).' He told Soutar also that he would reply to Hodge since much of the poetry he was then writing 'carries the sort of synthesis he seems to have in mind much further than it has yet been carried by anyone else known to me, and draws in this way on out-of-the-way originals — Gaelic, Russian, modern Greek sources, etc. — which few, if any, of the other practitioners of what may be called "the new plagiarism" cover at all'.

'The Eemis Stane' and 'Empty Vessel'

The best lyrics of *Sangschaw* and *Penny Wheep* testify to the import-ance of a sensitive and critically responsive medium, and Mac-Diarmid's self-dramatisation throughout his work is an integral part of his development, from his earliest writing onwards. In 'Focherty', when Duncan Gibb stands there like a bull in a sale-ring before the omnipotent judgement of God, MacDiarmid's voice merges in sympathy with the wronged lover who narrates the poem, who will laugh out loud until the giant bumpkin looks up to the austerity of judgement, unable to decide, 'whether it's God — or me!' And we nod assent to MacDiarmid's sympathies, as we enjoy the come-uppance of the ruddy loon whose gain 'was aye a weer man's loss'. In 'Crowdieknowe' also, we assent to the tone of voice. We can feel the fear, awe, and admiration that the poem registers, and we sympathise with the speaker, who tells us he cried at the sight of these huge, hairy 'men o' Crowdieknowe' when he was a child. Above all, 'Focherty' and 'Crowdieknowe' are superb comic poems. Their irony, careful swagger, infectious tones, and imaginative breadth are used humorously. (This is clear already in the half-serious, half mock-Romantic first line of 'Crowdieknowe'.)

In 'The Eemis Stane', in a similar way, MacDiarmid's 'I' is the medium by which *our* senses become involved in the depiction of an exterior setting and interior world of reflection, linked by the sensually perceived images of weather and environment.

The Eemis Stane

I' the how-dumb-deid o' the cauld hairst nicht
The warl' like an eemis stane
Wags i' the lift;
An' my eerie memories fa'
Like a yowdendrift.

Like a yowdendrift so's I couldna read
The words cut oot i the stane
Had the fug o' fame
An' history's hazelraw
No' yirdit thaim.

C.P., p.27

The first three lines seem not to suggest any 'self' involved in the poem at all. In the imagistic contexts of dark and light, cold and heat, night and day, unsteadiness and stability, ground and sky, we are given specific, sensually apprehensible images for dark, cold, night, unsteadiness, a backdrop of infinite sky (night sky), and the central image of the poem, the world. Who, then, is perceiving? Whose memories fall on these images like a snowdrift? The absence of any localising characteristics such as those that are present in 'Focherty' and 'Crowdieknowe' suggests that the poet's voice here has adopted a less individualised and local position. Yet it is unobtrusive and gentle. There are subtle and unspecified points of contact between the sensual perceptions the poet presents and the reader's understanding of the poem. The stone is a flat gravestone, covered with moss and lichen, and with the snow of memories drifting onto it, yet it is also a global image. More than one dimension is in play, and the duality of the planes alternates as the world 'wags i' the lift'. In the night sky, its inscription is concealed by a swirling (that is, circling *and* falling, spiralling down) blizzard of memories, but even if that were to clear, it would still be impossible to decipher under the curtains of fame and history. The poem is made more personal in tone by the vastness of the cosmic envelope around it. This simultaneous involvement of cosmic scale and intensely intimate human perception is a celebrated characteristic of these lyrics.

> Empty Vessel
>
> I met ayont the cairney
> A lass wi' tousie hair
> Singin' till a bairnie
> That was nae langer there.
>
> Wunds wi' warlds to swing
> Dinna sing sae sweet
> The licht that bends owre a'thing
> Is less ta'en up wi't.

C.P., p.66

Rural setting and universal significance are beautifully matched in the perception and experience of the first person. Two lines from the traditional ballad 'Jennie Nettles' are adapted and changed very slightly:

> I met ayont the Kairney
> Jenny Nettles, Jenny Nettles,
> Singing till her bairney,
> Robin Rattles bastard . . . [5]

But the change that comes in the fourth line of 'Empty Vessel' alters the poem entirely.

In the first stanza, the first person singular comes over a small hill, sees first the girl's tousled hair (already suggesting her distraction), then notices her singing (sweetly, we are to discover), then discovers this to be a register of her grief at the loss of the child she once carried. The reader's discovery of these things is exactly parallel with the growing awareness of the poem's first person (not an unusual process in first person 'narratives'). The second stanza comments on the picture from the point of view of one who has witnessed it. The *shape* of each image echoes the other: the light bends over the world and the winds rock it as the girl bends over and rocks the missing child. Would the cosmos be as indifferent were there no wailing world? The poem, at whose core is a living human expression (of love, of grief — 'singin''), suggests it might as well be. It is human beings who are 'taken up' with these things; only human beings.

To know that 'Jennie Nettles' provided the source for the first and third lines of the first stanza affirms the poem's rural setting, its linguistic and literary heritage, its 'traditional' quality (and the national literature it belongs to), its participation in a folk idiom dating back before the rise of capitalism, and the sense of the past as lived present experience. In 'Empty Vessel', the first person singular identifies itself as the voice which experiences, but it is also echoing the pre-existent 'I' of the ballad. Our knowledge of the ballad as source, therefore, drastically alters our sense of the 'I' in the poem. Moreover, one might press further to find an unstressed symbolism working in the poem. There is a sense in which the mother / child relationship is also one of nation / culture and culture / language, and none of these interpretations is entirely foreign to the poem. Indeed, if we think of other poems where similar associations are explicitly made, it would seem unlikely that MacDiarmid did not intend these senses to be present, at least implicitly. In 'The Glen of Silence' (*C.P.*, p.1310), for example, he asks where he has encountered such a silence as he finds in a desolate Highland glen, and equates the tragedy of foetal death with 'the tragedy of an unevolved people'. Or when, in 'A Vision of Scotland' (*C.P.*, p.1096), he evokes a girl throwing off her headsquare to reveal 'a mass / Of authentic flaxen hair', he links the image of the girl to specific aspects of Scotland's economic and social conditions through a brilliantly concise simile which does no damage to the striking beauty of the image the girl presents *as a girl* but supplements that image wonderfully by envisioning an actual Scotland with its immigrants and jute trade.[6] In 'O Jesu Parvule' (*C.P.*, p.31), the infant Christ is pictured drawn in towards his mother's breast: 'But the byspale's nae thocht o' sleep i' the least.' 'Byspale' the glossary gives as 'precocious, a child of whom wonderful things are predicted': but that child is not merely the child Christ — it is also the language in which the early lyrics are written. Thus, when the distracted mother sings to an absent child in 'Empty Vessel' there is also the sense of Scotland and the people of Scotland and their language being mourned.

In a letter to William Carlos Williams, Ezra Pound described his own lyric poems in the light of a 'surrounding text' which might also illuminate how we read 'Empty Vessel':

> To me the short so-called dramatic lyric — at any rate the sort of thing I do — is the poetic part of a drama the rest of which (to me the prose part) is left to the reader's imagination or implied or set in a short note. I catch the character I happen to be interested in at the moment he interests me, usually a moment of song, self-analysis, or sudden understanding or revelation, and the rest of the play would bore me and presumably the reader.[7]

Specifically with regard to lyric poetry, Pound's desire is to effect 'the maximum charge of verbal meaning'. But here, where Pound specifies 'the character', he is referring beyond his dramatic-theatrical metaphor to an essential characteristic of a revelatory moment or epiphany, a solitary perception which informs. In many of the best lyrics of *Sangschaw* and *Penny Wheep*, that essential interest is brought out through the mediation of a persona whose experience of events intricately follows the course of a reader's experience of the poem. This is the case with 'Empty Vessel' as it is with 'The Eemis Stane', where the revelations are simultaneously immediate and retrospective. The girl *was* singing, the child *was* gone, but the meaning of her song is unchanged by time; the inscription on the stone *has been* covered up, but the snow of responsive memories *still falls*. This is perhaps one reason why these lyrics seem never to grow tired; their immediacy always remains exact.

A Drunk Man Looks at the Thistle

One of the modernist or proto-modernist elements in *A Drunk Man Looks at the Thistle* is its use of a synthetic language. MacDiarmid's Scots is a peculiar linguistic medium, and the tendency to see it as a transcribed 'natural' language should be avoided. It is a consciously chosen and selectively used language in a way that the Scots of the ballads, for example, is not. It is grounded in rural Scots, but it is, above all, a literary language. Yet its fluent movement is often conversational and usually accommodative. There is a linear narrative in which the physical movements of the 'hero' are recorded: he has left the pub, fallen in a ditch, is lying on a hillside of bracken and heather looking at the moon, and finally looks forward to returning home to his wife. However, the physical world is important to the drunk man only in so far as it effects the movement of his mind and his roving imagination. Although the 'character' of the drunk man is more fully explored than the 'I' of any of the early lyrics, he remains a protean voice. Instead of a short lyric, with 'the maximum charge of verbal meaning', we have a long poem containing not only lyrics but also discussions, meditations, tirades, comic asides, political ballads, translations, and epigrams. Roderick Watson's essay on the symbolism of the poem concentrates on three central images and their counterparts: the thistle (and the rose), whisky (and moonlight), woman (and the sea serpent).[8] 'It will become apparent, however', he writes, 'that these groupings will not be stable, and that in keeping with the mobile character of the poem, some of the symbols interchange in value and effect.' The poem's mobile character is essentially that of the drunk man himself; by his mediation MacDiarmid can dramatically and poetically explore a range of intellectual, social, sexual, and political concerns. In striking contrast to MacDiarmid's later work, the one thing that is never dramatised in *A Drunk Man* is the act of writing.[9] The drunk man stands to MacDiarmid as Chaucer's first person stands to Chaucer in *The Canterbury Tales*: he is not an isolated persona, but not a completely autobiographical self-representation either. The poem is full, however, of self-proclamation. Its first word is 'I'.

Quotations are worked into the texture of the poem. From Shelley's *Prometheus Unbound* (ii.4.72),[10] for example:

> He gave man speech, and speech created thought
> Which is the measure of the Universe . . .

— a passage which had been quoted by Denis Saurat as a prefix to an essay in the influential journal *The New Age*, to which Grieve was contributing at the time — becomes in MacDiarmid:

> God gied man speech and speech created thocht,
> He gied man speech but to the Scots gied nocht
> Barrin' this clytach that they've never brocht

> To onything but sic a Blottie O
> As some bairn's copybook micht show . . .

C.P., p.115

Kenneth Buthlay glosses: 'Blotty O's: A schoolboys' game, played on slates or with pencil and paper. A certain number of "O"s are drawn and one boy, at the direction of another, joins up one to the other by lines, each "O" being "blotted" out as soon as it is touched. The object of the game is to join up every "O" as directed without intersecting any of the lines.'[11] MacDiarmid's gloss (in *The Complete Poems*) for 'clytach' is: 'balderdash' — and Buthlay gives 'inarticulate or childish chatter'. The irony in *A Drunk Man* is therefore deepened and enriched if we can add from the source that it is the 'measure of the Universe' which has been denied to Scots. In Shelley's lines 'thought' leads on to 'Which is the measure of the Universe'; but in MacDiarmid's lines, 'thocht' (by its Scots form in itself an example of 'this clytach') leads on to a banal rhyme and rhythmic repetition whose effect is bathetic, and the 'measure of the Universe' is not mentioned at all — as if, by the way in which the quotation lapses back into oblivion, what is left unsaid is literally left 'unthocht'.

A similar example, from Herman Melville's neglected epic poem *Clarel*:

> Old ballads sing
> Fair christian children crucified
> By impious Jews; you've heard the thing:
> Yes, fable; but there's truth hard by:
> How many Hughs of Lincoln, say
> Does Mammon in his mills to-day,
> Crook, if he does not crucify?[12]

MacDiarmid takes this over into a context where a near-acknowledgement and parenthetical aside add to the strength of the language a bitter power (particularly so when you consider the context in *Clarel*, where Melville is producing a vitriolic diatribe against the industrial misery perpetrated by those 'Mammonite freebooters' the Anglo-Saxons):

> Melville (a Scot) kent weel hoo Christ's
> Corrupted into creeds malign,
> Begotten strife's pernicious brood
> That claims for patron Him Divine.

(The Kirk in Scotland still I cry
Crooks whaur it canna crucify!)

C.P., p.135

The use of source-material here is an important part of the literary context which the concerns of the poem raise. But they are, characteristically in *A Drunk Man*, not primarily 'literary allusions' but appropriate examples for what the poem seeks to express. Though the act of writing is not foregrounded in the poem, a literary context is given to the consciousness the poem presents. The references link and align the poem with other works. But this is not to suggest that MacDiarmid's practice here is merely to incorporate blindly phrases from other writers. The point is rather that the implanting of such phrases produces a discursive texture in the poem which reveals how tone and ideology are affected by such 'incorporated' writing. The best example comes at the end of the poem, after the 'Great Wheel' turns. The 'Silence' into which the poem finally slides is a source of creative potential. By inverting the last lines of *King Lear*, MacDiarmid transforms the most abject tragic despair into a recognition of the possibility of return. Edgar closes Shakespeare's play with the words

> we that are young
> Shall never see so much, nor live so long.[13]

MacDiarmid describes the 'Silence' which is left with him at the end, as the silence of

> . . . Him, whom nocht in man or Deity,
> Or Daith or Dreid or Loneliness can touch,
> *Wha's deed owre often and has seen owre much.*

C.P., p.167
(MacDiarmid's italics)

This silence is the repository of ineffable experience, to which all surplus language is surrendered. Lear's 'nothing' is also a source of teeming possibilities, but where Lear makes the mistake of thinking that nothing will come of nothing, the drunk man is more cheerfully conscious of the miraculous capacities of life. The contrast is clearly marked in the shift from negation in Edgar's lines ('never' and 'nor') to excess in MacDiarmid's ('owre' and 'owre'). The drunk man is aware of the chaos within him; and the poem itself has a last laugh yet to play on the reader.

'The Old Laird'

Between *A Drunk Man Looks at the Thistle* and *To Circumjack Cencrastus*, the only poetry MacDiarmid published in a collection was in *The Lucky Bag* (1927), a Porpoise Press broadsheet.[14] The poems, sixteen in all, take up only eight pages in *The Complete Poems* and seem mainly to consist of short poems in Scots that were not as impressive as those of *Sangschaw* or *Penny Wheep*, or had been rejected from *A Drunk Man*. Of these, 'The Old Laird' shows clearly the use of Jamieson's *Dictionary* as source, and contrasts instructively with the poems we have been looking at.

> Moothlie as snails when they come snowkin'
> > Oot owre the drookit swaird
> > Cam' she in by to the drucken laird,
> Whaur he sat happy bowkin'.
>
> 'I'm no' fou eneuch for you,' quo' he,
> > Syne bawled for the room to catch it,
> > 'Awa' and mird wi' your maiks, ye smatchet,
> And mint nae mair wi' me!'

C.P., pp.172–3

Jamieson's *Dictionary of the Older Scottish Tongue* provides the source: 'To MIRD, v.n. 1. To make amorous advances; to toy amorously, Dumfr; as, "Mird wi' your maiks, ye smatchet" '.

Whether our appreciation should be focused on the event described in the poem or the language the poet employs to describe it seems here, unfortunately, a confused question. The failure of the poem lies, I think, in the fact that dramatic balance is not fully embodied in the relationship of the two figures so that only the language of the poem makes it texturally consistent. The language exerts its own fascination, of course, but that alone is insufficient. A mediating persona or consciousness depicted in the poem, which would help the reader interpret the event described and evaluate the relationship, is conspicuous by its absence.

'On a Raised Beach'

In 'On a Raised Beach' MacDiarmid is concerned with 'What happens to us' — plural — as at the same time he advocates 'self-purification and anti-humanity'. Although he is among others ('O we of little faith . . . '), he represents a humanity out of touch with the chthonic forces of existence; he is alone when he says, 'I am enamoured of the desert at last . . . '. These examples are typical of the shifting location of the poem's speaking voice. That voice

announces the conflict between the persistent egocentric consciousness and the various meanings of selfhood involved in the role of
the poet. A metaphysics that will work for society at large and not
merely cater to personal longing is invoked. As in 'On the Ocean
Floor', the short poem we looked at in Chapter 1, the impressions
of tidal movements, massy weights, and enormous pressures suggest
the difficult effort being made towards a reconciliation of self with
others.

> These bare stones brings me straight back to reality.
>   I grasp one of them and I have in my grip
> The beginning and end of the world,
> My own self, and as before I never saw
> The empty hand of my brother man . . .
>
> *C.P.*, p.432

It is reminiscent of the moment when King Lear flashingly contem-
plates the 'houseless heads' he long has been forgetful of.[15]

   Knowledge of MacDiarmid's use of sources in 'On a Raised Beach'
can enhance our appreciation of the single purpose driving the poem.
In the fifth verse-paragraph is a telling example:

> There are plenty of ruined buildings in the world but no
>   ruined stones.
> No visitor comes from the stars
> But is the same as they are.
> — Nay, it is easy to find a spontaneity here,
> An adjustment to life, an ability
> To ride it easily, akin to 'the buoyant
> Prelapsarian naturalness of a country girl
> Laughing in the sun, not passion-rent,
> But sensing in the bound of her breasts vigours to come
> Powered to make her one with the stream of earthlife round
>   her,'
> But not yet as my Muse is, with this ampler scope,
> This more divine rhythm, wholly at one
> With the earth, riding the Heavens with it, as the stones do
> And all soon must.
>
> *C.P.*, p.425

It is a pointedly awkward assimilation, with that pause before the
grandiose 'Nay' and the disturbed rhythm of 'But not yet as my
Muse is . . .'. We are alerted to the interpolation by MacDiarmid's
quotation marks (and they *are* MacDiarmid's), but we are unlikely

to guess the extent of his theft from F.R. Leavis's *New Bearings in English Poetry*,[16] where in the 'Epilogue', Leavis suggests that the modern tradition of English poetry shall be carried on by Ronald Bottrall — 'a very considerable poet indeed'. MacDiarmid makes use of both Leavis's critical prose and Bottrall's verse, running them into each other and altering the lineation of the verse. Leavis is talking about Bottrall's poem *The Loosening*:

> This poem, which is half a dozen or more pages long, is partly dramatic in presentment and exhibits great variety of theme, movement, and tone. The temptation to consider it in some detail must be resisted: the immediate point regards its end. The poet glimpses here a recovered spontaneity, a readjustment to life, an ability to ride it easily, analogous to the buoyant, prelapsarian 'naturalness' of the farm-girl who

> > Poised herself like a falcon at check
> > Amid the unfooted ploughland,
> > Laughter splashing from her mouth and
> > Rippling down her brown neck;
> > Not passion-rent she
> > But sensing in the bound
> > Of her breasts vigours to come, free
> > As air and powered to make her one
> > With the stream of earth-life around.

Leavis only adds: 'Must we despair of attaining a new naturalness at the far side of the experience of disharmony?' MacDiarmid, sensing the disharmony the interpolation creates in his own poem, goes on:

> But it is wrong to indulge in these illustrations
> Instead of just accepting the stones.

> > > > > *C.P.*, p.425

The passage transcribed from Leavis and Bottrall functions in 'On a Raised Beach' as one of these 'illustrations'. The quotation marks make that clear. But MacDiarmid has changed the text carefully, dropping the quotation marks from 'naturalness', compressing lines 3–4 of the Bottrall extract, altering 'the farm-girl' to 'the country girl', and dropping the phrase 'free / As air' which would have worked against the earth-bound, stony imagery of the poem and the earthy creaturality of the girl.

'On a Raised Beach' is a notoriously difficult poem. I have referred to a single purpose driving through it. In the illustration just given, this emerges not only in the rejection of the phrase 'free / As air' but also in the rejection of the interpolation itself as a mere 'illustration'. It might be helpful to suggest briefly the poem's structural coherence. The argument of the poem proposes a nexus of oppositions: meaning and meaninglessness, being and non-being, human life and geological time, 'intelligentsia' and 'the mob', profound conviction and direct expression, intellectual life and the life of 'mankind in the mass', 'great work' and 'popular appeal', arrogance and humility, self and others, Christianity and atheism, metaphysics and materialism. These are not simply parallel oppositions but intersect at various points in the text of the poem. MacDiarmid's philosophical drive is to find social meaning and value out of an individual's atheist and materialist position, but the struggle in which he engages raises more complicated metaphysical questions as it progresses.

Perhaps the central problem of 'On a Raised Beach' is that of the perspective from which the poem's own formal figuration can be discerned. In a determined attempt to take in the scale of an ultimate 'beginning and end', the poem confronts a logocentric universe with an atheist and materialist interpretation. One consequence of this is the rejection of anthropocentrism. Another is that the poem can be read as a critique and rejection of the possibility of the structurally and thematically delimited work of art. The 'general principle' cannot be guessed 'from these flashing fragments' of illumination in the text. If there is one it is not to be found as an abstractable truth, but *in* the struggle itself.

One theme of modern literature that emerges in the early days of Romantic writing and flows like a submerged river of meaning through practically all serious work in the nineteenth and twentieth centuries springs, as the American critic Guy Davenport has suggested, from the classical feeling that stone was a dead substance and therefore belonged to a separate realm of being from that which was living. 'Hades, for instance, was stone, as was the dead moon. The firm Greek sense that stone does not grow distinguished it radically from things that do. And yet it was of mineral substance that everything was made: an organism was an interpenetration of matter and spirit.'[17] Davenport continues: 'science and poetry from the Renaissance forward have been trying to discover what is alive and what isn't. In science the discovery spanned three centuries, from Gassendi to Niels Bohr and the answer is that everything is alive.' Poetry, he says, has had a similar search but has not yet formulated its answer. If that is so, MacDiarmid's must be one of the most sustained attempts, fully informed with scientific knowledge and a geologist's vocabulary, to bring out such an answer.

The poem is in eleven verse-paragraphs. The first proposes a basic opposition: 'All is lithogenesis — or lochia'. Everything is born from stones, or else it is a messy afterbirth: meaning exists in material omnitude or else it does not. The paragraph then goes on to present an alarming, attractive, curious, and forbidding display of words to depict and evoke the stones of the raised beach. MacDiarmid announces his student's apprenticeship to their existence and asks if the Christophanic rock — the stone moved by a miracle of love — is present. He never finds it; it is not there. But when the final paragraph recovers some of the strangeness of the first in its highly unusual vocabulary, the tone is one of triumph: the poem is a record of a struggle, and a victory through struggle, as deep and convincing as anything in modern poetry.

The balance of the first and last paragraphs is heightened by the use of the 'old Norn words' in the central paragraph, the keystone: paragraph six. Paragraphs two to five develop the oppositions mentioned above in a densely argued but coherent way. They depict a scene: the poet, the beach, the bird — which rescues the poem from being a piece of abstract philosophy. In the fourth stanza, from which the extract we discussed above was taken, the 'illustrations' of 'foam-bells on the currents of being' are dropped in an act of renewed concentration upon the stones, an attempt and a willingness to be 'chilled to the core'.

After the central paragraph, paragraph seven is where the argument reaches its fullest volume and strength, and the confrontation between ataraxia, fatalism, and suicide is rejected: the struggle the poem enacts goes deeper than that. 'It is reality that is at stake.' Paragraphs eight and nine are recapitulations and variations of the preceding arguments, and paragraph ten takes them forward to develop the final idea of the possibility of hope, the 'resurrection' of 'the masses'. Death itself is not to be feared for it holds no greater horrors than those already evoked in the poem; but one should beware of it, for it is certain. The certainty MacDiarmid achieves here to match it is a strength and conviction in the potential of humankind to get lives 'worth having'. If the meaning of death is to supply that meaning and value to life, then death is a material fact possessed by every living thing and no living thing can be deprived of it. The value and meaning of life which it supplies,

however, *can* be taken away from living things, and almost everywhere is. That is the certainty against which MacDiarmid dedicates
his life's work, and in that dedication, the poem closes in relief,
triumph, and provisional, tempered affirmation.

> '*Scotland*'
> It requires great love of it deeply to read
> The configuration of a land,
> Gradually grow conscious of fine shadings,
> Of great meanings in slight symbols,
> Hear at last the great voice that speaks softly,   5
> See the swell and fall upon the flank
> Of a statue carved out in a whole country's marble,
> Be like Spring, like a hand in a window
> Moving New and Old things carefully to and fro,
> Moving a fraction of flower here,   10
> Placing an inch of air there,
> And without breaking anything.
>
> So I have gathered unto myself
> All the loose ends of Scotland,
> And by naming them and accepting them,   15
> Loving them and identifying myself with them,
> Attempt to express the whole.
>
> C.P., p.652

This is a remarkably gentle poem, counterpointing the caustic survey
of his native land and its literature in which MacDiarmid indulged
in *Lucky Poet*, where it first appeared. The capitalisation of words
in lines 8 and 9 seems unusual, but the effect is to emphasise with
a tender pressure, to indicate quietly, without stridency. The poem
is almost confessional in tone. Despite the magnificence of the aspiration, there is no shouting, nothing shrill. It is a convincing and
coherent example of an old convention in poetry, identifying one's
self by naming places. It is surprising, then, to discover its source in
e.e. cummings, poem III from 'N &: seven poems' (which dates
from 1925):

> Spring is like a perhaps hand
> (which comes carefully
> out of Nowhere)arranging
> a window,into which people look(while
> people stare
> arranging and changing placing

carefully there a strange
thing and a known thing here)and

changing everything carefully

spring is like a perhaps
Hand in a window
(carefully to
and fro moving New and
Old things, while
people stare carefully
moving a perhaps
fraction of flower here placing
an inch of air there)and

without breaking anything.[18]

We bring to 'Scotland' certain assumptions about the ways in which it is related to its author. The name 'MacDiarmid' provides coherence for the poem, integrating the words from cummings with both a vision of Scotland and MacDiarmid's praxis as a writer in Scotland. And the poem returns an affirmation of that praxis. That praxis cannot be taken out of the poem. Moving things from here to there, changing the places of new and old things, applies to MacDiarmid's technique: in a sense, the poem exemplifies the advice it gives ('Be like Spring'), and the word 'So' in MacDiarmid's poem applies to the technique as much as it does to the matter. This is made clear as the first person singular appears only *after* the paraphrase. Even if we juxtapose these two texts, the achievement of MacDiarmid's poem cannot be simply dismissed. In *Lucky Poet*, MacDiarmid introduced the poem by saying 'I almost always bring the matter of my poetry home to Scotland and one of the principal elements in my view of life is expressed in these lines' (p.324).

'Beyond Desire' and 'A Language Not To Be Betrayed'

'Beyond Desire' was the short poem in the 1967 *Collected Poems* which replaced 'Perfect' (both originally from *The Islands of Scotland*, 1939), after a sensational correspondence in the *Times Literary Supplement* had (temporarily) discredited the latter poem as being plagiarised from the prose of the Welsh writer Glyn Jones.[19] If 'Perfect' created such controversy, 'Beyond Desire' is even more of a liability, for in 'Perfect', typographical rearrangement of prose material brings out a degree of assonance and rhythm to effect a meaning we can justifiably ascribe to 'MacDiarmid', as Kenneth

Buthlay has shown.[20] But with 'Beyond Desire', the typographical arrangement of the words was already there. In Hart Crane's *The Bridge* (1930), the final stanza of the first section, 'Ave Maria', runs thus:

> White toil of heaven's cordons, mustering
> In holy rings all sails charged to the far
> Hushed gleaming fields and pendant seething wheat
> Of knowledge, — round thy brows unhooded now
> — The kindled Crown! acceded of the poles
> And biassed by full sails, meridians reel
> Thy purpose — still one shore beyond desire!
> The sea's green crying towers a-sway, Beyond
>
> And kingdoms
>> naked in the
>>> trembling heart —
> Te Deum Laudamus
>> O Thou Hand of Fire.[21]

This is taken over into the 'Introductory' chapter to MacDiarmid's *The Islands of Scotland* and appears just after the end of 'Island Funeral' in a cluster of quotations:

> In the Hebrides at any rate — although one may not
> agree that
>> Nature's herself turned metaphysical —
> the main thing is undoubtedly
>> the subtler music, the clear light
> Where time burns back about th'eternal embers,
> and one can always see
>> . . . still one shore beyond desire!
>> The sea's green crying towers a-sway, Beyond
>> And kingdoms
>>> naked in the
>>>> trembling heart —
>> Te Deum Laudamus
>>> O Thou Hand of Fire!

Whether MacDiarmid himself or an anonymous typesetter reconstructed the 'poem' from this fragment I do not know, but this was published in MacDiarmid's *Collected Poems* (1967) as

BEYOND DESIRE

One can always see
Still one shore beyond desire!
The sea's green crying towers a-sway, Beyond
And kingdoms
                    naked in the
                              trembling heart —
Te Deum Laudamus
                    O Thou Hand of Fire!

Ironically enough, 'Beyond Desire' was silently dropped from *The Complete Poems* (1978) and replaced by 'Perfect'. A similar case of direct transcription is 'A Language Not To Be Betrayed' from *Lucky Poet*, which is indeed included in *The Complete Poems*:

I should use . . .
A language not to be betrayed;
And what was hid should still be hid
Excepting from those like me made
Who answer when such whispers bid.

C.P., p.665

There is no acknowledgement at all of Edward Thomas (1878–1917), the Anglo-Welsh poet who was among the first to recognise Pound and whose finely-honed 'nature' poetry includes one work, 'I Never Saw that Land Before', in which this stanza occurs:

I should use, as the trees and birds did,
A Language not to be betrayed;
And what was hid should still be hid
Excepting from those like me made
Who answer when such whispers bid.[22]

'Verses Written during the Second World War'

At last! Now is the time with due intensity
    To hew to what really matters — not
'Making the world safe for democracy!',
    'Saving civilization', or any such rot.
But what there was about the Welsh handling, say,   5
        Of Arthur and Merlin (as good an example as may
    be got)
That conquered the imagination of Europe in a way
        Conchobhar and Cuchulainn did not.

Let it at least be said of us when we die:
  'Of all the slogans to which mass-man clings   10
Only a Chinese could have thought more lightly than they
  — They had so much love for real things.'

C.P., p.603

At first sight, the poem is laboured, the rhyme awkward and imposed, the rhythm difficult and clumsy.

In John Cowper Powys's *Obstinate Cymric: Essays 1935–47*, in an essay called 'Welsh Culture — Inclusive or Exclusive', we find the following:

> Nor does Sir John Rhys help us much by interpreting Arthur and Merlin and all their cycle from what he calls their 'congeners' in Ireland. What, it seems to me, we Anglo-Welsh ought to press the scholars to reveal to us is not how the Welsh Arthur resembles the Irish Airem, or how the Welsh Merlin might be equated with the Irish Conchobhar, but *what there was* about the Welsh handling of Arthur and Merlin that conquered the imagination of Europe in a way Conchobhar and Cuchulainn did not.
>
> There must be some sort of 'struggle for existence' among these mythical heroes. What was there about the Welsh ones that carried them so far afield?[23]

Perhaps the poem is not quite so forced as it seems. The rhyme-scheme is constricting: abab / cbcb / dede. However, those catch-rhymes — the isolated monosyllabic words 'not' and 'say'; the long phrase 'as good an example as may be got' taking up two-thirds of line 6 — have their own effect. That line's ponderous movement, for example, is justified by the resonance and authority the rhythmic stress beats into the last line of that stanza with its all-too predictable rhyme but perhaps surprising negative. MacDiarmid is concerned here with the historical process of imaginative conquest and domination. In 1943, after Yeats, Lady Gregory, and Joyce, it might have been debatable whether the Irish heroes had not conquered the imagination of Europe. However, there is a sense that Arthur and Merlin actually *did* conquer Europe in a far more effective way than all the armed forces of the Second World War ever could. And the distinction made between the first person plural of the poem (implicitly, the author and the reader — and perhaps John Cowper Powys) and the general notion of 'mass man' might well suggest the fact that the function of mythology has been superseded by the function of ideology, and that only poets (who help create and sustain such mythology) and their readers (who, in some degree, understand its working) can see beyond the slogans to the world where imaginative realities work.

'Third Hymn to Lenin'

Four lines from the 'Third Hymn to Lenin' (first published in Mac-Diarmid's magazine *The Voice of Scotland*, in 1955):

> On days of revolutionary turning points you literally
>   flourished,
> Became clairvoyant, foresaw the movement of classes,
> And the possible zig-zags of the revolution
> As if on your palm . . .

C.P., p.894

come from a speech delivered by Stalin at a Memorial Meeting of the Kremlin Military School, 28 January 1924 (published in *Pravda*, 34, 12 February 1924, and in Stalin's *Works*, VI, Moscow, 1953). Its title was 'The Genius of Revolution' and the relevant passage runs:

> In times of revolution he literally blossomed forth, became a seer, divined the movement of classes and the possible zig-zags of the revolution, seeing them as if they lay in the palm of his hand.[24]

Again in the same poem, MacDiarmid uses quotation marks to describe 'the logic of your speeches':

> — 'like some all-powerful feelers
> Which grasp, once for all, all sides as in a vice,'
> And one has 'no strength left to tear away from their
>   embrace;
> Either one yields or decides upon complete failure'.

C.P., p.894

He is quoting from a quotation by Stalin. In the same speech, in the section called 'Force of Logic', there is a recollection of the effect of Lenin's speeches:

> I was captivated by that irresistible force of logic in them which, although somewhat terse, gained a firm hold on his audience, gradually electrified it, and then, as one might say, completely overpowered it. I remember that many of the dele-

gates said: 'The logic of Lenin's speeches is like a mighty tentacle which twines all round you and holds you as in a vice and from whose grip you are powerless to tear yourself away: you must either surrender or resign yourself to utter defeat.'[25]

Not all of the 'Third Hymn' is blank verse — rhyming stanzas take up much of its length — but the structure of the opening stanzas, with their elementary abcbdefe rhyme-scheme and variable stresses, allows considerably more freedom than that of 'Verses Written during the Second World War'. This loosening of formal restrictions occurs in MacDiarmid's work simultaneously with an increase in the extent of the use of source-material so that the texture of the poetry becomes changed. Unlike the other two Hymns and unlike 'Verses Written During the Second World War', the 'Third Hymn to Lenin' employs an irregularly metrical blank verse, and the open-ended line can accommodate convolutions of syntax and interruptions of prose passages into the verse.

'Island Funeral'

In 'Island Funeral' a connection is made between the spiritual core of the Gaelic islands, as MacDiarmid sees it, and (unexpectedly) the sound of Bix Beiderbecke's cornet. This connection, which at first seems arbitrary, suggests a kind of optimistic resignation when Mac-Diarmid begins to use a series of quotations to echo and fill out the sense of the unique beauty of the islands and cornet solo alike:

> Panassié speaks of it as 'full and powerful,'
> But also as 'so fine
> As to be almost transparent,'
> And there is in fact
> This extraordinary delicacy in strength.
> He speaks of phrases that soar;
> And this, too, is in fact
> A remarkable and distinguishing quality.
> Otis Ferguson speaks of 'the clear line
> Of that music', of 'every phrase
> As fresh and glistening as creation itself,'
> And there is in fact
> This radiance, and simple joyousness.
> These terms tell a great deal, but there remains
> Much that eludes words completely
> And can only be heard.   *C.P.*, p.581

It becomes evident that he is using these descriptions to create a feeling of essential value and he closes the poem with a reference to the 'cornet solo of our Gaelic islands'.

Through the poem, the shifts from narrative description to speculative reminscence, quotation, and announcement of faith, move the tone from a grimly realistic symbolism to a remarkable assertion of hope. In the course of the poem, MacDiarmid develops a mythic system which is, he asserts, in agreement with his materialism and his Marxism. That the declaration of hope he makes seems thoroughly improbable to us now is not to deny the force of that declaration in the poem. The system has its aberrant and fictitious logic, just as the systems evolved by Eliot or Pound have theirs. It is, MacDiarmid says, 'A logical deduction from thoroughgoing materialism' that all possible developments of matter in all its possible formations shall take place throughout eternity. It is, rather, a logical decantation from J.B.S. Haldane. In his essay 'Some Consequences of Materialism', Haldane wrote that in the course of eternity any event with a finite probability must occur an infinite number of times. 'Hence every human type has occurred already, and will occur again. Of course, the particular kind of material structure called the human body would be evolved in an infinitesimal fraction of those cycles in which intelligent life occurs. But the fraction would be finite, and that is all matters.' Haldane goes on in his next paragraph:

> Now, if the nature of the mind is determined by that of the body (and I think that one may hold a view substantially equivalent to this without being a fullblown materialist), it follows that every type of human mind has existed an infinite number of times, and will do so. If, then, the mind is determined by the body, Materialism promises something hardly to be distinguished from eternal life. A mind or soul of the same properties as my own has existed during an eternal time in the past, and will exist for an eternal time in the future. Of course, this time is broken up by enormous intervals of non-existence, but it is an infinite time. Such a view differs from the theory of reincarnation in two fundamental respects. In the first place, the mind, though the same in different lives, is new each time and does not carry over any trace of memory or experience from one to the other. Secondly, there is no reason for supposing it to exist apart from the body of which it is an aspect.[26]

He goes on to insist this does not entail either cyclical recurrence, regularity, or the inevitability of predestination, since reconstituted matter offers an opportunity to develop potential denied to matter constituted in the same way, but in a different era.

> . . . I presume that continued existence without memory is generally felt to be better than nothing. And if one regards one's personality as possessing some value, there is a certain satisfaction in the thought that in eternity it will be able to develop in all possible environments, and to express itself in all the ways possible to it. Those who have died prematurely will be able, under other conditions, to live out complete lives. Our social organization of to-day is so rudimentary that one feels justified in hoping that our present lives are very poor samples . . .

He says with regard to these ideas: 'I believe that they are a logical deduction from thoroughgoing Materialism' and that he is using the word in the widest sense, irrespective of the precise type of Materialism involved:

> I have taken the word in its widest sense, to denote the view that all occurrences depend on phenomena obeying definite mathematical laws, which it is the business of physics to discover. It is quite unimportant whether we call our ultimate reality matter, electric charge, ψ-waves, mind-stuff, neural stuff, or what not, provided that it obeys laws which can, in principle, be formulated mathematically.

From the beautifully drawn sketch of the procession through the description of the islanders mourning at the graveside, 'Island Funeral' moves to reflections on the peculiar quality of island life evanescently perceptible in the houses and homes of the islands, many of which are empty now, and so to the unique beauty of their character, the life and work of the islanders. This passage itself is made up of extensive quotations. The startling juxtaposition of the uniquely clear beauty of the sound of the phrase from Bix Beiderbecke's cornet leads to the lowest point of the poem, immediately following the list of quotations from Panassié, Ferguson, and 'others'. The last islander, the last vestige or trace of this 'quality', will soon be gone.

> — One will listen, and one's face will never
> Light up with recognition and appreciation again.
>
> *C.P.*, p.582

Then comes the transcription:

Yet if the nature of the mind is determined
By that of the body, as I believe,
It follows that every type of human mind
Has existed an infinite number of times
And will do so. Materialism promises something
Hardly to be distinguished from eternal life.
Minds or souls with the properties I love
— The minds or souls of these old islanders —
Have existed during an eternal time in the past
And will exist for an eternal time in the future.
A time broken up of course
By enormous intervals of non-existence,
But an infinite time.
If one regards these personalities
As possessing some value
There is a certain satisfaction
In the thought that in eternity
They will be able to develop
In all possible environments
And to express themselves
In all the ways possible to them
— A logical deduction from thoroughgoing Materialism
And independent of the precise type
Of materialism developed.
It is quite unimportant whether we call
Our ultimate reality matter, electric charge,
ψ-waves, mind-stuff, neural stuff, or what not,
Provided it obeys laws which can, in principle,
Be formulated mathematically.

C.P., pp.582–3

The secular, fantastically optimistic conclusion follows immediately:

The cornet solo of our Gaelic islands
Will sound out every now and again
Through all eternity.

I have heard it and am content for ever.

C.P., p.583

If the poem is finally resigned to deference, that is perhaps much more than might have been expected under the circumstances. It is a triumphant complement to the very immediate propositions for materially changing the conditions of island life for the better, which were put forward in the book in which the poem was first published.[27] For the resignation of the poem is not one of rejecting the physical world in the hope of a better non-material one; the poem emphasises above all the life left undeveloped and dying. The changes of tone are exquisitely registered and superbly controlled by the voice of the first person singular, who is both witnessing one of the last funerals and whose own funeral will be one of these last.

'Dìreadh III'

In 'Dìreadh III' MacDiarmid presents himself as the representative of his nation's 'changeless element' and sets himself in a natural, country place, a 'simple place of clean rock and crystal water' near the summit of Sgurr Alasdair, in Skye. He pictures himself in concretely physical terms, lighting his pipe, looking round him. But he is, it seems, as much a part of the essential Scotland this landscape represents as he is part of the landscape itself. 'I lie here like the cool and gracious greenery . . . '. The poem is visionary through his presence, his mediation:

> I am possessed by this purity here
> As in a welling of stainless water . . .
>
> C.P., p.1187

His memory of a line of poetry and the flight of a bird he actually sees are drawn together; his vision is the real experience of the poem. He asserts that 'every loveliness Scotland has ever known' flies to him as the bird flew 'up-in-under' to the shelter of the overhanging cliff. There follows a particularly direct equation of the first person singular and the autobiographical poet:

> And remembering my earlier poems in Scots
> Full of my awareness 'that language is one
> Of the most cohesive or insulating of world forces
> And that dialect is always a bond of union,'
> I covet the mystery of our Gaelic speech . . .
>
> C.P., p.1191

The changes of perspective contribute to our awareness of the scale of the vision of Scotland MacDiarmid describes. The location of the poem works with the open and ingenuous statements about Gaelic culture in an immediately effective way.

> It is easy here to accept the fact
> That that which the 'wisdom' of the past

> And the standards of the complacent elderly rulers
> Of most of the world to-day regard
> As the most fixed and eternal verities —
> The class state, the church,
> The old-fashioned family and home,
> Private property, rich and poor,
> 'Human nature' (to-day meaning mainly
> The private-profit motive), their own race,
> Their Heaven and their 'immortal soul' —
> Is all patently evanescent . . .
>
> C.P., p.1188

This is from a book of speculative essays by the scientist H.J. Muller, entitled *Out of the Night: A Biologist's View of the Future*, published in the Left Book Club Editions series in 1936:

> . . . The mind of man must more and more become the master, not only of the outer material world, but also of the genetic thread of life within him. Thus there will come an even greater freedom.
>
> That which the 'wisdom' of the past and the standards of the complacent elderly rulers of most of the world to-day regard as the most fixed and eternal verities: the class state, the church, the old-fashioned family and home, private property, rich and poor, 'human nature' (to-day meaning mainly the private-profit motive), their own race, their heaven and their 'immortal soul' — all this is patently evanescent. But that which the daring and science of the young-minded realists (whether physically young or old) have projected as a practicable though never finished ideal — this becomes, as we watch, the ever more solid and substantial.[28]

'The ideal', Muller concludes, is 'the product of aspiration and of controlled creative imagination based on knowledge of the real material world', and it is 'an object to be worked for', not relegated as in the mystical sense of 'philosophical idealism' or immaterial reality and pure contemplation. H.J. Muller was a U.S. citizen of German descent who worked as a scientist in the fields of genetics, evolution, and eugenics. He became famous early in his life for his imaginative theorising and ingenious experimental design. He was a full Professor at the University of Texas, went to Berlin on a Guggenheim Grant in 1932, and when Hitler rose to power, travelled to the Soviet Union because he considered it to be an experimental society that would support his research in genetics and eugenics. In 1938 he spent some time in Scotland at the University of Edinburgh and returned finally to the United States in 1939.

In 'Dìreadh III', the very clarity of vision imparted by MacDiarmid's location is the product of a careful assemblage of texts. The first person singular is not simply the editor of these pieces, however; it imbues the poem with a single and unifying character.

> I am with Alba — with Deirdre — now
> As a lover is with his sweetheart when they know
> That personal love has never been a willing and efficient slave
> To the needs of reproduction, that to make
> Considerations of reproduction dictate the
>   expression of personal love
> Not infrequently destroys the individual at
>   his spiritual core,
> Thus 'eugenic marriages' cannot as a whole
> Be successful so far as the parents are concerned,
> While to make personal love master over reproduction
> Under conditions of civilization is to degrade
> The germ plasm of the future generations,
> And to compromise between these two policies
> Is to cripple both spirit and germ,
> And accept the only solution — unyoke the two,
> Sunder the fetters that from time immemorial
> Have made them so nearly inseparable
> And let each go its own best way,
> Fulfilling its already distinct function,
> An emancipation the physical means for which
> Are now known for the first time in history!

C.P., p.1193

This too is from Muller's book. In the chapter 'Birth and Rebirth' it is argued that only social inertia and popular ignorance are restraining a limited practical experiment involving the severance of the function of reproduction from the personal love-life of the individual. He writes:

> Personal love, on the one hand, which is largely a matter of imperative emotions, that do not readily wait for the approval of expedience and foresight — or, if they do, tend thereby to become thwarted, perverted, and cankerous — has in the past never been a willing and efficient slave to the needs of repro-

duction. Make considerations of reproduction dictate the expression of personal love, and you not infrequently destroy the individual at his spiritual core; thus 'eugenic marriages' cannot as a whole be successful, so far as the parents are concerned. On the other hand, make personal love master over reproduction, under conditions of civilization, and you degrade the germ plasm of the future generations. Compromise between these two policies, and you cripple both spirit and germ. There is only one solution — unyoke the two, sunder the fetters that from time immemorial have made them so nearly inseparable, and let each go its own best way, fulfilling its already distinct function. The physical means for this emancipation are now known for the first time in history.[29]

The 'Dìreadh' poems, for all their abstractions, are unmistakably Scottish poems. They could not be set anywhere else. If the light of the vision remains with us longer than the argument about eugenics, we should remember that the poem is attempting an integration of material fact and visionary perception in an 'act of surmounting'; it seeks to affirm the practical value of such a vision and challenges the reader on more than one level. The poem's epigraph comes from Muller's grim exclamation made in the face of the entropic nature of the universe: 'So, in the sudden light of the sun, has man stopped, blinded, paralysed, and afraid!' In MacDiarmid's hands, that final exclamation mark is changed to an altogether more challenging — and more demanding — question.

Form and Voice

These examples illustrate all three of the ways in which, Kenneth Buthlay suggested, MacDiarmid's appropriations are worth studying. There is some intrinsic interest in the material taken from Haldane and Muller, for example, which students of the history of science would share. There is, secondly, in MacDiarmid's use of the e.e. cummings poem, a transcription making something quite different in effect from that which cummings envisaged. And, in most cases, there is considerable interest in *how* MacDiarmid transferred the material — not only in specific terms of prosody and lineation but also in the larger terms of how the transcribed material is recontextualised in MacDiarmid's *œuvre*. Although 'Beyond Desire' and 'A Language Not to be Betrayed' may be merely mnemonic oversights, their significance as functions of *MacDiarmid's œuvre* illustrates the distinct quality of the mode of circulation of texts peculiar to our culture: the commodification of the author. At the same time, the notion of authorial 'originality' has been undermined. This is true of all the examples we have examined. They each imply a community of insight, a vision to be shared, a kind of participation.

It is now time to bring our reckoning of MacDiarmid's epic poetry to a final account. How does our experience of the protean forms taken by MacDiarmid's first person through the course of his career lead us to account for the formal, epic character of *In Memoriam James Joyce*? And what is the relation between that formal character and the quality of voice which animates the work? For without a vocal component of some kind poetry fails. Without the living energy of vocal tone, poetry of any kind ceases to be essential. If I have argued at length that MacDiarmid's later work deserves our attention, it is at least partly because I remain convinced by the voice which runs through it. It should be clear by now that I do not mean a sustained, unitary, lyrical ego identifiable as that metaperson, 'the poet' but rather a vitality which is sometimes startlingly present and never completely absent, and which requires the participation of the reader to be experienced.

Three interwoven areas of enquiry come together at this point; three dimensions of argument which have been informing the course of the book so far. Specifically, these are:

1. the epic as a formal principle, an attempt to bring together in one generic unit the countless social discourses which are normally assigned to discrete functionaries (the priest, the politician, the philosopher, etc.) and to present them in such a way as to reclaim them as areas within the provenance of poetry;
2. language as the 'subject' of MacDiarmid's epic, as well as its medium; the innumerable varieties of language and linguistic forms as they effect all kinds of organised and disorganised communication, and take effect in every sphere of activity, visceral and cerebral, academic and anti-academic, cultured and philistine, since it is in terms of language control that the struggle for political and social forms is ultimately fought;
3. the first person, MacDiarmid's 'I', which is constructed out of the formal requirements of the epic *and* the linguistic requirements of his medium and subject.

The most compelling essay in which the last two of these questions are addressed is Tom Leonard's 'The Locust Tree in Flower, and

Why it Had Difficulty Flowering in Britain'.[30] Leonard designates three separate components of language and identifies three modern British poets who have 'most consistently' followed the tracks opened up by an awareness of each specific component: (1) syntax: the chief practitioner of 'Concrete Poetry' in Britain has been Ian Hamilton Finlay; (2) phonology: in 'Sound Poetry', phonology ('as a fact rather than as a factor') has its most creative poet in Bob Cobbing; (3) lexis: 'anti-existential in its insistence on the validity of the naming process, and through this process deliberately and constantly ignoring the boundaries of what would be considered "correct" lexis for poetry', the poet whose work is 'a consistent assertion of the primacy of lexis, is Hugh MacDiarmid.'

In a primary form (to move back from the trees to look at the forest), naming, lexis, is an act of appropriation in which an object is taken for use. One picks up a stone to use as a tool or to throw in an enemy's face. The identity of the object and that of the act are not to be confused, and even a series of such acts will not be confused with the things they put to use. The ways in which labour, through industry and technology, produces commodities, are not to be confused with the commodities themselves. But at a certain stage of capitalist production, labour itself becomes a commodity. When language is caught up in capitalist modes of production and distribution, there is a marked development of the tangibility of the word, and an increase in the descriptive and narrative capacities of language. In English literature the clearest example of this is the transformation in lyric poetry which took place through the Renaissance, from a pre-Renaissance lyric poetry whose primary dynamic might be described as musical (disembodied, enacted in air) to a post-Renaissance lyric poetry whose primary dynamic might be described as verbal (embodied and enacted in utterance). What this process does is confirm the illusion of realities, identities, and objects as units for capitalist thought to manœuvre. And these developments are clearly tied to the nature of reference in language.[31]

Tom Leonard's identification of the component parts of language effectively catapults MacDiarmid into the role of a self-appreciative 'cultural and linguistic monopoly capitalist', and makes of his referentiality an acquisitive and greedy perversion. This, it seems to me, is an accurate description of how MacDiarmid might appear to those who equate culture with desirable property, who might (as Leonard says) then interpret MacDiarmid's own work as a commodity which is to be appropriated and not used but stored. However, it seems to me a mistaken description of MacDiarmid's work because it fails to take into account those operations of Mac-Diarmid's first person which undermine that secure identity of self-hood. This is a project doomed to 'failure', of course. For a 'success-ful' dissolution of identity would necessarily result in babble or silence. The success MacDiarmid achieves is of a less absolute, more pragmatic order. His work demonstrates the activities it is engaged in, and in so doing shows the extent to which there is room for strategic movement between the social and linguistic structures which form identities in capitalist societies and the identities which are thereby formed. This demonstration is, clearly, not consistently 'self-appreciative' (Leonard's term), because it is at times capable of becoming inchoate and confused. Yet wherever this happens (as we have seen, for instance, in 'Plaited Like the Generations of Men'), some form of recuperation allows for the growth and reconstitution of an energy which cannot be simply identified in an authorial position. That authorial position is never allowed consistent credi-bility in the course of the text. It was never allowed consistent credibility in the course of MacDiarmid's (or C.M. Grieve's) lifetime, either. In the Introduction to this book we stated that MacDiarmid's 'status' has never been absolutely secure amongst poets, critics, and teachers. It was never really secure in his own life, as his biography shows: he was not steadily employed throughout a career, though he was, at different times, a journalist, lecturer, publisher, professional writer, and soldier. He was engaged in almost as many professions in the course of his long life as you will find in a novel by Smollett. But this is not to be understood as merely an inability to sustain responsibility and attention. We have seen his powers of concen-tration and application yielding rich rewards in philosophical poetry, while one needs to look no further than *To Circumjack Cencrastus* to see how those abilities were thwarted and frustrated in the mun-dane world. So we cannot make any *absolute* divisions between the performance of the poetry and the biography of the man: we must affirm the notion that there are varying degrees of identity in the behaviour of both, and that both deserve the recognition of certain qualities of integrity (if not others).

What Leonard does not address in his essay is the first area of our enquiry noted above: the epic. Leonard is able to accuse MacDiarmid in the manner he does by reference to a single poem of MacDiarmid's, 'My Songs are Kandym in the Waste Land' (he even locates its place of publication). It is not his prerogative to discuss MacDiarmid's epic work as a whole, either in social terms or in terms of a developing poetic practice. And yet, it is only by paying due attention to the formal qualities the epic confers that we can appreciate the function of the first person singular running through it (from its very first word).

Michael Bernstein, in *The Tale of the Tribe: Ezra Pound and the Modern Verse Epic*,[32] suggests a number of qualities by which epic works might be seen to share a family likeness. Of the four propositions by which he characterises epic verse (based upon an admittedly uneasy combination of a priori conditions and a posteriori conclusions), the second deserves to be quoted in full:

> The dominant voice narrating the poem will . . . not bear the trace of a single sensibility; instead, it will function as a spokesman for values generally acknowledged as significant for communal stability and social well-being. Within the fiction of the poem, the dominant, locatable source of narration will not be a particular individual (the poet), but rather the voice of the community's heritage 'telling itself'.

The ellipsis covers the word 'therefore': this is the second proposition Bernstein offers because it follows logically from the first, which is that the epic provides its audience with its own collective cultural heritage. It is consequent upon the narrator being a spokesperson for a community that (in Bernstein's third proposition) 'the proper audience of an epic is not the *individual* in his absolute inwardness but the *citizen* as participant in a collective linguistic and social nexus.'

> Whereas a lyric is addressed to the purely private consciousness of its hearer apart from all considerations of his class, circumstances, or social bonds, the epic speaks primarily to members of a 'tribe', to listeners who recognize in the poem, social (in the broadest sense, which here includes political) as well as psychological, ethical, emotional, or aesthetic imperatives.

Bernstein's fourth proposition is that the element of instruction, which is arguably present in some degree in any kind of poetry, is foregrounded in epic because the epic offers its audience lessons 'presumed necessary to their individual and social survival'.

It was Maxim Gorky, writing in 1909, and well aware of how literature could help individual and social survival, who argued that the contrast between the collective symbolised by the concept of 'We' and that symbolised by the concept of 'They' arose from 'a struggle among clans'.

The process of the emergence of the 'I' is analogous to that of the appearance of the epic hero; the collective felt it imperative to create personality because the need had arisen to share out the various functions of the struggle against them and against Nature; the need arose for specialization, for the distribution of the collective experience among the members; this moment was the commencement of the splitting up of the collective's integral energy.[33]

The first person of MacDiarmid's poetry is ultimately a summation of a collective's strengths and resiliences, its specialisations and ambitions. As such, it is peculiarly adapted for the struggle it engages in by preserving the virtue of anonymity, the ability to quote opinion and use masks, offer fictional identities, divert and direct our critical attention. If the later poetry is centripetal it is also afferent, and the process goes on through as well as in its medium. In other words, MacDiarmid has it both ways. He accepts a public role but remains a private man, and not at the same time but according to the time and place. As one journalist put it, at a celebration held in his honour in the 1970s he rose to address the audience and mild Chris Grieve melted away until before the lectern stood the fiery and declamatory tub-thumper, Hugh MacDiarmid.[34] This, however, raises once again the question of 'sincerity' and 'authenticity' which we encountered earlier, in reference to plagiarism. Are we not entitled to ask of a poem describing the flight of a bird, did the poet actually see that happen?

In his Journal for 1840, Emerson wrote 'There is no deeper dissembler than the sincerest man', and, in 1841, 'Many men can write better in a mask than for themselves.'[35] Nietzsche, whose admiration of Emerson is always an engaging surprise, says with much the same intention 'Every profound spirit needs a mask.' It is paradoxical, but none the less true, that the expression of sincerity, the 'authentic call' is best heard through a mask. Perhaps the reason for this is to be found in the social or public nature of such expression. The 'authentic call' finds its apotheosis in the fulfilment of a social role. That is one of the reasons why 'British Leftish Poetry, 1930–40' (*C.P.*, p.1060; first published in *Lines Review* in January 1954) is such a successful combination of two lines of MacDiarmid, followed by thirteen lines of Aristophanes, and concluded by a final line by MacDiarmid. The poem is balanced by the pronouncements in the first and the last lines, and the distant rhyme of the first couplet with the last line. The passage from *The Acharnians* between them, from the Everyman edition (volume I, first published in 1909 without identifying the translator), is from the first speech in the play, and is spoken by Dicaeopolis, the principal actor. The name Dicaeopolis, we are told in an Introductory Note, 'may be interpreted as conveying the idea of honest policy . . . He is represented as a humorous, shrewd countryman (a sort of Athenian Sancho), who (in consequence of the war, and the invasion of Attica by the Peloponnesian Army) had been driven from his home to take shelter in the city.' He is regretting lost comforts and is first presented seated at the Palace of Assembly, alone, a misfit, remembering the stifling shortcomings of more modern theatre. This is the Everyman Aristophanes:

But again I suffered cruelly in the Theatre
A tragical disappointment. There was I
Gaping to hear old Aeschylus, when the Herald
Called out, 'Theognis, bring your chorus forward.'
Imagine what my feelings must have been!   5
But then Dexitheus pleased me coming forward
And singing his Boetian Melody:
But next came Chaeris with his music truly,
That turned me sick, and killed me very nearly.
But never in my lifetime, man or boy,   10
Was I so vexed, as at this present moment;
To see the Pnyx, at this time of the morning,
Quite empty, when the Assembly should be full.

MacDiarmid makes minor changes. In line 11, 'this' becomes 'the'. 'Gaping' in line 3 becomes 'Hoping' in MacDiarmid, referring back to the poem's second line:

> Auden, MacNeice, Day Lewis, I have read them all
> Hoping against hope to hear the authentic call.

C.P., p.1060

The authentic call was to be heard in 'old Aeschylus' and we might recall those other lines in 'The Kind of Poetry I Want':

> As Aeschylus in his new drama
> Gave form and voice
> To the Greek liberation from Persia.
> This is the poetry that I want.

C.P., p.627

But that was clearly not what he was getting from MacSpaunday, any more than Dicaeopolis was from Theognis (who is described in a footnote simply as 'A bad tragic poet'). MacDiarmid assumes, to some extent, the character of Dicaeopolis as it is presented in the speech, but there is juxtaposition as well as similarity in the situations, as the final pronouncement makes clear. For, instead of a play in which these problems can be explored and may be resolved in comedy and satire, we are left only with the 'explanation' that 'must' be passed: 'You cannot light a match on a crumbling wall.' Though the poem, in a striking image, conveys disgust, and despair, and contempt, it is also a condemnation of particular poets and implicitly, kinds of poetry, in a particular place and time.[36] Its title emphasises its specificity. In this poem, the posture is not itself heroic — though there is something grand implied in the 'call' — but there is confrontation and conflict. MacDiarmid, wishing to light that match, ranges himself implicitly with Aeschylus in a way that Dicaeopolis does not.

What is this sense of the heroic? Discussing the question, Lionel Trilling quoted Margaret Bieber, who, in her book on Greek theatre, said that the hero is primarily an actor — he acts out his own high sense of himself.[37] The ancient Greek heroes were often possessed of some divinity. Aristotle suggested that the virtuous man's perfection lies in his megalopsychia — great-souledness — aristocratic pride; and the fact that this has to be exhibited makes an actor of him. A role played becomes a function performed. And other actors are their own audience; the notion of passive spectator has not arisen. It is to this experience of wealth as life, of culture as being and becoming rather than having or storing, that MacDiarmid makes his 'authentic call'. Yet, if he shares some of these ancient heroic qualities, he is a twentieth-century man. Consider the 'hero' of 'The Poet as Prophet' (subtitled 'The Man for whom Gaeldom is Waiting'): he is, like the third person of 'The Kind of Scot I Want', 'King Over Himself', 'A New Scots Poet', 'The Poetic Faculty', and 'The Kulturkampf' — 'the ideal figure of whom Mr Power [William Power, dedicatee of the last poem], the author himself, and all the others associated in the new Scottish Literary Movement, form parts.' He is, in other words, the Supreme Faction personified. And the choice he makes in 'The Poet as Prophet' is one of 'A Communist Europe' whose centre is Moscow and whose prophet is Marx, in preference to a liberal parliamentary Europe whose centre is 'the English tradition' and whose prophet is Rousseau, or a federative, corporative Europe whose centre is Rome.

His sympathies were wholly with the first of these
Which alone, he knew, had anything of value
To say to Gaeldom . . .

C.P., p.1374

He is immersed in company, individual but also — in the original meaning of the word — indivisible. As the individuals of the Trinity were inseparable from each other, so MacDiarmid's 'hero' is indivisible from his nation's people and culture, and his choice reflects the depth of his conviction that Marxism is capable of encouraging in all of them 'more fruitful modes of production'.

The Vision of Desire

Encouraging 'more fruitful modes of production' may be, however, a thankless task. Encouraging a particular vision of the world may be even more thankless, when the whole dynamic of that world is shifting in another direction. Communism in Eastern Europe appears to be, in the early 1990s, increasingly on the retreat. MacDiarmid, by contrast, appears to be increasingly on the syllabus. A perhaps surprising literary comparison will emphasise the point. To Edmund Spenser, writing on the periphery of the Elizabethan world, stasis was a higher state than movement. The nine-lined stanzas of *The Faerie Queen* suggest this — they hang self-enclosed. They do not run on in the manner of, for example, the couplets of Marlowe's 'Hero and Leander'. The reader of Marlowe is more rapidly excited than tranquilly observant. A poetry designed to affirm stasis is therefore also antithetical to the drama of the time because theatre, by its very medium, breaks down the idea of a still centre, focusing on more than one figure on the stage. Spenser was writing at the edge of the Elizabethan world (in Ireland) and looking towards the centre (London), while in London itself drama was flourishing. *The Faerie Queen* might then be read not as a dramatic or narrative poem at all, for its many stanzas all ask to be held in the mind to perceive the vision the poem offers in stillness. The poem asks to be looked through, as opposed to at; it promises to lead you to see through its totality to a truth beyond. That truth is not the poet, but rather a metaphysical and sacral vision of the world, revealed through pattern, exempla, and feelings of delight (in a religious, sacral, beatific sense) and conveniency (oneness with the world).

There are two crises threatening this world. If the poet, like the priest, holds up a poem or a vision which compels the populace into an order, then what can be done if the populace refuses to be drawn? The music of transcendental poetry becomes insistent, it loses its tranquillity, it becomes something else. The poet continues his flight unaccompanied, with violence and cruelty in the land below. Secondly, the 'changelessness that lies behind change' can be felt *only* by the mind. Its presence is not implicit in the words, which can be seen and felt sensually. The cancelled stanzas at the end of *The Faerie Queen* (about desire seeking gratification — to Spenser, a base emotion here uncharacteristically beautified) suggest the incompatibility of sensual gratification and the sacral world.

MacDiarmid's world is not sacral and his vision is not one of stasis or rigid order. Yet his epic poetry has things in common with Spenserian as well as Marlovian poetry. As with Spenser, for MacDiarmid 'The supreme reality is visible to the mind alone.' The changelessness behind change can be contemplated only in a cerebral way. The indications he makes towards what lies beyond expression, beyond human experience even, hint at the changelessness behind the 'frenzied and chaotic age' he lived through. The crisis which we have discussed in Chapter 2, of materialist conviction and Marxist method confronting 'mystical perception', is essentially similar to the crisis in *The Faerie Queen*. MacDiarmid's verse-paragraphs are not to be held in the mind as Spenser's are; despite syntactic instabilities, they run on with an energy and rhythmic consistency only clearly felt if they are read quickly and at length. But, as with Spenser, they ask to be looked *through* to a vision of a world that is desirable and inevitable but needs to be struggled towards. As with Spenser, violence and cruelty endanger the unwilling populace — though MacDiarmid is aware of the cost of that violence and cruelty, and accepts the price to be paid. In the text itself, the price is paid where the verse becomes inchoate and assertion overrides sensitive apprehension.

It was one of the most remarkable characteristics of Scottish poetry from 1920, that not only a cultural but a political Renaissance was involved in its production. Instead of the Spenserian élite, poets, priests, and sovereigns, MacDiarmid rallies poets, philosophers, and politicians. As MacDiarmid said himself, very early in the development of the Scottish literary movement of the 1920s, the poets and writers involved in that movement realised that it could not reach its fullest fruition 'unless it was accompanied by a corresponding political movement. That took longer to effect, but I don't think that any student of the matter, viewing the enormous escalation of the Scottish National Movement in the last few years [he

was speaking in 1968] will deny that the instigation of that movement lay in the work of a few writers like myself.'[38] A later statement
on the matter in an essay 'Scotland: Full Circle'[39] (in 1971) was a
further endorsement of separatist policies. He advocated 'the John
MacLean line of Scottish Separatism, Republicanism and anti-
Imperialism' and pointed to the repercussions of the teaching of
Scottish literature and history and the importance of the fact that
'a new image of Scotland is being projected'. That image is, he says,
of increasing importance as England's decline to 'fifth or sixth-
rate status' marks the imminent truth: 'The whole situation has
changed — and will change a great deal further in the very near
future'.

If contemporary forms of ideology have taken over the functions
of mythology, purging alternative possibilities and ambiguities, and
naturalising social constructs, then certain politically committed
texts will interrogate that ideology and reject it. This takes place
irrespective of the political allegiance of the authors of such texts.
If we compare MacDiarmid's élitism with that of T.S. Eliot, which
itself attacked the ideology of middle-class liberalism, and in author-
ising 'the tradition' revealed its imperious (and rigorous) denial of
alternative possibilities — we shall find MacDiarmid's Marxism
equally rigorous, but innately more susceptible of constant revision
(in the sense in which Lenin meant the word, and not, as it is so
often pejoratively used, as 'revisionism'). Moreover, MacDiarmid's
élite, his Supreme Faction, loads social consequence and political
responsibility upon its members. Unlike the symbolic systems
developed by Yeats, Graves, Eliot, Lawrence, and Pound, Mac-
Diarmid's Gaelic Idea, his Scotland indeed, is not a flight from
contemporary history but an attack upon it.

But as for the poetry, who reads it? As Brecht once said: 'You
cannot just "write the truth"; you have to write it *for* and *to*
somebody, somebody who can do something with it.'

Terry Eagleton describes the kind of 'super-reader' posited by
structuralism as a transcendental subject absolved from all limiting
social determinants.[40] The kind of reader MacDiarmid wants is
perhaps similarly 'fully equipped with all the technical knowledge
essential for deciphering the work', and who would need 'to be
faultless in applying this knowledge, and free of any hampering
restrictions . . . stateless, classless, ungendered, free of ethnic characteristics and without limiting cultural assumptions. It is true that
one does not tend to meet many readers who fill this bill entirely
satisfactorily, but the structuralists conceded that the ideal reader

need not do anything so humdrum as actually exist. The concept was merely a convenient heuristic (or exploratory) fiction for determining what it would take to read a particular text "properly". The reader, in other words, was just an ideal function of the text itself: to give an exhaustive description of the text was really the same thing as to give a complete account of the kind of reader it would require to understand it.' MacDiarmid would share some of these requirements, but there would remain the most important differences. The reader Eagleton depicts is both a mythical projection and a direct result of a particular branch of literary theory (structuralism), which, through its isolation of the purely cerebral response had no concrete means with which to react against the control and constraint of the prevailing ideologies to which it found itself susceptible. Mac-Diarmid's intended reader is a 'function of the text' in a very real way, for the text posits social change as a necessity *and ideal* which will bring such a reader into being, or at least bring about the material conditions in which such a reader might more completely belong.

> Poetry of such an integration as cannot be effected
> Until a new and conscious organisation of society
> Generates a new view
> Of the world as a whole
> As the integration of all the rich parts
> Uncovered by the separate disciplines.
> That is the poetry that I want.

C.P., p.1025

Here we are being asked to imagine a poetry that cannot be written *until* there is a general social adjustment sufficient to allow its being written. The poetry MacDiarmid wants is finally to be understood as something inseparable from the society in which it would be read. This, as we have seen, is the condition *In Memoriam James Joyce* attempts to make for itself. What we realise as we read through the various texts which constitute the work is that the world, as far as we can comprehend it, is determined by the kinds of discourse we use to comprehend it with. And there is no final, fixed discourse which comprehends it all completely. The attempt to assert that such a thing exists falls back to the assertion that it *will* exist or that it *might* exist. The 'Idea and Word Chart' is imaginatively *present* at the beginning of 'The World of Words' but it can be present only in the imagination, and it can be represented only in fictive terms, in poetry.

The poetry itself, moreover, is so much a constitution of various discourses that our attempt to infer an identity we can work with depends, ultimately, on the sanction of print and binding. The text cuts across and transgresses from that identity so frequently that it threatens the stability of our description of it as an object. If the text disappears, then, logically, the critic disappears too. A great deal lies behind Edwin Morgan's comment: 'the critic's pen has been inhibited, uncertain whether it would be praising (or dispraising) MacDiarmid or someone else.'[41]

We have seen how *In Memoriam James Joyce* interrogates the notion of identity by its formal practice. The struggle against that interrogation is necessarily difficult, and criticism — especially in Scotland — has hardly begun to work on it. Edwin Morgan himself is the most notable exception, but it is telling that his readings of MacDiarmid's later poetry are written as essays, their acuity matched by their brevity. We might conclude from this that the text creates plural readings. The critic, or reader, is no longer in a position of dominance from which he or she extracts the 'entire' meaning from the text; nor is he or she even on an equal plane, sharing the experience of the text (as we saw was the case with the early Scots lyrics). Rather, the reader of 'Plaited Like the Generations of Men', for example, is asked to 'follow me' — where 'me' is a confused term. Do we understand it to mean MacDiarmid or Busoni? Or do we take it to refer to the text itself?

If we do take it to mean the text, then the contradictions within that text seem all the more open and declared. The distance that is thereby created clears the space for new things to be articulated. This is the political nature of the text: it is itself a *polis*, a site where a number of voices are interchanging. As such, it is distinct from mere pluralism, by which one thing might be interpreted in a number of different ways. The desire at the heart of pluralism is for the 'one thing' to be seen from all angles and identified. That is logocentrism. It is possible to see that desire working to devastating effect in Ezra Pound. But it is not the same thing with MacDiarmid.

The moral sense which comes through MacDiarmid's poetry involves a different kind of personal engagement (or disengagement) from that involved in the poetry of Pound and Eliot. The pluralism I mentioned — whereby an event or thing is seen from various different perspectives — has a clear lineage from Browning to Pound. It resulted in Pound's enormous exhaustion at the fragmentation and disintegration of his work. We quoted in Chapter 2 Pound's reference to *The Cantos* as a 'rag-bag' — which supplied Mac-

Diarmid with the term to use in the text of *In Memoriam* to refer to itself (*'this* rag-bag'). But Pound's attitude to the term was critical: it was not, he said in later years, the way to make 'a work of art'. MacDiarmid's attitude was more cheerful. He was happy, and resigned, to refer to *In Memoriam* as a rag-bag. Furthermore, he disagreed with Pound's opinion of *The Cantos*, saying that the regret Pound felt because he could not bring the whole project to resolution and coherent completion was unwarranted. In MacDiarmid's opinion, the achievement of *The Cantos* was sufficient. It was good enough as it was.

This points to a final set of considerations. If MacDiarmid comes out from a Victorian sensibility, he also stretches forward towards a 'post-modern' one. The theorists of post-structuralism, Jacques Derrida and Lacan, would be very familiar with the kind of struggle we have been looking at in MacDiarmid, and my discussion has been informed by their writings. The struggle against logocentrism and anthropocentrism (as they have described it) takes a shape determined by those opposing forces. Consequently, a struggle to disengage from that struggle ensues. It is possible to see this beginning to happen in 'On a Raised Beach'. It has already happened in *In Memoriam James Joyce*, but it is enacted again in passages and moments in the course of the verse. It is never completely over and done with in MacDiarmid's work.

In post-structuralist literary theory, great importance is attached to the words difference, deference, and desire. It is not my purpose to develop an introductory explication of post-structuralism at this point and then graft it back onto our reading of MacDiarmid. Rather, I wish to make some acknowledgement of those theorists whose work has underwritten a great deal of my approach to Mac-Diarmid. In so doing, I might also be able to suggest ways in which a more exclusively theoretical approach could yield valuable readings.

The Kind of Poetry I Want is predicated on desire. Desire functions through and across individuals: it does not exist singly, in a unitary self. The first person singular in the title is, as we have seen, a compositional figure comprising self *and others*. MacDiarmid 'projects' a poetry that cannot be fully 'present'; and this projection is an attempt to articulate itself. This takes place across and through individual publications. The poetry, therefore, is a demonstration of its own inadequacy: its plenitude is never enough to exhaust its resources. Paradoxically, its failure reveals its accomplishment. It is *directly* demonstrative. By contrast, for example, there is a famous moment in Shakespeare's *Troilus and Cressida* where the Greeks hear the Trojans brass accolade announcing the arrival of Cressida. They cry out: 'The Trojans' trumpet!' And what we hear, of course, is 'The Trojan strumpet.' Shakespeare presents characters whose language is working tricks on them, showing them up to be incapable of controlling even their own articulation, let alone a military campaign. MacDiarmid's 'presentation' is different: he gives us a fictive poet, 'himself', and discloses his methods as he practises them.

> — And all this here, everything I write, of course
> Is an extended metaphor for something I never mention.
>
> C.P., p.745

The recurrence of submerged thoughts and, by extension, the continual use of metaphor in language, is the enactment of desire. The sexual implication is clear: the repression of sexuality and of thoughts related to sexual identity is what allows apparent selfhood to function. But the force of desire always allows those repressed thoughts to return. In Shakespeare, and especially in *Troilus and Cressida* (a play very much about political identity, repression, and sexuality), these thoughts intrude upon characters' speeches in puns and slips. In the later MacDiarmid, the entire process of writing is revealed working according to this law. Instead of dealing authoritatively with characters and their language, 'MacDiarmid' is an extension of the language of his own works. And instead of dealing with the working of desire in sexuality, MacDiarmid is concerned with its function in poetry and in politics.

Jacques Lacan has described the development of the human infant into language in terms which are richly suggestive of ways we might read MacDiarmid. The human child comes to understand him or herself as an individual, sexed identity separate from the world and others, at the same time as she or he begins to speak. This happens with the recognition of absent things: the departure, for example, of the child's mother from the room. The sense of identity characteristic of adulthood is the recognition of unrepeatability: absences that can never be restored. In the process of this development, the child realises it can be decentred: 'I' or 'you' can become 'he' or 'she', and thereby *excluded* from discourse. So the child's growth into language parallels the recognition of difference and identity. The early, self-centred world Lacan calls 'imaginary'. He terms the new world the 'symbolic': it is unstable, always volatile, and in it all meanings — including meanings for the self — have to be created.

The extent to which people develop their own significant personality varies, of course. Identity in such terms is constructed by imposing different versions of 'other' identities across the gaps and exclusions between them. This is the operation of desire: not desire for a specific thing but part of the formative human structure. It can be attached to local sexual and other goals and aims, but at a deeper level it is directed towards an unremediable absence in our earliest formation as human beings.[42]

In our reading of MacDiarmid, the importance of Lacanian theories is directly political. The constitution of the idea of the individual in the eighteenth century was a progressive stage in the movement by which the bourgeoisie (often led by radical intellectuals) rejected corrupt aristocratic rule and established the rights of each person (or at least each European male) to pursue their own ends rationally. In crude and general terms, the establishment of the individual pre-empts political objectives which require solidarity with a class or group. 'Public' discourses could contribute little to those of the individual mind, just as the individual mind holds itself aloof from public discourses. The legacy of this situation can be felt in the conflicting notions of selfhood and solidarity which are re-enacted in 'Plaited Like the Generations of Men'.

What is at stake in such a conflict, as MacDiarmid puts it in 'On a Raised Beach', is reality itself. Belief in selfhood is reciprocal with belief in an ultimate reality. The question arises, then, whether there is any such thing or if it has any secure referent. For Lacan, as we have seen, the self is acquired, received from the world it grows into. As for MacDiarmid, we have seen the ways in which language operates in the later poetry, in the functions of transcription, and in the movement of the verse: our reading underscores the Lacanian idea of how selfhood is constructed. With MacDiarmid's texts, however, that construction is politically engaged in a thoroughly uncommon way.

What makes it uncommon is not only its mixed strategies but also its preference for those aspects of a culture which are not, habitually, favoured. To help us with this, we might enlist the theorist of 'deconstruction': Jacques Derrida. Derrida has argued that the history of Western thought shows a number of attempts to construct centres of meaning by devising systems of metaphysics. Metaphysical systems are based on favoured 'sources' of meaning: God, truth, reason, man, nature, speech. These systems depend upon the foundational belief in a *source* of truth, which is most often located 'beyond' humanity, in divine wisdom for example. The history of

Western thought is, therefore, a history of logocentrism. The consequence of such a history is that in Western society a number of cultural identities are favoured over their binary opposites. Reason is preferable to madness; Nature to culture; Man to woman; Theory to practice. (This is clear enough if you notice how appropriate the capitalisation is to the first but not the second term.)

The binary relationship of these sets of terms is undermined by Derrida's theoretical approach to language and thought. Destabilise the 'full meanings' which keep logocentric systems of thought and order in place and you can then reinstate those things traditionally subordinated or suppressed. Your faith in the systems as such is also profoundly shaken. What is opened up is the possibility of the 'radical freeplay' of language and thought, without access to identity or certitude.

This stops short of determination and the possibility of real change which Marxism would insist upon. There is an ambivalence to deconstruction which is problematic. This 'radical freeplay' can be liberating or restrictive, empowering or debilitating. Like pleasure, it can serve *any* political purpose. A deconstructive reading of MacDiarmid might show his work to be unstable quite easily. We have already indicated instabilities of syntax, debilitating contradictions in arguments, and we could point to places where the versification departs from any 'normal' practice altogether. But it is also possible to recognise in MacDiarmid's work a reading that is *already* deconstructive: an understanding of language and literature which is working through its own instabilities to present a record of its dynamic and direction. Deconstruction tests to the limit the systems and formations by which we construct meanings and values. MacDiarmid certainly engages in such testing, but, although they do not exert their usual dominance, he never completely abandons notions of identity and certitude.

At the beginning of this chapter, I referred to notions of selfhood and sincerity, the tradition of 'dramatic monologue' which runs from Donne to Pound, and breaks up to present a version of MacDiarmid whose radicalism extends into a destabilised world. If I have presented MacDiarmid as a poet in whom a Victorian moral conscience evolved into a post-modern questioning of self and identity, it is, perhaps, only to recognise the extent of his achievement, and to take the senses of delight and exhilaration I mentioned in the Introduction to this book further. MacDiarmid is very clear about particular meanings and values. He is committed to pragmatic political intervention and strategic acts. He is not totally devoted to 'radical freeplay'.

> — If the book's ultimate realisation
> Is the impotence of language
> In the face of the event,
> This abdication is announced
> With a power of words wholly inaccessible
> To those never overpowered and speechless.
>
> *C.P.*, p.776

He believes that certain things have a curative, restorative value. As a Marxist, he is sure to insist upon certain relations of language to matter, and that it would be unwise to deny the pressures of identity and certitude possessed by matter. Matter will always exert them upon you. But an essential quality of MacDiarmid's activity points forward to, or overlaps with, deconstruction: his willingness, or indeed compulsion, to carry things through to extremes. It is fitting to conclude with the famous stanza inscribed on the poet's tombstone:

> I'll ha'e nae hauf-way hoose, but aye be whaur
> Extremes meet — it's the only way I ken
> To dodge the curst conceit o' bein' richt
> That damns the vast majority o' men.
>
> *C.P.*, p.87

This kind of extremism has made MacDiarmid sometimes appear outrageous and irresponsible, and he has risked his credibility as well as his credentials. The overall result is a practice which, in some ways, resembles sawing off the branch on which you are sitting. And there is an appropriateness in that image which can be explained in the terms Jonathan Culler used to describe the practice of deconstruction: if unusual, and somewhat risky, it is manifestly something that is possible.

> One can and may continue to sit on a branch while sawing it. There is no physical or moral obstacle if one is willing to risk the consequences. The question then becomes whether one will succeed in sawing it clear through, and where and how one might land. A difficult question: to answer one would need a comprehensive understanding of the entire situation — the resilience of the support, the efficacy of one's tools, the shape of the terrain — and an ability to predict accurately the conse-

206 Hugh MacDiarmid's Epic Poetry

quences of one's work. If 'sawing off the branch on which one is sitting' seems foolhardy to men of common sense, it is not so for Nietzsche, Freud, Heidegger, and Derrida; for they suspect that if they fall there is no 'ground' to hit and that the most clear-sighted act may be a certain reckless sawing, a calculated dismemberment or deconstruction of the great cathedral-like trees in which Man has taken shelter for millennia.[43]

Culler's terms are clearly appropriate for Nietzsche, Freud, Heidegger, and Derrida. They might also be considered appropriate for Brecht, for Joyce, and for Hugh MacDiarmid.

Notes

1. Cf. Tony Lopez, *The Poetry of W.S. Graham* (Edinburgh: Edinburgh University Press, 1989), p.125, where Lopez makes a similar distinction between Graham's first person and Pound's and Eliot's. It seems to me that Graham and MacDiarmid might be considered as poets whose enquiry into the nature and function of language is equally essential, but which led them to develop completely different poetics.

2. Harvey Oxenhorn, *Elemental Things: The Poetry of Hugh MacDiarmid* (Edinburgh: Edinburgh University Press, 1984), p.vii. I applaud Oxenhorn's presentation of the 'gentle, vital visionary man' and I agree that it was necessary to move on from the image of the kilted terror. Yet to leave those two aspects of one man separate is not sufficient, and, perhaps consequently, what is conspicuous by being absent from Oxenhorn's book is any sustained analysis of *In Memoriam James Joyce*.

3. Kenneth Buthlay, *Hugh MacDiarmid (C.M. Grieve)* (Edinburgh: Scottish Academic Press, 1982), p.102.

4. *The Letters*, p.168.

5. Cf. Kenneth Buthlay, op. cit, pp.20–2. And Kenneth Buthlay, *Hugh MacDiarmid (C.M. Grieve)* (Edinburgh: Oliver & Boyd, 1964), pp.32–3.

6. See Peter McCarey, *Hugh MacDiarmid and the Russians* (Edinburgh: Scottish Academic Press, 1987), pp.126–7.

7. Ezra Pound, *Selected Letters*, ed. D.D. Paige (London: Faber & Faber, 1951).

8. Roderick Watson, 'The Symbolism of *A Drunk Man Looks at the Thistle*', in *Hugh MacDiarmid: A Critical Survey*, ed. Duncan Glen (Edinburgh: Scottish Academic Press, 1972), pp.94–116 (p.101).

9. Though there are the lines 'We wha are poets and artists / Move frae inklin' to inklin' . . . ', there is nothing to compare with 'I have known all the poets of the world, I think' in *The Kind of Poetry I Want* (C.P., p.1032).

10. P.B. Shelley, *The Complete Poetical Works*, ed. Thomas Hutchinson (London: Oxford University Press, 1987), p.237.

11. Hugh MacDiarmid, *A Drunk Man Looks at the Thistle*, ed. Kenneth Buthlay (Edinburgh: Scottish Academic Press, 1986), p.237.

12. Herman Melville, *Clarel: A Poem and Pilgrimage in the Holy Land*, Part IV, Section 9, in the Standard Edition of the *Works of Herman Melville* (London: Constable, 1922–9), II, pp.192–3.

13. William Shakespeare, *King Lear*, v. iii.325–6 (Arden edn), ed. Kenneth Muir (London and New York: Methuen, 1985), p.206.

14. See Alistair McCleery, *The Porpoise Press 1922–39* (Edinburgh: Merchiston Publishing, 1988), especially pp.48–9, for background to this publication.

15. When we regard King Lear as a character we witness the internalising of the most powerful natural and cosmic influences, and this implosive factor is part of the titanic scale of his passions even when the basis of the conflict seems hardly to warrant them. MacDiarmid's poetry is a repository of this essential aspect of theatre: being so largely metaphorical, it expands the immediate meaning and action of the poet and implies a world of chthonic forces and metaphysical contexts. In this world the poet is man's representative. The function of the dramatic protagonist is thus, to a degree, taken over by the poet, the fiction created by the poetry as a whole; that the name *Hugh MacDiarmid* has and was meant to have a specific author-function is an aspect of this.

16. F.R. Leavis, *New Bearings in English Poetry* (London: Chatto & Windus, 1923; repr. Harmondsworth: Penguin/Pelican, 1979), p.154. This source has been noted by Ruth McQuillan, in her essay 'Hugh MacDiarmid's "On a Raised Beach"', *Akros*, 12 (34–5) (August 1977), pp.87–97.

17. Guy Davenport, 'Olson', in *The Geography of the Imagination: Forty Essays* (London: Pan, 1984), pp.80–99 (pp.97–8).

18. e.e. cummings, *Complete Poems*, I, 1913–35 (London: MacGibbon and Kee, 1968), p.124.

19. See 'Mr MacDiarmid and Dr Grieve', in *TLS Essays and Reviews from The Times Literary Supplement* 4 (1965) (London: Oxford University Press, 1966), pp.176–95.

20. Kenneth Buthlay, 'Some Hints for Source-Hunters', *Scottish Literary Journal*, 5(2) (December 1978), pp.50–66 (pp.60–5).

21. Hart Crane, *The Complete Poems and Selected Letters and Prose*, ed. Brom Weber (London: Oxford University Press), pp.51–2.

22. Edward Thomas, *The Collected Poems of Edward Thomas*, ed. R. George Thomas (London: Oxford University Press, 1978), p.311.

23. John Cowper Powys, *Obstinate Cymric: Essays 1935–47* (Carmarthen: The Druid Press, 1947; reissued London: Village Press, 1973), p.42.

24. Stalin, *Works*, VI (Foreign Language Publishing House, Moscow, 1953), p.63.

25. Ibid., p.57.

26. J.B.S. Haldane, 'Some Consequences of Materialism', in *The Inequality of Man and other Essays* (Harmondsworth: Penguin/Pelican, 1932: repr. 1937), pp.157–70 (p.167).

27. Hugh MacDiarmid, *The Islands of Scotland* (London: Batsford, 1939). A ψ-wave (pronounced as 'sigh' after the Greek letter, psi) signifies the concept of electrical flux, the energy of repulsion and attraction between charged particles. The term 'psi-phenomena' as applied to extra-sensory perception is recorded in the *Oxford English Dictionary* as being mentioned first in 1942 by a certain R.H. Thouless, following the suggestion of a Dr Wiesner. True to form, MacDiarmid's poem appeared years before this.

28. H.J. Muller, *Out of the Night: A Biologist's View of the Future* (London: Victor Gollancz, 1936), p.159.

29. Ibid., pp.139–40.

30. Tom Leonard, 'The Locust Tree in Flower, and Why it Had Difficulty Flowering in Britain' (from *Poetry Information*, 16, Winter 1976–7), in *Intimate Voices: Selected Work 1965–1983* (Newcastle: Galloping Dog Press, 1984), pp.95–102.

31. Cf. Ron Silliman, 'Disappearance of the Word, Appearance of the World', in *The L=A=N=G=U=A=G=E Book*, ed. Bruce Andrews and Charles Bernstein (Carbondale and Edwardsville: Southern Illinois University Press, 1984), pp.121–32. A sidelight on this matter would be a consideration of the poetry of Louis Zukovsky (1904–78), a New Yorker of Russian-Jewish parentage, a friend of Williams, cummings, and Pound, and thoroughly unlike them in being a committed Marxist and in bringing to *completion* his masterwork, the poem 'A', which took him over forty-six years. He more than any other single person attempted to regain for poetry the condition of music that had gone out with the Elizabethans.

32. Michael André Bernstein, *The Tale of the Tribe: Ezra Pound and the Modern Verse Epic* (Princeton, NJ: Princeton University Press, 1980). Quotations come from the Introduction, pp.3–25 (p.14).

33. Maxim Gorky, 'The Disintegration of Personality' (1909), in *On Literature* (Moscow: Progress Publishers, n.d.), pp.71–137 (p.75).

34. Duncan MacLaren, 'MacDiarmid', *Q. Question: An Independent Political Review for Scotland. Arts, Business, Science*, 34 (26 August 1977), pp.10–11.

35. R.W. Emerson, quoted in Lionel Trilling, *Sincerity and Authenticity* (London: Oxford University Press, 1972), p.119.

36. See, for example, W.R. Aitken 'On Editing MacDiarmid's *Complete Poems*' (a paper read at the conference organised by Richard Demarco in Edinburgh in August 1988, but as yet unpublished). Aitken records

that when the poem was published in the *Nation* (NY) on 5 January 1957, the contents list on the front cover of that issue listed the poem as 'British Leftist Poetry, 1930–40' and this is the title Aitken later found over the draft and fair copy of the poem among MacDiarmid's papers. But over the poem as printed in the *Nation* (and as reprinted in the *Collected Poems* of 1962 and 1967) the title is given as 'British Leftish Poetry, 1930–40'. When Aitken asked MacDiarmid, he confirmed that Leftish was a printer's error, a misprint he had not intended, but when asked if he wanted his original title restored in the *Complete Poems*, he said 'with an amused twinkle in his eye, "No. Leave the misprint. 'Don't you think 'Leftish' is just a bit more pejorative?"'

37. Lionel Trilling, *Sincerity and Authenticity* (London: Oxford University Press, 1972), p.84.
38. Hugh MacDiarmid, on the LP *Hugh MacDiarmid Reads His Own Poetry* (Dublin: Claddagh Records, 1968).
39. Hugh MacDiarmid, 'Scotland: Full Circle', in Duncan Glen (ed.), *Whither Scotland?* (London: Victor Gollancz, 1971), pp.233–50.
40. Terry Eagleton, *Literary Theory* (Oxford: Basil Blackwell, 1983), pp.121–2.
41. Edwin Morgan, *Hugh MacDiarmid* (Harlow: Longman, 1976), p.24.
42. Perhaps the best introductory handbook to this and many other related matters is Alan Durant and Nigel Fabb, *Literary Studies in Action* (London and New York: Routledge, 1990), passages of which I have paraphrased here.
43. Jonathan Culler, *On Deconstruction* (London: Routledge & Kegan Paul, 1983) p.149.

Bibliography

This bibliography is divided into four sections. In each one I have included only those works which, though not necessarily mentioned in the book, were essential to its composition. The first section deals chronologically with MacDiarmid's own work, including journals and papers edited by MacDiarmid (or C.M. Grieve); the second deals with critical and biographical work on MacDiarmid; the third lists source-texts for MacDiarmid's work; and the fourth collects all other material. A full bibliography has not been attempted. I am indebted to W.R. Aitken's 'A Hugh MacDiarmid Bibliography', in *Hugh MacDiarmid: A Critical Survey*, ed. Duncan Glen (Edinburgh, 1972); 'Hugh MacDiarmid's "Unpublished" Books: A Bibliographical Exploration', in *Of One Accord: Essays in Honour of W.B. Paton*, ed. Frank McAdams (Glasgow, 1977); and 'Hugh MacDiarmid's Recent Bibliography', *Akros*, 12 (34–5) (August 1977). These are supplemented by 'A Bibliography of Hugh MacDiarmid', in *Hugh MacDiarmid: Man and Poet*, ed. Nancy K. Gish. Duncan Glen's 'Hugh MacDiarmid: A Chronological Bibliography', in *Hugh MacDiarmid and the Scottish Renaissance* (Edinburgh, 1964) contains a useful 'select list' of MacDiarmid's numerous contributions to periodicals. I have included a number of such contributions here, but my list is by no means exhaustive. I am also indebted to Michael K. Glenday's 'Hugh MacDiarmid: A Bibliography of Criticism, 1924–78', *Bulletin of Bibliography*, 36(2) (1979).

My list of MacDiarmid's sources is also select; many others are not noted here. There is, as yet, no bibliographical index of all the known and recorded sources of MacDiarmid's work.

The Works of Hugh MacDiarmid (C.M. Grieve)

'The Young Astrology', *The New Age*, 7(12) (July 20, 1911)
The Dunfermline Press (a series of articles, 1922–3)
(ed.), *Northern Numbers* (first and second series, Edinburgh, 1920, 1921; third series, Montrose, 1923)
(ed.), *The Scottish Chapbook* (monthly, 1922–3)
Annals of the Five Senses (Montrose, 1923; reissued, ed. Alan Bold, Edinburgh, 1983)

(ed.), *The Scottish Nation* (weekly, 1923)

The New Age (a series of articles, 1924–31)

(ed.), *The Northern Review* (monthly, 1924)

The Scottish Educational Journal (a series of articles, 1925–7)

Sangschaw (Edinburgh, 1925)

Penny Wheep (Edinburgh, 1926)

A Drunk Man Looks at the Thistle (Edinburgh, 1926; reissued, ed. Kenneth Buthlay, Edinburgh, 1987)

Contemporary Scottish Studies (London, 1926; reissued Edinburgh, 1976)

(ed.), *Robert Burns, 1759–1796* (London, 1926)

Albyn, or Scotland and the Future (London, 1927)

The Pictish Review (a series of articles, 1927–8)

The Lucky Bag (Edinburgh, 1927)

The Scots Observer (a series of articles, 1928–34)

Vox (a series of articles printed under A.K.L., Stentor and unsigned, 1929–30)

To Circumjack Cencrastus or The Curly Snake (Edinburgh, 1930)

The Modern Scot (a series of articles, 1930–4)

(transl.), *The Handmaid of the Lord* by Ramon Maria Tenreiro (London, 1930)

'Clainn Albainn and Other Matters', *The Modern Scot*, 1(2) (Summer 1930)

The Scottish Educational Journal (a series of articles printed under James Maclaren and A.K.L., 1931–4)

First Hymn to Lenin, and Other Poems (London, 1931)

(ed.), *Living Scottish Poets* (London, 1931)

The Free Man (a series of articles, 1932–4)

Scots Unbound and Other Poems (Stirling, 1932)

'Not Merely Philosophical Piety. Communism Means a Clean Sweep', *Scots Observer*, 7(334) (25 February 1933)

Scottish Scene, with Lewis Grassic Gibbon (London, 1934; reissued Bath, 1974)

Stony Limits, and Other Poems (London, 1934)

At the Sign of the Thistle (London, 1934)

Second Hymn to Lenin, and Other Poems (London, 1935)

'Scotland, France and Working Class Interests', *New Scotland (Alba Nuadh)*, 1(3) (October 1935)

'Communism and Literature', *New Scotland (Alba Nuadh)*, 1(9–10) (December 1935)

Scottish Eccentrics (London, 1936; reissued, with 'A Note on the Author' by Norman MacCaig, New York, 1972)

'Scottish Culture and Imperialist War', in *Eleventh Hour Questions* (Edinburgh, 1937) (ed.), *The Voice of Scotland* (issued irregularly, 1938–9; 1945–9; 1955–8)

The Islands of Scotland (London, 1939)

(ed.), *The Golden Treasury of Scottish Poetry* (London, 1940)

'Scottish Art and Letters: The Present Position and Post-War Prospects', in *The New Scotland: 17 Chapters on Scottish Reconstruction* (Glasgow, 1942)

'Foreword', in *Auntran Blads* by Douglas Young (Glasgow, 1943)

Lucky Poet: A Self-Study in Literature and Political Ideas (London, 1943; reissued London, 1972)

'Poetry in Scotland Today', *Poetry Scotland*, 1 (Glasgow, 1944)

'Signposts in Scottish Poetry Today', *Scots Independent*, 222 (February 1945)

'Pages from Hugh MacDiarmid's Notebook', *Poetry Scotland*, Third Collection (Glasgow, July 1946)

A Kist of Whistles (Glasgow, 1947)

'Films and the Scottish Novelist', in *Arts Review*, ed. Robin Russell (Edinburgh, 1947)

'Scottish Workers' Republic', *Forward*, 42(46) (13 November 1948)

The National Weekly (a series of articles, 1948–52)

'Introduction', in *Uranium 235* by Ewan MacColl (Glasgow, 1948)

'A Birthday Wish to T.S. Eliot', *Adam: International Review*, 186 (September 1948)

(ed.), *Poetry Scotland*, 4 (Edinburgh, 1949)

(ed.), *Robert Burns: Poems* (London, 1949)

'Making the Deserts Grow Fruitful. A Defence of Lysenko', *Forward*, 43(26) (25 June 1949)

(ed.), *Scottish Art and Letters*, Fifth Miscellany (Glasgow, 1950)

'Impressions of the U.S.S.R.', *The New Alliance and Scots Review*, 11(12) (March 1951)

Scottish Journal (a series of articles, 1952–4)

(ed.), *Selections from the Poems of William Dunbar* (Edinburgh, 1952)

Cunninghame Graham: a Centenary Study (Glasgow, 1952)

'The Key to World Literature', *Scottish Journal*, 4 (1954)

'Scottish Poetry 1923–1953', *Lines Review*, 4 and 5 (1954)

Francis George Scott: An Essay on the Occasion of his Seventy-Fifth Birthday, 25th January 1955 (Edinburgh, 1955)

'Jerqueing Every Idioticon: Some Notes on MacDiarmid's Joyce Poem' by Arthur Leslie, *The Voice of Scotland*, 6(2) (July 1955)

(ed.), *Selected Poems of William Dunbar* (Glasgow, 1955)

In Memoriam James Joyce (Glagow, 1955; reprinted 1956)

'Reply to Criticism', *The Voice of Scotland* 7(1) (April 1956)

Stony Limits and Scots Unbound, and Other Poems (Edinburgh, 1956)

Three Hymns to Lenin (Edinburgh, 1957)

'Why I Rejoined', *The Daily Worker* (28 March 1957)

The Battle Continues (Edinburgh, 1957)

'The Scottish Tradition', *Saltire Review*, 5(16) (Autumn 1958)

'Foreword', in *Poems* by Boris Pasternak, transl. L. Slater (Sussex, 1959)

Burns Today and Tomorrow (Edinburgh, 1959)

'Poets on Poetry', *X: A Quarterly Review*, 1(2) (March 1960)

'The Art of William McCance', *Saltire Review*, 6(22) (Autumn 1960)

The Kind of Poetry I Want (Edinburgh, 1961)

'The Wrong Turning in Scottish Poetry', *New Saltire*, 1 (Summer 1961)

the ugly birds without wings (Edinburgh, 1962)

David Hume — Scotland's Greatest Son (Edinburgh, 1962)

The Man of (almost) Independent Mind (Edinburgh, 1962)

(ed.), *Robert Burns: Love Songs* (London, 1962)

Collected Poems (New York and Edinburgh, 1962; revised and reissued New York and London, 1967)

(transl. with Elspeth Harley Schubert) *Aniara* by Harry Martinson (London, 1963)

Poems to Paintings by William Johnstone 1933 (Edinburgh, 1963)

'Foreword', in *Carotid Cornucopius* by Sydney Goodsir Smith (Edinburgh, 1964)

'The Return of the Long Poem', in *Ezra Pound: Perspectives*, ed. Noel Stock (Chicago, 1965)

The Company I've Kept (London, 1966)

'Foreword', in *Poems of Love* by Lilias Scott Chisholm (Edinburgh, 1966)

A Lap of Honour (London, 1967)

'Scotland', in *Celtic Nationalism*, with Owen Dudley Edwards, Gwynfor Evans, and Ioan Rhys (London, 1968)

Early Lyrics of Hugh MacDiarmid, ed. J.K. Annand (Preston, 1968)

The Uncanny Scot, ed. Kenneth Buthlay (London, 1968)

'Slàinte Chùramach, Seán', in *Sean O'Casey: Modern Judgements*, ed. Ronald Ayling (London, 1969)

'Introduction', in *Witdom* by Oliver Brown (Glasgow, 1969)

A Clyack-Sheaf (London, 1969)

Selected Essays, ed. Duncan Glen (London, 1969)

'Satori in Scotland' and 'Growing Up in Langholm', in *Memoirs of a Modern Scotland*, ed. Karl Miller (London, 1970)

More Collected Poems (London, 1970)

'Preface', in *The Collected Poems of Burns Singer*, ed. W.A.S. Keir (London, 1970)

'The Esemplastic Power' [on Ezra Pound], *Agenda*, 8(3–4) (Autumn/Winter 1970)

'Foreword', in *The Scottish Insurrection of 1820* by P. Berresford Ellis and Seamas Mac a' Ghobhainn (London, 1970; reissued London, 1989)

The MacDiarmids — A Conversation, with Duncan Glen, Arthur Thompson, and Valda Grieve (Preston, 1970)

Selected Poems, ed. David Craig and John Manson (Harmondsworth, 1970)

'Scotland: Full Circle', in *Whither Scotland?*, ed. Duncan Glen (London, 1971)

A Political Speech (Edinburgh, 1972)

The Hugh MacDiarmid Anthology, ed. Michael Grieve and Alexander Scott (London, 1972)

'The Master-Voyager of Our Age' [on Ezra Pound], *Agenda*, 10–11(4–1) (Autumn-Winter 1972–3)

'Introduction', in *John Maclean* by John Broom (Loanhead, 1973)

(ed.), *Henryson* (Harmondsworth, 1973)

Song of the Seraphim (London, 1973)

(transl.), *The Threepenny Opera* by Bertolt Brecht (London, 1973)

Direadh I, II and III (Frenich, Foss, 1974)

'Foreword', in *Poets to the People: South African Freedom Poems*, ed. Barry Feinberg (London, 1974)

'Foreword', in *The Art of J.D. Fergusson: A Biased Biography* by Margaret Morris (Glasgow and London, 1974)

Metaphysics and Poetry, with Walter Perrie (Hamilton, 1975)

'Sydney', in *For Sydney Goodsir Smith* (Loanhead, 1975)

'Introduction', in *Collected Poems* by Sydney Goodsir Smith (London, 1975)

'The Foundation Stone of the New Scotland' [on *The Scottish National Dictionary*], *The Scottish Review*, 1(2) (Winter 1975)

'Our Brecht', the *Guardian* (Thursday, 6 May 1976)

'Knox, Calvinism and the Arts', in *John Knox*, with Campbell Maclean and Anthony Ross (Edinburgh, 1976)

'Previews', *The Radio Times* (a series of articles, 1976–8)

'Introduction to Volume I' and 'Introduction to Volume II', in *Scotland in Europe* by Olive M. Squair (second edn, Inverness, 1977)

Cornish Heroic Song for Valda Trevlyn and Once in a Cornish Garden (Cornwall, 1977)

The Socialist Poems of Hugh MacDiarmid, ed. T.S. Law and Thurso Berwick (London, 1978)

The Complete Poems of Hugh MacDiarmid: 1920–1976, ed. Michael Grieve and W.R. Aitken (2 vols, London, 1978; reissued with corrections and appendix, 2 vols, Harmondsworth, 1985)

The Thistle Rises: An Anthology of Poetry and Prose, ed. Alan Bold (London, 1984)

Aesthetics in Scotland, ed. Alan Bold (Edinburgh, 1984)

The Letters of Hugh MacDiarmid, ed. Alan Bold (London, 1984)
The Langholm and Eskdale Connection, ed. Bill Vevers (Langholm, 1985)
'Some Uncollected Poems by Hugh MacDiarmid', ed. Kenneth Buthlay, *Scottish Literary Journal*, 12(1) (May 1985)
'Hugh MacDiarmid's Flytin Againss W.D. Cocker', 'Yae MacDiarmid Fuitnote' by T.S. Law, *Chapman*, 45(9, 2) (Summer 1986)
'Question to Edwin Morgan', 'MacDiarmid and the Beatniks' by Hamish Whyte, *Scottish Literary Journal*, 13(2) (November 1986)
Hugh MacDiarmid: Saltire Self-Portraits, arr. Henry Stamper (Edinburgh, 1986)
The Hugh MacDiarmid-George Ogilvie Letters, ed. Catherine Kerrigan (Aberdeen, 1988)
'Two Poems and a Fragment', intro. Patrick Crotty, *Scottish Literary Journal*, 15(2) (November 1988)

Critical and Biographical Works on Hugh MacDiarmid

Ackerman, Diane, 'Hugh MacDiarmid's Wide-angle Poetry', *Parnassus*, 9 (1981)
Agenda, 5(4–6, 1) (Autumn/Winter 1967–8)
Akros, 5(12–14) (April 1970)
— 12(34–5) (August 1977)
Aquarius, 11 (1979)
Ascherson, Neil, 'MacDiarmid the Brave: Last of the Giants', *The Sunday Times* (London) Magazine Supplement (14 May 1978)
Baglow, John, *Hugh MacDiarmid: The Poetry of Self* (Kingston and Montreal, 1987)
Bold, Alan, 'MacDiarmid: The Man Himself', *Chapman*, 22 (1978)
— *MacDiarmid: The Terrible Crystal* (London, 1983)
— *MacDiarmid. Christopher Murray Grieve. A Critical Biography* (London, 1988; reissued with corrections, London, 1990)
Boutelle, Ann Edwards, *Thistle and Rose: A Study of Hugh MacDiarmid's Poetry* (Loanhead, 1980)
Bunting, Basil, 'Thanks to the Guinea-Worm', *Agenda*, 8(3–4) (Autumn/Winter 1970)
— 'Hugh MacDiarmid Lost', *Agenda*, 16(3–4) (1978)
Burgess, Anthony, 'Hugh MacDiarmid: A Tribute', *Scottish Review*, 12 (1978)
Buthlay, Kenneth, 'What's Your Line', *Scottish Journal*, 9 (1953)
— *Hugh MacDiarmid (C.M. Grieve)* (Edinburgh, 1964)
— 'The Appreciation of the Golden Lyric', *Scottish Literary Journal* 2(2) (July 1975)

— 'The Complete Poems of Hugh MacDiarmid' (review), *Scottish Literary Journal Supplement*, 10 (Summer 1979)

— *Hugh MacDiarmid (C.M. Grieve)* (Edinburgh, 1982)

— 'An Awkward Squad: Some Scots Poets from Stevenson to Spence', in *Scotland and the Lowland Tongue*, ed. J. Derick McClure (Aberdeen, 1983)

Campbell, Ian, 'Gibbon and MacDiarmid in the German Democratic Republic', *Books in Scotland*, 6 (1979–80)

Chiari, Joseph, *Impressions of People and Literature* (London, n.d.)

Cox, Kenneth, 'The Poetry of Hugh MacDiarmid', *Agenda*, 24(4), 25(1) (1987)

Craig, David, 'Hugh MacDiarmid's Poetry', *The Voice of Scotland*, 7(1) (April 1956)

— 'The Radical Literary Tradition', in *The Red Paper on Scotland* (Edinburgh, 1975)

Crawford, Robert, 'A Drunk Man Looks at the Waste Land', *Scottish Literary Journal*, 14(2) (November 1987)

Crawford, Tom, 'Autobiographical Anatomist: Notes on the Collected MacDiarmid', *Chapman*, 23–4 (1979)

Cribb, T.J., 'The Cheka's Horrors and "On a Raised Beach"', *Studies in Scottish Literature*, 20 (1985)

Crotty, Patrick, 'Alan Bold, *MacDiarmid, Christopher Murray Grieve. A Critical Biography*' (review), *Scottish Literary Journal Supplement*, 30 (Spring 1989)

Daiches, David, 'Hugh MacDiarmid and the Scottish Renaissance', *Poetry* (Chicago), 72(3) (June 1948)

— 'MacDiarmid and Scottish Poetry', *Poetry* (Chicago), 72(4) (July 1948)

— 'Introduction', in *A Drunk Man Looks at the Thistle* (Glasgow, 1953)

— 'MacDiarmid's New Poem', *Lines Review*, 9 (August 1955)

— 'Diversity in Unity', *Scottish Field* (August 1962)

— 'Vision and Reality', *Lines Review*, 67 (December 1978)

— 'Types of Vision: Edwin Muir and Hugh MacDiarmid', in *God and the Poets* (Oxford, 1984)

Davie, Donald, '"A'e Gowden Lyric"', in *The Poet in the Imaginary Museum* (Manchester, 1977)

— 'MacDiarmid and MacCaig', in *Under Briggflatts* (Manchester, 1989)

Davie, George Elder, *The Crisis of the Democratic Intellect* (Edinburgh, 1986)

— 'On Hugh MacDiarmid', *Cencrastus*, 25 (1987)

Duval, K.D. and Smith, S.G. (eds), *Hugh MacDiarmid: A Festschrift* (Edinburgh, 1962)

Fisher, Allen, 'The Manners of Society. Homage to Hugh MacDiarmid', in *Unpolished Mirrors* (London, 1985)

Fraser, G.S., 'Hugh MacDiarmid, *In Memoriam James Joyce*' (review), *The New Statesman and Nation* (10 September 1955)

Gish, Nancy K., 'An Interview with Hugh MacDiarmid', *Contemporary Literature*, 20(2) (1979)

— 'Reality at Stake: Hugh MacDiarmid's early long poems', *Chapman*, 30 (1981)

— *Hugh MacDiarmid: The Man and His Work* (London, 1984)

Glen, Duncan, *Hugh MacDiarmid and the Scottish Renaissance* (Edinburgh, 1964)

— *The Literary Masks of Hugh MacDiarmid* (Glasgow, 1964)

— *The Individual and the Twentieth-Century Scottish Literary Tradition* (Preston, 1971)

— (ed.), *Hugh MacDiarmid: A Critical Survey* (Edinburgh, 1972)

Graham, Cuthbert, 'MacDiarmid and the North', *Leopard*, 43 (October 1978)

Hall, J.T.D., 'Hugh MacDiarmid, Author and Publisher', *Studies in Scottish Literature*, 21 (1986)

Harvie, Christopher, 'MacDiarmid the Socialist', *Scottish Labour History Journal*, 16 (1981)

Herbert, W.N., 'To Circumjack MacDiarmid', *Verse*, 2 (1985)

Johnstone, William, *Points in Time: An Autobiography* (London, 1980)

Kerrigan, Catherine, *Whaur Extremes Meet: The Poetry of Hugh MacDiarmid 1920–1934* (Edinburgh, 1983)

— 'MacDiarmid's Early Poetry', in *The History of Scottish Literature: Volume 4. Twentieth Century*, ed. Cairns Craig (Aberdeen, 1987)

Kocmanova, Jessie, 'Art and Revolution in the Poetry of Hugh MacDiarmid', *Philologica Pragensia*, 5 (1962)

Leavis, F.R., 'Hugh MacDiarmid — Second Hymn to Lenin', *Scrutiny*, 4(3) (December 1935)

Leonard, Tom, 'The Locust Tree in Flower, and Why it Had Difficulty Flowering in Britain', in *Intimate Voices: Selected Work 1965–1983* (Newcastle upon Tyne, 1984)

Lindsay, Maurice, 'Appendix D: The Scott/MacDiarmid Letters', in *Francis George Scott and the Scottish Renaissance* (Edinburgh, 1980)

Milner, Ian, 'The Poetic Vision of Hugh MacDiarmid', *Landfall* (New Zealand), 64 (December 1962)

Milton, C., 'Hugh MacDiarmid and North-East Scots', *Scottish Language*, 5 (1986)

Montague, John, 'Hugh MacDiarmid: A Parting Gloss', in *The Celtic Consciousness*, ed. Robert O'Driscoll (Edinburgh, 1982)

Montgomerie, William, 'Hugh MacDiarmid's "Empty Vessel"', *Akros*, 51 (1983)

Morgan, Edwin, 'Modern Makars Scots and English', *Saltire Review*, 1(2) (August 1954)

— 'Jujitsu for the Educated', *Twentieth Century*, 160(955) (September 1956)

— 'Who Will Publish Scottish Poetry?', *New Saltire*, 2 (Autumn 1961)

— 'MacDiarmid and Sherrington', *Notes and Queries*, 10(10) (October 1963)

— *Essays* (Cheadle Hulme, 1974)

— *Hugh MacDiarmid* (Harlow, 1976)

— *Provenance and Problematics of 'Sublime and Alarming Images' in Poetry* (London, 1977)

— 'On Hugh MacDiarmid's *Complete Poems 1920–1976*', *Comparative Criticism*, 3 (1981)

— 'James Joyce and Hugh MacDiarmid', in *James Joyce and Modern Literature*, ed. W.J. McCormack and Alistair Stead (London, 1982)

— 'The poet as letter-writer: Edwin Morgan finds a fuller picture of the age – and the man' (review of *The Letters of Hugh MacDiarmid*, ed. Bold and *The Thistle Rises*, ed. Bold), *The Guardian* (23 August 1984)

Murphy, Hayden, 'An Irish View of MacDiarmid', *Books in Scotland*, 4 (1979)

Mackenzie, Compton, *My Life and Times. Octave Six: 1923–1930* (London, 1967)

Mackinnon, R.M., 'Conclusion', in *The Problem of Metaphysics* (London, 1974)

Maclaren, Duncan, 'MacDiarmid', *Q. Question: An Independent Review for Scotland. Arts, Business, Science*, 34 (26 August 1977)

MacLean, Sorley, 'Lament for the Makar', in *Ris a' Bhruthaich. The Criticism and Prose Writings* (Stornoway, 1985)

— 'The Drunkard and the Thistle', *Margin*, 3 (Summer 1987)

McCleery, Alistair, 'MacDiarmid and the Porpoise Press', *Books in Scotland*, 28 (1988)

McCarey, Peter, *Hugh MacDiarmid and the Russians* (Edinburgh, 1988)

McCulloch, Margery G., 'Hugh MacDiarmid: A Study of Three Major Poems' (unpublished m.litt. dissertation, University of Glasgow, 1977)

— 'Modernism and the Scottish Tradition: The Duality of *A Drunk Man Looks at the Thistle*', *Chapman*, 25 (1979)

— 'The Undeservedly Broukit Bairn: Hugh MacDiarmid's *To Circumjack Cencrastus*', *Studies in Scottish Literature*, 17 (1982)

McQuillan, Ruth, 'MacDiarmid's Other Dictionary', *Lines Review*, 66 (September 1978)

— 'In Memoriam Alister K. Laidlaw', *Lines Review*, 67 (December 1978)

— and Shearer, Agnes, *In Line With the Ramna Stacks* (Edinburgh, 1980)

— 'The Complete MacDiarmid', *Studies in Scottish Literature*, 18 (1983)

Oxenhorn, Harvey, *Elemental Things: The Poetry of Hugh MacDiarmid* (Edinburgh, 1984)

— 'Yowdendrift: Gerard Manley Hopkins and Hugh MacDiarmid', in *Hopkins Among the Poets*, ed. Richard F. Giles (Hamilton, Ont., 1985)

Pacey, Philip, *Hugh MacDiarmid and David Jones: Celtic Wonder-Voyagers* (Preston, 1977)

Perrie, Walter, *Out of Conflict* (Dunfermline, 1982)

— 'Calling (Out) MacDiarmid', *Chapman*, 35–6 (July 1983)

Riach, Alan, 'On the Death of Hugh MacDiarmid', *Gallimafray* (Cambridge, 1978)

— 'The Complete Hippopotamus', *Cencrastus*, 23 (1986)

— '"The present is prologue": Postmodernist Scotland', *Verse*, 4 (June 1987)

— 'The Later MacDiarmid', in *The History of Scottish Literature: Volume 4. Twentieth Century*, ed. Cairns Craig (Aberdeen, 1987)

— 'T.S. Eliot and Hugh MacDiarmid', *Literary Half-Yearly*, 29 (1988)

— 'Plagiarism and MacDiarmid', *Edinburgh Review*, 83 (Summer 1990)

Rosenthal, M.L. and Gall, Salley M., 'Hugh MacDiarmid's *A Drunk Man Looks at the Thistle*', in *The Modern Poetic Sequence* (New York, 1983)

Ross, Raymond, J., 'Hugh MacDiarmid and John Maclean', *Cencrastus*, 11 (1983)

— 'Marx, MacDiarmid and MacLean', in *Sorley MacLean: Critical Essays*, ed. R.J. Ross and Joy Hendry (Edinburgh, 1986)

— 'The Russians Are Coming', *Cencrastus*, 30 (1988)

Roy, G. Ross, 'Hugh MacDiarmid (1892–1978)', *Studies in Scottish Literature*, 15 (1980)

Scott, P.H. and Davis, A.C. (eds), *The Age of MacDiarmid: Essays on Hugh MacDiarmid and his influence on contemporary Scotland* (Edinburgh, 1980)

Scottish Literary Journal: MacDiarmid Memorial Number, 5(2) (December 1978)

Scottish Literary Journal (MacDiarmid number), 15(2) (November 1988)

Silver, R.S., 'Student Culture in the 1930s and acquaintance with C.M. Grieve', *Edinburgh Review*, 74 (1986)

Smith, Iain Crichton, *Towards the Human: Selected Essays* (Edinburgh, 1986)

Smith, Sydney Goodsir, 'The Last Word', *The Saltire Review*, 4(12) (1957)

Thomas, R.S., 'A Welsh View of the Scottish Renaissance', *Wales*, 8(30) (November 1948)

'Mr MacDiarmid and Dr Grieve', in *TLS: Essays and Reviews from the Times Literary Supplement. Volume 4: 1965* (London, 1966)

Wang Zuoliang, 'Reflections on Hugh MacDiarmid', *Studies in Scottish Literature*, 19 (1984)

Watson, Roderick, 'Hugh MacDiarmid and the "Poetry of Fact"', *Stand* 9(4) (1968)
    — *Hugh MacDiarmid* (Milton Keynes, 1976)
    — 'The Licht that Bends Owre A' Thing', *Lines Review*, 67 (December 1978)
    — *MacDiarmid* (Milton Keynes, 1985)
    — 'Seminars in the Glen of Silence', *Cencrastus*, 25 (1987)

White, Kenneth, 'Taking Off from Hugh MacDiarmid', *Scottish Literary Journal*, 17(1) (May 1990)

Whyte, Christopher, 'Construction of Meaning in MacDiarmid's "Drunk Man"', *Studies in Scottish Literature*, 23 (1988)

Wright, Gordon, *MacDiarmid: An Illustrated Biography* (Edinburgh, 1977)

MacDiarmid's Sources

Aristophanes, *Plays*, I (Everyman edn), intro. Maine, anonymous transl. (London, 1909)

Buchan, John, *A Prince of the Captivity* (London, 1933)

Busoni, Ferruccio, *Letters to His Wife*, transl. Rosamond Ley (London, 1939)

Chardin, Teilhard de, *The Phenomenon of Man*, transl. Bernard Wall (London and New York, 1959)

Crane, Hart, 'The Bridge', in *The Complete Poems and Selected Letters*, ed. Brom Weber (New York, 1966)

cummings, e.e., 'N&: seven poems', in *Complete Poems*, I, 1913–35 (London, 1968)

Flaubert, Gustave, *Bouvard and Pécuchet*, trans. T.W. Earp and G.W. Stonier, intro. G.W. Stonier (London, 1936)

Haldane, J.B.S., *The Inequality of Man and other essays* (London, 1932; reissued Harmondsworth, 1937)

Herd, David, *Ancient and modern Scottish Songs, Heroic Ballads, etc.*, 2 vols (Edinburgh, 1776)

Herrigel, Eugen, *Zen in the Art of Archery* (London, 1953)

Jamieson, John, *Dictionary of the Older Scottish Language* (London and Edinburgh, 1885)

Leavis, F.R., *New Bearings in English Poetry* (London, 1932)

Lewis, Wyndham, *The Wild Body* (London, 1927)

Malraux, André, *Days of Contempt*, transl. Haakon M. Chevalier (London, 1936)

Melville, Herman, *Clarel: A Poem and Pilgrimage to the Holy Land* (standard edn., London, 1922–4, 15)

Muller, H.J., *Out of the Night* (London, 1936)

Nietzsche, Friedrich, *Thus Spoke Zarathustra*, transl. R.J. Hollingdale (Harmondsworth, 1961)

Powys, J.C., *Autobiography* (London, 1934; reissued London, 1982)
  — *The Pleasures of Literature* (London, 1938; reissued London, 1975)
  — *Obstinate Cymric* (Carmarthen, 1947; reissued London, 1973)

Raymond, Marcel, *From Baudelaire to Surrealism* (London, 1947)

Shakespeare, William, *The Works* (Alexander edn., London, 1951)

Shelley, P.B., *The Complete Poetical Works*, ed. Thomas Hutchinson (London, 1956)

Sherrington, Charles, *Man On His Nature* (London, 1940)

Stalin, J.V., *Lenin* (Moscow, 1953; reissued Peking, 1977)

Suckling, Norman, *Paul Valéry and the Civilized Mind* (London, 1954)

The Times Literary Supplement, 10 June 1939, 'De Quincey's Retreat: The Uncharted Lands of Dream', p.340
  — 6 July 1951, 'Christian Morgenstern', p.420
  — 21 March 1952, 'Dry Soul and Spun Fate', pp.197–8
  — 15 August 1952, 'Growth and Consummation', p.532
  — 8 May 1953, 'Satirist in the Modern World', pp.293–5

Thomas, Edward, *The Collected Poems of Edward Thomas*, ed. George Thomas (London, 1978)

White, T.H., *The Sword in the Stone* (London, 1939)

Material Not Directly Related to MacDiarmid

Agutter, Alex, 'Middle Scots as a Literary Language', in *The History of Scottish Literature: Volume 4. Origins to 1660 (Medieval and Renaissance)*, ed. R.D.S. Jack (Aberdeen, 1988)

Althusser, Louis, *For Marx* (London, 1969)
  — *Lenin and Philosophy* (London, 1971)

Andrews, Bruce and Bernstein, Charles (eds), *The L=A=N=G=U=A=G=E Book* (Carbondale and Edwardsville, 1984)

Arnold, Matthew, *On the Study of Celtic Literature* (London, 1910)
— *Selected Prose*, ed. Keating (Harmondsworth, 1970)
Arnold, Thurman, *The Folklore of Capitalism* (New Haven, 1961)
Auerbach, Erich, *Mimesis. The Representation of Reality in Western Literature* (Princeton, NJ, 1953)
Bakhtin, Mikhael, *Rabelais and his world* (Cambridge, Mass., 1968)
— *Problems of Dostoevsky's Poetics* (Michigan, 1973)
— *The Dialogic Imagination* (Texas, 1981)
Bann, S. and Bowlt, S. (eds), *Russian Formalism* (Edinburgh, 1973)
Barthes, Roland, *Writing Degree Zero* (London, 1967)
— *Elements of Semiology* (New York, 1968)
— *Mythologies* (London, 1972)
— *The Pleasure of the Text* (London, 1976)
— *Image–Music–Text* (Glasgow, 1977)
Benjamin, Walter, *Illuminations* (London, 1970)
— *Charles Baudelaire: A Lyric Poet in the Era of High Capitalism* (London, 1973)
— *Understanding Brecht* (London, 1977)
— *One-Way Street* (London, 1979)
Bennett, Tony, *Formalism and Marxism* (London, 1979)
Beowulf (Berkeley, 1952)
Bernstein, Michael André, *The Tale of the Tribe: Ezra Pound and the Modern Verse Epic* (Princeton, NJ, 1980)
Berger, John, 'In Defence of Art', *New Society*, 45(834) (28 September 1978)
Beveridge, Craig and Turnbull, Ronald, *The Eclipse of Scottish Culture. Inferiorism and the Intellectuals* (Edinburgh, 1989)
Biebuyck, Daniel and Mateene, Kahombo C. (eds), *The Mwindo Epic* (Berkeley and Los Angeles, 1977)
Bloch, Ernst and Lukács, Georg, Brecht, Bertolt, Benjamin, Walter, Adorno, Theodor, *Aesthetics and Politics* (London, 1977)
Borges, J.L., *Labyrinths* (Harmondsworth, 1970)
Bowra, C.M., *Heroic Poetry* (London, 1952)
Bradbury, Malcolm and MacFarlane, James (eds), *Modernism* (Harmondsworth, 1976)
Brecht, Bertolt, *The Life of Galileo* (London, 1963)
— *Brecht on Theatre*, ed. Willett (London, 1964)
— *The Messingkauf Dialogues* (London 1964)
— *The Mother* (New York, 1965)
— *Parables for the Theatre: The Good Woman of Setzuan and The Caucasian Chalk Circle* (Harmondsworth, 1966)
— *Poems 1913–1956*, ed. Willett and Manheim (London, 1976)
— *The Measures Taken and Other Lehrstücke* (London, 1977)
— *Mr Puntila and his Man Matti* (London, 1977)

Brewster, B., 'From Shklovsky to Brecht: A Reply', *Screen*, 15(2) (Summer 1974)

Bunting, Basil, *Collected Poems* (Oxford, 1978)

Burns, Robert, *Poems and Songs*, ed. Kinsley (London, 1968)

Cardenal, Ernesto, *Homage to the American Indians* (London, 1973)
— *Marilyn Monroe and Other Poems* (London, 1975)

Caudwell, Christopher, *Illusion and Reality. A Study of the Sources of Poetry* (London, 1946)

Cesaire, Aimé, *Return to My Native Land* (Harmondsworth, 1969)
— *Discourse on Colonialism* (New York and London, 1972)

Chadwick, H.M., *The Heroic Age* (Cambridge, 1912)

Chiari, Joseph, *Art and Knowledge* (London, 1977)

Cohen, J.M., *Poetry of This Age* (London, 1959)

Coleridge, S.T., *Biographia Literaria* (London, 1975)

Corkery, Daniel, *The Hidden Ireland* (Dublin, 1924)

Cory, Daniel, 'Ezra Pound: A Memoir', *Encounter*, 30(5) (1968)

Coward, R. and Ellis, J., *Language and Materialism: Developments in Semiology and the Theory of the Subject* (London, 1977)

Craig, Cairns (ed.), *The History of Scottish Literature: Volume 4. Twentieth Century* (Aberdeen, 1987)

Culler, Jonathan, *On Deconstruction* (London, 1983)

Dante, *The Divine Comedy*, 3 vols (London, 1971)

Davenport, Guy, *The Geography of the Imagination: Forty Essays* (London, 1984)

Davie, George Elder, *The Democratic Intellect* (Edinburgh, 1961)

Deane, Seamus, *Celtic Revivals: Essays in Modern Irish Literature* (London, 1985)

Derrida, Jacques, *Of Grammatology* (Baltimore and London, 1976)
— *Writing and Difference* (London, 1978)

Donne, John, *Poems*, ed. l'Anson Fausset (London, 1958)

Donoghue, Denis, *We Irish: Essays on Irish Literature and Society* (New York, 1986)

Doughty, Charles M., *Travels in Arabia Deserta* (Cambridge, 1888)
— *The Dawn in Britain*, 6 vols (London, 1906)
— *Selected Passages from 'The Dawn in Britain'*, arr. Barker Fairley (London, 1935)

Durant, Alan and Fabb, Nigel, *Literary Studies in Action* (London and New York, 1990)

Durking, R.M., *The Figure of the Poet in Renaissance Epic* (Cambridge, Mass., 1965)

Eagleton, Terry, *Marxism and Literary Criticism* (London, 1976)
— *Literary Theory* (Oxford, 1983)

Easthope, Antony, *Poetry As Discourse* (London, 1983)

Eliot, T.S., *Complete Poems and Plays* (London, 1969)
— *Selected Prose*, ed. Kermode (London, 1975)

Ellmann, Maud, *The Poetics of Impersonality: T.S. Eliot and Ezra Pound* (Brighton, 1987)

Ellmann, Richard, *James Joyce* (Oxford, 1966; revised and reissued London, 1983)

Emerson, Ralph Waldo, *Essays and Poems*, ed. Maine (London and Glasgow, 1954)

— *The Portable Emerson*, ed. van Doren (Harmondsworth, 1977)

Evans, Ifor, *Literature and Science* (London, 1954)

Ewen, Frederic, *Bertolt Brecht: His Life, His Art and His Times* (New York, 1967)

Fanon, Frantz, *The Wretched of the Earth* (Harmondsworth, 1970)

Fender, Stephen (ed.), *The American Long Poem* (London, 1977)

Fernando, Lloyd, 'Joyce and the Artist's Quest for a Unviersal Language', in *Cultures in Conflict: Essays on Literature and the English Language in South East Asia* (Singapore, 1986)

Forrest-Thomson, Veronica, *Poetic Artifice* (Manchester, 1978)

Foucault, Michel, *The Order of Things* (London, 1970)

— *Power/Knowledge* (Brighton, 1980)

Gilkes, Michael, *Cultural Schizophrenia. The Caribbean Cultural Challenge* (Coventry, 1986)

Gombrich, E.H., *In Search of Cultural History* (Oxford, 1969)

Gorky, Maxim, *On Literature* (Moscow, 1960)

Gray, Alasdair, *Lanark: A Life in Four Books* (Edinburgh, 1981)

Gray, Ronald, *Brecht* (Edinburgh, 1961)

Greene, Thomas, *The Descent from Heaven: A Study in Epic Continuity* (New Haven and London, 1963)

Hallberg, Robert von, *American Poetry and Culture, 1945–1980* (Cambridge, Mass. and London, 1985)

Hamburger, Michael, *The Truth of Poetry* (Harmondsworth, 1972)

Harari, Josué V. (ed.), *Textual Strategies* (London, 1980)

Havelock, Eric, *A Preface to Plato* (Cambridge and London, second printing, 1982)

Heath, Stephen, 'Lessons from Brecht', *Screen*, 15(2) (1974)

— 'Language, Literature, Materialism', *Sub-Stance*, 17 (1981)

Hobsbaum, Philip, 'Robert Lowell: The Mask Behind the Face', *Lines Review*, 58 (June 1976)

Holloway, John, *Widening Horizons in English Verse* (London, 1966)

Homer, *The Odyssey* (Harmondsworth, 1946)

— *The Iliad* (Harmondsworth, 1950)

Hulme, T.E., *Speculations* (London, 1924)

Hume, David, *Essays: Moral, Political and Literary*, ed. Greene and Grose (London, 1975)

Huxley, Aldous, *Music at Night and Other Essays* (London, 1931)

Jameson Fredrick, *The Prison-House of Language* (Princeton, NJ, 1972)

Johnson, Samuel, *The History of Rasselas, Prince of Abissinia*, ed. Enright (Harmondsworth, 1976)

Jones, David, *In Parenthesis* (London, 1937)
— *The Anathemata* (London, 1952)

Joyce, James, *Ulysses* (Harmondsworth, 1971)
— *Finnegans Wake* (London, 1975)
— *Letters*, ed. Gilbert, I (London, 1957)
— *James Joyce in Padua*, ed. Berrone (New York, 1977)
— *The Critical Writings of James Joyce*, ed. Mason and Ellmann, Foreword by Guy Davenport (New York, 1989)

Ker, W.P., *Epic and Romance* (New York, 1897)

Korsch, Karl, *Marxism and Philosophy* (London, 1970)
— *Three Essays on Marxism* (London, 1971)

Kristeva, Julia, *Desire in Language* (Oxford, 1980)
— *Revolution in Poetic Language* (New York, 1984)

Lacan, Jacques, *Ecrits* (London, 1977)

Laing, R.D., *The Divided Self* (London, 1960)

Langbaum, Robert, *The Poetry of Experience* (New York, 1963)

Lenin, V.I., *On Literature and Art* (Moscow, 1967)
— *Collected Works: Vol 20, December 1913–August 1914* (London and Moscow, 1972)
— *Materialism and Empirio-Criticism* (Peking, 1972)

Lopez, Tony, *The Poetry of W.S. Graham* (Edinburgh, 1989)

Lord, Albert D., *The Singer of Tales* (London, 1960)

Lyotard, J.F., *The Postmodern Condition* (Manchester, 1984)

Manganiello, Dominic, *Joyce's Politics* (London, 1980)

Mao Tse-Tung, 'On Contradiction', in *Four Essays in Philosophy* (Peking, 1966)

Marcuse, Herbert, *Soviet Marxism* (London, 1958)
— *An Essay on Liberation* (London, 1969)
— *Negations* (Harmondsworth, 1972)

Marx, Karl and Engels, Friedrich, *Ludwig Feuerbach and the End of Classical German Philosophy, with Theses on Feuerbach* (Moscow, 1946)
— *The Communist Manifesto* (Harmondsworth, 1967)
— *On Literature and Art*, ed. Baxandall and Morawski (New York, 1974)
— *Selected Letters* (Peking, 1977)

Medawar, P.B., *The Hope of Progress* (London, 1972; revised edn, 1974)

Meir, Colin, *The Ballads and Songs of W.B. Yeats* (London, 1974)

Melville, Herman, *Moby-Dick; or, The Whale*, ed. Beaver (Harmondsworth, 1972)

Merchant, Paul, *The Epic* (London, 1971)

Milton, John, *Paradise Lost and Other Poems* (London, 1961)

Mirsky, D.S., *A History of Russian Literature* (London, 1927)
— *Lenin* (London, 1931)
— 'James Joyce', *International Literature* 1(7) (April 1934)

Morgan, Edwin, *Nothing Not Giving Messages*, ed. Hamish Whyte (Edinburgh, 1990)

McCabe, Colin, *James Joyce and the Revolution of the Word* (London, 1979)
— (ed.), *James Joyce: New Perspectives* (Brighton, 1982)
— '"So truth be in the field": Milton's Use of Language', in *Teaching the Text*, ed. Kappeler and Bryson (London, 1983)
— *Theoretical Essays: film, linguistics, literature* (Manchester, 1985)

McCleery, Alistair, *The Porpoise Press 1922–39* (Edinburgh, 1988)

McGrath, John, *A Good Night Out* (London, 1981)
— *The Bone Won't Break* (London, 1990)

Maclean, John, *In the Rapids of Revolution*, ed. Milton (London, 1978)

McLuhan, Marshall, *The Gutenburg Galaxy* (London, 1962)

Neruda, Pablo, *The Heights of Macchu Picchu* (London, 1966)

Ngũgĩ wa Thiong'o, *Homecoming* (London, 1972)
— *Writers in Politics* (London, 1981)
— *Decolonizing the Mind* (London, 1986)

Nietzsche, Friedrich, *The Birth of Tragedy and the Genealogy of Morals* (New York, 1956)
— *Beyond Good and Evil* (Harmondsworth, 1973)

O'Casey, Sean, *The Story of the Irish Citizen Army* (Dublin and London, 1919)

Oinas, Felix, *Heroic Epic and Saga: An Introduction to the World's Great Folk Epics*, intro. Richard Dorson (Bloomington and London, 1978)

Olson, Charles, *Charles Olson and Ezra Pound: An Encounter at St Elizabeths*, ed. Catherine Seelye (New York, 1975)
— *Muthologos: The Collected Lectures and Interviews*, ed. Butterick, 2 vols (Bolinas, Calif., 1979)
— *The Maximus Poems*, ed. Butterick (Berkeley, Los Angeles, and London, 1983)

Paulin, Tom, *Ireland and the English Crisis* (Newcastle upon Tyne, 1987)

Perloff, Marjorie, *The Dance of the Intellect: Studies in the Poetry of the Pound Tradition* (Cambridge, 1985)

Plekhanov, Georgi, *Fundamental Problems of Marxism* (Moscow, 1962)
— *Art and Social Life* (London, n.d.)

Potts, Willard (ed.), *Portraits of Artists in Exile. Recollections of James Joyce by Europeans* (Seattle, 1979)

Pound, Ezra, *Letters 1907–1941*, ed. Paige (London, 1951)
— *Guide to Kulchur* (London, 1952)
— *ABC of Reading* (London, 1961)
— *Literary Essays*, ed. Eliot (London, 1963)
— *Pound/Joyce; The Letters of Ezra Pound to James Joyce with Pound's Essays on Joyce*, ed. Read (London, 1968)
— *Selected Prose 1909–1965*, ed. Cookson (London, 1973)
— *The Cantos* (London, 1975)

Power, Arthur, *Conversations with James Joyce*, ed. Hart (London, 1974)

Prawer, S.S., *Karl Marx and World Literature* (Oxford, 1978)

Richards, I.A. and Ogden, C.K., *The Meaning of Meaning* (London, 1923)

Richards, I.A., *Principles of Literary Criticism* (London, 1924)
— *Science and Poetry* (London, 1926)
— *Practical Criticism* (London, 1929)
— *The Philosophy of Rhetoric* (Oxford, 1936)
— *Basic English and Its Uses* (London, 1943)
— *Complementarities*, ed. Russo (Manchester, 1977)

Robertson, J.M., *Montaigne and Shakespeare* (London, 1897; revised and reissued 1909)

Said, Edward W., *The World, the Text and the Critic* (London, 1984)
— *Orientalism* (Harmondsworth, 1985)

Sartre, J.P., *What Is Literature?* (London, 1967)
— *Politics and Literature* (London, 1973)

Saurat, Denis, *Modern French Literature, 1870–1940* (London, 1946)

Saussure, Ferdinand de, *Course in General Linguistics*, intro. Jonathan Culler (revised edn, London, 1974)

Scully, James (ed.), *Modern Poets on Modern Poetry* (London and Glasgow, 1966)

Segel, Harold B., *Twentieth-Century Russian Drama: From Gorky to the Present* (New York, 1979)

Sélincourt, Basil de, *Pomona: or, the Future of English* (London, n.d. but pre-1927)

Shklovsky, Victor, *Mayakovsky and His Circle* (London, 1974)

Sinfield, Alan (ed.), *Literature and Society: 1945–1970* (London, 1983)

Smith Jr., G. Grover, *T.S. Eliot's Poetry and Plays: A Study in Sources and Meaning* (Chicago, 1950)

Solomon, Maynard (ed.), *Marxism and Art, Essays Classic and Contemporary* (Brighton, 1979)

Soloviev, Vladimir, *War, Progress and the End of History* (London, 1915)

Soyinka, Wole, *Myth, Literature and the African World* (Cambridge, 1976)

Spenser, Edmund, *Poetical Works* (Oxford, 1912)

Stalin, J.V., *Works. Volume 6: 1924* (London, 1953)
— *Marxism and the Problem of Linguistics* (Peking, 1972)
— *Marxism and the National Question* (Tirana, 1979)

Stevens, Wallace, *Collected Poems* (New York, 1954)

Timpanaro, Sebastiano, *On Materialism* (London, 1975)

Thomson, George, *Marxism and Poetry* (London, 1975)

Trilling, Lionel, *Sincerity and Authenticity* (London, 1972)

Trotsky, Leon, *Literature and Revolution* (Michigan, 1960)

Valéry, Paul, *The Collected Works*, ed. Matthews, 15 vols (London, 1958–75)

Vansina, Jan, *Oral Literature* (London, 1965)

Volosinov, V.N., *The Marxist Philosophy of Language* (Seminar Press, 1979)

Weber, Betty Nance and Heinen, Hubert (eds), *Bertolt Brecht: Political Theory and Literary Practice* (Manchester, 1980)

West, T.G. (ed.), *Symbolism: An Anthology* (London, 1980)

Whitehead, A.N., *Adventures of Ideas* (Harmondsworth, 1948)

Whitman, Walt, *Complete Poems and Selected Prose and Letters*, ed. Holloway (London, 1938)

Whyte, J.H. (ed.), *Towards a New Scotland: Being a Selection from 'The Modern Scot'* (London, 1935)

Willett, John, *The Theatre of Bertolt Brecht* (London, 1959)

Williams, Raymond, *Drama from Ibsen to Brecht* (Harmondsworth, 1973)
— *Marxism and Literature* (Oxford, 1977)
— *Politics and Letters* (London, 1979)

Williams, William Carlos, *Paterson* (Harmondsworth, 1983)

Wittgenstein, Ludwig, *Tractatus Logico-Philosophicus*, intro. Bertrand Russell (London, 1971)

Womack, Peter, 'Brecht: The Search for an Audience', *Cencrastus*, 1 (Autumn 1978)

Woroszyski, Wiktor, *The Life of Mayakovsky* (London, 1972)

Yeats, W.B., *The Collected Poems* (London, 1978)

Young, Robert (ed.), *Untying the Text* (London, 1981)

Zamyatin, Evgeny, 'On Literature, Revolution and Entropy', in *Dissident Voices in Soviet Literature*, ed. Blake and Hayward (London, 1964)

Zhdanov, A.A., *On Literature, Music and Philosophy* (London, 1950)

Zis, Avner, *Foundations of Marxist Aesthetics* (Moscow, 1977)

Index

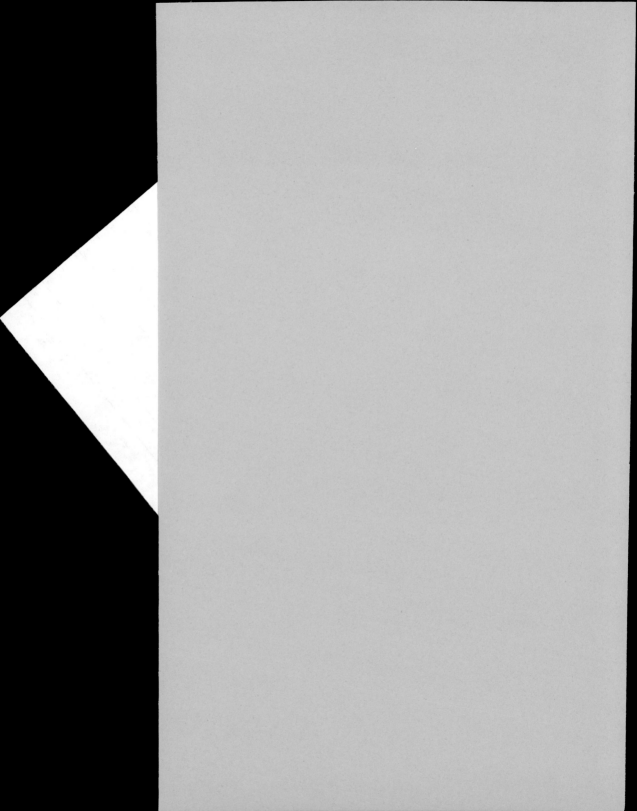

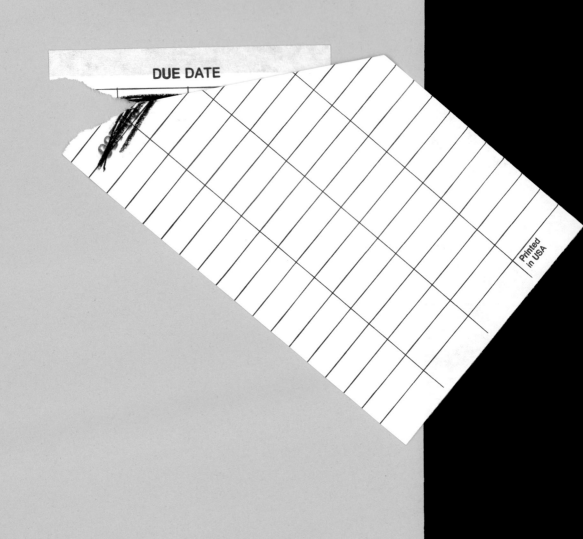

DUE DATE

Printed
in USA